THE GENESIS
OF GOD

Also by Thomas J. J. Altizer
and published by Westminster/John Knox Press

Genesis and Apocalypse:
A Theological Voyage Toward Authentic Christianity

THE GENESIS
OF GOD

A Theological Genealogy

Thomas J. J. Altizer

Westminster/John Knox Press
Louisville, Kentucky

© 1993 Thomas J. J. Altizer

Book design by Susan E. Jackson

First edition

Published by Westminster/John Knox Press
Louisville, Kentucky

This book is printed on acid-free paper that meets the American National Standards Institute Z39.48 standard. ∞

PRINTED IN THE UNITED STATES OF AMERICA

9 8 7 6 5 4 3 2 1

Library of Congress Cataloging-in-Publication Data

Altizer, Thomas J. J.
  The genesis of God : a theological genealogy / Thomas J. J. Altizer. — 1st ed.
        p.   cm.
  Includes bibliograpical references and index.
  ISBN 0-664-21996-9 (cloth)

  1. God.   2. Beginning.   3. Theology—20th century.   I. Title.
BT102.A47 1993
231—dc20   93-10748

For
Katharine Blake Altizer

CONTENTS

Contents

PREFACE

Nothing is more forbidden today than thinking about God, perhaps
nothing else so clearly witnesses to the deep fragility of our institutions and life, and just as this is a prohibition which is embodied in
virtually every twentieth century philosopher, it is now one which is fully
manifest in theologians and Biblical scholars. If Judaism can exercise an
authentic witness by its refusal to pronounce the name of God, contemporary Christianity would appear to be attempting a comparable witness by
dissolving the very possibility of thinking about God, a dissolution which
might be interpreted as a contemporary iconoclasm, but which could also
be interpreted as a flight from our deepest and most ultimate ground. How
ironic that ours is an era when radical thinking would appear to be the
norm of thinking itself, but seldom if ever is such thinking directed to an
ultimate or absolute ground, and at no other point is there such a chasm
between contemporary and pre-contemporary thinking, or between the
"postmodern" and modernity itself. All too significantly, a thinking
refusing all thinking about God, which is perhaps the purest such refusal
in our history, is occurring at a time when there is a greater distance than
ever before between pure thinking and all institutional or manifest power,
just as there is a comparable distance between the imagination and all such
power, as for the first time all "higher" culture is fully divorced from the
public realm, thereby bestowing upon that culture a new and radical
freedom if only because it can threaten or affect no one whatsoever.

Nothing could be a greater theological irony, for even as theology could
only come into existence and realize itself as genuine thinking by way of an
inevitable conflict with all institutional power, at the very time when
thinking as such is seemingly free of every institutional repression, it is
most liberated from the very possibility of theological thinking, as though
it were freedom itself which inevitably dissolves all theological thinking.
But it is not only theological thinking which has been eroded in our world,

1

so likewise has been annulled a "metaphysical" thinking, and this even in a pre-Christian sense. And in a world in which Marxism and Freudianism are disappearing, a modern radicalism directed to interior and exterior actualities, is now divorced from all human actuality whatsoever, or can survive as such only in a purely utopian or fantasy form. So that the contemporary dissolution of theological thinking is inseparable from the dissolution of pure thinking itself, a situation which is clearly an apocalyptic situation, and apocalyptic if only because it is such a deep and ultimate ending. Yet Christian theological thinking was originally an apocalyptic thinking, as present not only in Paul but in that conflict with Gnosticism which so dominates the New Testament itself, a conflict which can be understood as the origin of Christian theological thinking, and one which even now is being reborn. For Gnosticism is a total isolation of faith from every possible human or historical actuality, an isolation which is clearly all powerful today, and perhaps most powerful in the very refusal to think about God.

This book may be understood as an assault upon a uniquely contemporary "spiritualism" or Gnosticism, it is certainly directed against a contemporary refusal to think theologically, and with a recognition that genuine theological thinking can now only be a transgressive thinking, and perhaps most deeply transgressive as a thinking which is a theological thinking. Furthermore, this book presumes that theological thinking is inevitably philosophical and imaginative thinking at once, thus it seeks a deep ground both in the Christian epic tradition from Dante through Joyce and in that radically modern philosophical thinking occurring between Spinoza and Hegel, with the presumption that both of these grounds are deeply and ultimately theological, and are so above all in centering upon Godhead or absolute ground. Surely one reason why theology has become so peripheral in our time is that it has withdrawn itself from our deeper traditions, and above all so from our deeper modern traditions, so that conservative theologians can now laud the advent of a "postmodernity" which is seemingly a dissolution of the modern world. But the simple truth is that a fully modern theology has not yet been written or conceived, so that there cannot yet be a postmodern theology, but only a renewed medieval, or patristic, or pagan theology, even if such a renewal forecloses all possibility of either a truly imaginative or a genuinely philosophical ground.

This book is in full continuity with my previous book, *Genesis and Apocalypse: A Theological Voyage Toward Authentic Christianity*. Nevertheless, *The Genesis of God* can be read independently of that book, none

2

of its expositions presuppose the expositions of the earlier book, and each of its voyages is an independent voyage in its own right. Once again scholarly documentation is absent, for this is not a scholarly book, it is a fully theological book, and it intends to realize a meaning that is wholly confined within its own language, even if the potentialities of such meaning go far beyond this book. When necessary, exact citation does occur, but this occurs within the text itself. Unfortunately, we still lack a truly critical edition of Joyce's *Ulysses,* and the page references to that epic are to the Modern Library edition. The numerical references to Hegel's *Phenomenology of Spirit* are to its paragraphs, and are contained as such in A. V. Miller's translation (Oxford, 1977). The Blake references are to plate and line numbers, and occur in all critical editions of Blake. In the past two generations we have been blessed with rich and extraordinary studies of Dante, Milton, Blake, and Joyce, studies which have wholly transformed our understanding of the Christian epic, and so likewise have we been given a vast and exciting body of interpretations of Spinoza, Hegel, and Nietzsche. Never before has the theologian been blessed with such riches, and while these might appear as a curse to the conservative theologian, it is no longer possible to believe that modernity is theologically inferior to any previous age.

Once again I am deeply indebted to my wife, Barbara Walters Altizer, and not least for her critical response and support. Mark C. Taylor, Ray L. Hart, Charles E. Winquist, Richard Underwood, Edith Wyschogrod, and D. G. Leahy have been enriching theological partners, and Leahy's *Foundation: Matter the Body Itself,* soon to be published by The State University of New York Press, includes a chapter which is a profound critique and transformation of my theological thinking. And yet again, Davis Perkins and Danielle Alexander of the Westminster/John Knox Press have given invaluable editorial assistance.

PROLOGUE

Nothing is more alien to our thinking than the very possibility of the genesis of God, and even if a truly contemporary thinking is precisely that thinking which cannot think God, that is the thinking which is most open to a subversion of our given identity of God. An affirmation of the genesis of God is just such a subversion, and here it is vitally important to distinguish subversion from dissolution; for subversion inverts or reverses a given identity, whereas a dissolution simply dissolves it. Modern Christian radical thinking is a subversive thinking, and if that thinking occurs in Luther, Kierkegaard, and Dostoyevsky, that is a thinking subverting a given Christianity, and subverting it so as to invert or reverse the apparent or manifest or public identity of Christianity. Such a subversion occurred in the prophets of Israel, even as it is also present in Paul and the Fourth Gospel, and this Biblical subversion is even a subversion of God, or a subversion of that God which is manifest or real apart from what is here realized as faith itself. Such subversion is necessary and essential to what the Christian most deeply knows as faith, even as offense is necessary to that faith, an offense that inevitably occurs in a proclamation of the Christian faith. Surely an affirmation of the genesis of God is an offense to faith, but whether or not that offense is necessary to faith itself is a question which will be prosecuted in this book.

While it is true that philosophical and theological thinking have long known an eternal genesis of God which is identical with the eternal act of God, no such thinking has affirmed a once-and-for-all genesis of God, or a genesis of God which is a unique and once-and-for-all beginning, or a genesis of God which is a real and actual beginning. Blake alone among our visionaries has envisioned such a beginning, and just as Blake is our most radical Christian poet and visionary, he is nowhere more subversive than in envisioning the origin of Urizen or the Creator. But Blake is also our most apocalyptic Christian visionary, and that apocalypse which he knew

4

as the "Self-Annihilation" of God is an apocalypse which is a self-annihilation or self-negation of the Creator. That self-annihilation is not unlike that kenotic emptying of the Godhead which is so deeply present in Eckhart's thinking, just as it fully parallels Hegel's philosophical understanding of the absolute self-negation of Absolute Spirit, a self-negation which many critics have unveiled as being fully present in many of the deepest imaginative expressions of full or late modernity.

It would not be amiss to interpret the opening of *Finnegans Wake* as an enactment of the genesis of God, a genesis of God which is here a fall of God, even as a Blakean genesis of God is such a fall. A symbol or vision of total fall has always been essential to apocalyptic faith and vision, for even as apocalyptic vision has known Satan more fully than any other form of Christian vision, such a vision of total darkness is inseparable from an apocalyptic celebration of total light. The final victory of that light is inseparable from the actual ending of a total darkness, and that is an ending of the deep ground of that darkness, a ground which is named in the naming of Satan.

Even if a uniquely modern Christianity has been unable to name Satan, the naming of Satan in the modern imagination has gone far beyond its Biblical source, a movement already beginning with Milton, but one going beyond Milton in Blake and Joyce, and perhaps beyond Joyce in Kafka and Beckett. Such an ultimate naming of darkness is finally a naming of God, and perhaps the naming of an alien God which is manifest and real in modernity alone, and there most fully manifest in the deepest expressions of modernity itself. Certainly that modernity has undergone a historical genesis, and even as alien images of God are wholly absent from Aquinas and Dante, they are fully present in Luther and Boehme, and perhaps nothing is more historically distinctive of the Reformation. While it may be difficult today to understand how an original Protestantism could so deeply identify the Papacy and the Antichrist, it should not be difficult for us to grasp the necessity of understanding ultimate evil. And that evil must have a real and actual origin, for if it is eternal then we must be without an ultimate hope.

So it is that the question of evil in the context of faith is inevitably the question of genesis, the question not only of why there is evil at all but why evil has come into existence. That question has simply been unanswerable in classical philosophy and theology, but even as a uniquely modern thinking and a uniquely modern imagination have most deeply posed that question, that very questioning has inevitably evoked a truly new understanding of genesis itself.

Yet no such understanding has been incorporated into our theological thinking, or not openly or systematically, and just as the very question of the genesis of God is alien to our theological thinking, it is just the question of the genesis of evil which has again and again shattered and deconstructed that thinking. But if the question of the genesis of evil is inseparable from the question of the genesis of God, and, indeed, is only finally meaningful in the context of the question of a divine genesis, then the ultimate mystery of evil can only be broached by broaching the ultimate mystery of God. Our ancient Western mythologies could know the genesis of deity, and nothing is more distinctive of the Greek gods and goddesses than their actual origin, an origin which the ancient Greeks could know as the origin of light. While destiny or *ananke* is deeper than that light, a destiny or darkness which is triumphant in the deepest expressions of Greek tragedy, that is a darkness which is thereby affirmed, and affirmed in the very enactment of tragedy. But tragedy is not confined to ancient Greece, and just as the Christian world is that historical world which has known the deepest epiphany of darkness, that is an epiphany that begins with an original Christianity, and with an original Christian naming of Satan. Jesus named Satan more fully and more continually than did any earlier prophet, and that naming is inseparable from his eschatological proclamation and parabolic enactment, an enactment which is a disenactment of an ultimate evil.

But that evil can come to an end only because it has an actual origin; it is precisely because evil is not an eternal evil that it can come to an end, an ending which is the apocalyptic triumph of the Kingdom of God. Now just as Christian theology has yet to evolve a truly or fully apocalyptic theology, Christian theology has yet to evolve a full understanding of evil, and a full understanding of that ultimate evil which is shattered by the actual advent of the Kingdom of God. It is precisely the absence of a theological understanding of the Kingdom of God which is the absence of a theological understanding of ultimate evil, and the scholastic understanding of evil as the privation of Being was possible only in the context of a dissolution of the original apocalyptic identity of the Kingdom of God, a dissolution which is the advent of what we have known as Christianity. Just as it is apocalyptic movements which have most profoundly challenged the dominant expressions of Christianity, it is apocalyptic faith and vision which have most profoundly subverted the given Christian identity of God, even as the modern historical discovery of an original Christianity as an apocalyptic Christianity has been the deepest and most unanswerable challenge to modern theology itself. But the refusal to meet this challenge is also the refusal to meet the challenge of ultimate evil, an evil that has only actually been named by apocalypticism, and there so named only by an apprehension that it even now is coming to an end.

Nothing is more important in apocalypticism than its envisionment and enactment of ultimate ending, an ending that is the ending of evil itself. That ending is simultaneously the final realization of the Kingdom of God so that the ending of evil and the eschatological embodiment of the Kingdom of God are one event. But that ending and that embodiment are an actual ending and an actual embodiment, an actuality that is inseparable from genesis itself, for an actual ending is inseparable from an actual beginning. So it is that evil can finally end only insofar as it has actually begun, and if fall is a primal symbol in all genuine apocalypticism, that is a fall that is inseparable from apocalypse itself. For an apocalyptic apocalypse is not an eternal apocalypse of the Godhead, but rather a final and eschatological act, and an act that is a final enactment of the original act of genesis. Just as that act is the ultimate origin of apocalypse, apocalypse is the final ending of that creation enacted in genesis, a creation which itself is consummated in apocalypse. And just as the creation is a consequence of a once-and-for-all and irreversible beginning, apocalypse is the embodiment of a once-and-for-all and irreversible ending. That ending is not simply and not only a catastrophic ending, but far rather a triumphant ending, an ending of everything whatsoever that is intrinsically "other" than the Kingdom of God. Therefore the full actualization of that "otherness" is necessary and essential for the realization of apocalypse itself, an apocalypse that is apocalypse only insofar as it is the actual ending of the totality of evil.

That actual ending is the very center of apocalypse, but it is that center only as a consequence of genesis, or only as the consequence of an ultimate and actual beginning. Thus that beginning cannot be an eternal beginning, not a beginning which is the eternal genesis of the Godhead, but rather a beginning which is the beginning of actuality itself, or the actual beginning of that actuality which is consummated in apocalypse itself. For just as an apocalyptic apocalypse is not an eternal apocalypse, an apocalyptic genesis is not an eternal genesis, and cannot be if apocalypse is an actual ending. Only the actuality of that ending calls forth the full actuality of evil itself, so that full visions of Satan are inevitably apocalyptic visions, just as a full naming of Satan is inevitably an apocalyptic naming. That naming itself is inseparable from an apocalyptic naming of the Godhead, and if that naming in the New Testament is the naming of the Kingdom of God, a naming which never occurs in the Hebrew Bible, that is the naming of an ultimate evil which occurs in no other horizon of vision or speech.

Nothing is more historically distinctive of the New Testament itself than its continual naming of demonic power, a power that is manifest and real only in the context of an apocalyptic ending, and therefore only in the context of the actual advent of the Kingdom of God. Jesus was the first prophet to proclaim that actual advent, just as Jesus was the first prophet who is recorded as having seen the fall of Satan (Luke 10:18), a final fall of Satan which is an apocalyptic epiphany, and an apocalyptic epiphany which is the epiphany of the Kingdom of God. So it is that a naming of Satan and a naming of the Kingdom of God are inseparable in Jesus' eschatological proclamation, a naming which is the naming of ultimate evil and of apocalyptic Godhead at once.

The gospel or "good news" of Jesus is the gospel of the final ending of evil, an ending that even now is occurring with the advent of the Kingdom of God, and an ending that is the ending of an evil that has actually begun. Nothing could be further from that gospel than an acceptance of the eternity or ultimacy of evil, and if evil is not eternal then it has undergone an actual genesis, for only that which has actually begun can actually come to an end. Paradoxically, and not so paradoxically, it is an apocalyptic naming of evil which is our deepest naming of evil, nowhere else is there a naming of total evil, just as nowhere else is there a true naming of Satan.

But that naming of evil is the naming of an evil that is the consequence of fall, a fall that apocalyptically is the fall of the creation itself, and thus a fall that is comprehensive or all in all. Paul could celebrate that Godhead that will be all in all (I Cor. 15:28), an apocalypse that is clearly an absolute reversal of fall, and an absolute reversal of total fall. For it is total fall that is the arena of apocalypse, and if it is apocalypticism alone which knows total fall, it is apocalypticism alone which knows a Godhead that will be all in all. This is an essential and integral correlation which is absolutely necessary to full apocalypticism, an apocalypticism that can know the triumph of Godhead only by knowing an all comprehending darkness. Nothing is more fundamental in both Paul and the Fourth Gospel than a realization of that darkness, and an epiphany of that darkness is inseparable from an epiphany of apocalyptic light.

Thus both Paul and the Fourth Gospel can know the crucifixion and the resurrection of Christ as one event, and as that one event which is the *event* of salvation, that once-and-for-all and irreversible act which is the *act* of Godhead itself. That is the act which ends the power of evil, or the ultimate power of evil, and that is the ending of that total fall embodying a total darkness. Indeed, only that ending truly makes manifest a total fall, so that the naming of that ending is the naming of total fall, and a total fall which is not an irrevocable fall precisely because it is a consequence of an actual genesis. That is the genesis which is an apocalyptic genesis insofar as it is consummated in apocalypse, and the once-and-for-all actuality of genesis is inseparable from the once-and-for-all actuality of apocalypse. But that is precisely a genesis which has never truly entered our theological thinking, and if this is because our theological thinking has never been a truly apocalyptic thinking, we have theologically failed to understand genesis just because we have failed to understand apocalypse itself.

Yet we have been given imaginative visions of apocalypse, and most clearly so in the Christian epic tradition, a tradition which itself is an apocalyptic tradition, just as it has been enacted by Christian apocalyptic seers. The vision of those seers is in manifest continuity with the Bible, as witness the visions of Dante, Milton, and Blake, and even as the Christian epic tradition is a historically evolving tradition, that evolution is an apocalyptic evolution, for it becomes ever more fully and more finally apocalyptic as it evolves.

Surely the time is at hand for a theological understanding of an apocalyptic genesis, which as a theological understanding could only be an understanding of the genesis of God, and of the apocalyptic genesis of God. While that is the goal of this book, it is a goal which here can only be approached and not fulfilled, an approach which at most would be the beginning of an apocalyptic theology. Accordingly, this book is in full continuity with *Genesis and Apocalypse*, attempting to press forward the problems that are posed in that book, but now with full attention being given to genesis itself. The problems therein and thereby arising are virtually innumerable, only a few of which will here be examined, and these never so as to effect anything like a full resolution. Theology in the past has often effected full resolutions, but never has it done so when entering truly new arenas or fields, and just as Augustine is our most original and creative theologian, Augustine's most systematic thinking is his thinking which is most closed to the future, and which most demanded a subsequent theological transformation. Such transformations have again and again occurred in the history of theological thinking, and they are commonly the consequence of the advent of truly new historical and cultural worlds, historical worlds demanding the transformation of theology itself, for it is an unmoving theology which is a dead theology, and that is the very theology which is most closed to a uniquely Christian redemption and faith. Certainly theology is now in a state of deep crisis, and if a truly new theology is not possible for us, then that would be nothing less than a decisive and perhaps even ultimate sign of the dissolution of Christianity itself.

1

THE LOGIC
OF GENESIS

Hegel's science of logic is the purest and most comprehensive system of thinking which has evolved in the Western world, and if logic is the realm of pure thought, here this realm is truth as it is without veil and in its own absolute nature, as Hegel declares in its introduction, so that the content of pure logic is the exposition of God as He is in His eternal essence before the creation. Yet nothing is more elusive in the *Science of Logic* than the identity of God, for even if Hegel can initially declare that God is the absolute, that absolute idea with which this work concludes is not only *all* truth, but its essential nature is to return to itself through its own "self-determination." That return is a circle returning upon itself, the end being wound back into the beginning, for teleologically the end is the beginning, and the whole of the science of logic is within itself a circle in which the first is also the last and the last is also the first. Here, an original *logia* of Jesus becomes pure logos or pure logic, and if Hegel's dialectical system is the first and only fully philosophical realization of an original apocalyptic negation, apocalyptic negation logically reveals or unveils itself as an eternal circle of return. Therein and thereby alpha and omega are ultimately and essentially identical, even as genesis and apocalypse are so identical, and are identical in that absolute actuality which is the negative return of the absolute into itself.

Kierkegaard could respond to Hegel's system and to Hegel's God as the pure antithesis of the Christian God, a judgment which is echoed again and again in twentieth century theology, but that judgment is precarious if only because of the elusive identity of the Hegelian God, a God who is absolute Idea but nevertheless and even thereby pure personality, a "personality" which is not exclusive identity but rather universality itself. That universality in the *Science of Logic* is an eternal circle of return, a circle in which genesis is apocalypse even as apocalypse is genesis, therefore genesis is an eternal genesis even as apocalypse is an eternal apocalypse, and both are united in the eternal cycle of return. Thus eternal return is the innermost center of the life and movement of the Godhead, a Godhead which quite simply *is* eternal return, an eternal return in which ending is essentially and necessarily an eternal beginning. While Hegel can remark that the sections and headings of the *Science of Logic* are strictly only of historical value, there can be little doubt that here ending can only be beginning, and that in the strictest and most logical sense. So it is that the ending of eternal return is indistinguishable from its beginning, even as the beginning of eternal return is indistinguishable from its ending. Nevertheless, genesis or absolute beginning is the deepest problem posed by the *Science of Logic,* and that problem is inseparable from the problem of the identity of the Hegelian absolute.

The science of logic and not only the *Science of Logic* begins with the problem of beginning, a seemingly insoluble problem which at once impels the realization that in pure or abstract thinking the method must be united with the content, and that union unveils the absolute truth that there is nothing which does not equally contain both immediacy and mediation, so that these two determinations reveal themselves to be inseparable and the apparent opposition between them to be a nullity. Whereas in the phenomenology of spirit or the science of consciousness or manifested spirit, the beginning is made from empirical or sensuous consciousness and this is immediate knowledge, in that pure science which is logic itself, that immediate beginning is a fully and wholly mediated beginning. Now simple immediacy is itself an expression of reflection, and therefore is "pure being." Therefore that beginning is an absolute, and even if it is only an abstract beginning, and as abstract beginning an unmediated and groundless beginning, that beginning is nevertheless the ground of the science of logic, and is so as mere immediacy itself. But that mere immediacy is necessarily pure being, and is necessarily pure being because here it is apprehended through pure thinking or pure knowledge.

Now the science of logic is a science in which advance is retreat into the ground, that is the ground from which originates that with which the beginning occurs, and absolute knowledge is the innermost truth of that ground. This is the ground from which the beginning proceeds, a beginning which at first appears as immediacy, but which finally appears as absolute spirit, the concrete and final truth of all being. At the end of the science of logic, absolute spirit is finally known as freely abandoning and externalizing itself, even abandoning itself to sheer immediacy, an abandonment which religious or mythical thinking knows as the creation. Thus the beginning is the pure immediacy of absolute spirit, an immediacy which is not only pure being, but is that pure being which is an immediate form and manifestation of absolute spirit. Therefore the first is the last, even as the last is the first, and this *coincidentia oppositorum* of immediacy and mediation is not simply a coincidence of opposites, for absolute immediacy and absolute mediation are one and the same, an identity which is the nullity of the apparent opposition between them. That nullity is manifest in consciousness, and is pure in pure consciousness, but is realized only in the negative movement of consciousness itself, a movement which is finally the movement of absolute spirit itself. That is the movement which begins with sheer immediacy, and ends with an absolute and total mediation, a mediation which is the absolute *kenosis* or self-emptying of absolute spirit itself.

If it belongs to the very nature of beginning that it must be being and nothing else, that beginning in its very identity as beginning is the unity of being and nothing, a unity in which being and nothing are distinguished from each other in the beginning. That is the distinction which is absolutely essential to beginning itself, for the beginning as such is only on the way to being, a being which is the "other" of non-being. For only non-being is the other of being, and therefore the being embodied in the beginning is a being which removes itself from non-being, or which negates non-being as something opposed to and other than itself. That negation is genesis or the beginning, and therefore the opposites of being and non-being are united in that beginning, a beginning which is the undifferentiated unity of being and nothing. But absolute beginning embodies mediation within itself, a mediation between the opposites of being and nothing, and a mediation that is known or manifest in the knowledge that being *is* nothing. This occurs in the realization that pure being, or being without any further differentiation, or that being which is the indeterminate immediate, is in fact "nothing," and neither more nor less than nothing. It is a wholly empty intuition which presents us with the thought of both pure being and pure nothing, and that is an emptiness in which pure nothing is the same as pure being, and it is the vanishing of that pure being and pure nothing which is the advent of becoming. Hegel challenges his reader to state what is the absolute difference between being and nothing, insisting that the impossibility of meeting that challenge makes manifest the truth that such a difference is unknowable, and it is the unknowability of that difference which most clearly makes manifest that immanent dialectic in which apparent opposites realize their unity.

Becoming is the unity of being and nothing, but not a unity which abstracts from being and nothing, but rather a determinate unity in which there is both being and nothing. Now being and nothing are actually unseparated from each other, and insofar as each is, each is not. Therefore they exist in this unity only as vanishing or negated moments, as each negates itself in itself if only because in becoming each is in actual union with its other, and that unity can only be the vanishing of being in nothing and of nothing in being. This is that uniquely Hegelian negation or sublation (*Aufhebung*) in which something is truly negated only insofar as it has entered into union with its opposite, that is the union which is the Hegelian "moment," and that is a moment in which immediacy is lost but is not for that reason annihilated. Now world or determinate being (*Dasein*) is at hand, a determinate being which is the simple oneness of being and nothing, as nonbeing is now taken up into simple unity with being. This is the clearest and most decisive point at which Hegel solved or resolved the deepest metaphysical problem of Christendom, the seemingly ultimate or irresolvable problem of the relation between being and nothing in becoming. But that is a solution which is the end of metaphysics, as metaphysics is now fully transposed into the objective logic of the science of logic. No thinker, not even Nietzsche, is finally as anti-metaphysical as Hegel, but in Hegelian thinking metaphysics is negated by way of its own integral and necessary transition into pure logic, and therein its actuality is not annihilated, but is rather preserved by way of its own transcending movement into a higher and truer actuality.

It is the uniquely Hegelian movement of pure negation which annuls and transcends all given distinctions and divisions, including that primal division between being and nothing. If every distinction which is present in consciousness is a consequence of the act and activity of consciousness itself, then those distinctions have no final ground in "being in-itself," but rather are a consequence of "being for-itself," a for-itself which is the negation of an abstract being in-itself. That negation is genesis or the beginning, and it is a negation which necessarily must occur, and must occur if only because of the actuality of consciousness itself, an actuality which is undeniable, and an actuality which is inseparable from the movement and activity of consciousness. This is the Hegelian answer to the metaphysical question of why is there any being at all, why not far rather nothing?

Yet this Hegelian answer disguises a cypher which is perhaps the one inexplicable category of the science of logic, and that is *Trieb,* a primal urge or instinct or drive, which Hegel can finally identify as the sole and absolute force of pure reason, its supreme and sole *Trieb* to find and cognize itself by means of itself in everything whatsoever. That *Trieb* is present in the beginning, and present as the beginning, for the immediacy of the beginning is deficient in its own immediacy, and as such is endowed with the *Trieb* to carry itself further. But the origin of that *Trieb* is an inexplicable mystery, for even if it is the very center of the absolute Idea or the Notion, and is itself the final source of all movement and process, it cannot have an origin in a purely abstract and inactive being in-itself, and cannot do so if only because being in-itself is a wholly inactual passivity.

Finally, nothing is a deeper mystery in the *Science of Logic* than absolute origin or genesis, and if that origin is a mystery then so likewise is the final ending or apocalypse of the science of logic, for if that apocalypse is genesis, it is precisely a mystery because of that. While we could join a Heidegger or a Derrida in looking upon the Hegelian system as the end of metaphysics, which is in fact a Hegelian judgment, in this perspective it would be far more than that, for it would be the end of pure thinking itself if its necessary resolution of that thinking is both grounded in and culminates in an inexplicable mystery. Then Marx and Kierkegaard would be the true inheritors of the Hegelian system, the one inverting pure reason so as to transpose it into the dark mystery of a purely material ground, and the other reversing pure reason so as to transpose it into the equally dark mystery of the absolutely transcendent God. Each of these reversals of Hegelian thinking is an absolute reversal of the Hegelian method and movement of pure negation, and even if such reversal is inseparable from a Hegelian ground, and must inevitably perish apart from that ground, it is nonetheless a reversal which annuls that ground, so that each of these reversals has culminated in our own time with a dissolution of itself. That culmination could be the end of pure thinking, and if that end is apocalypse, it is itself an ultimate mystery which an original apocalypse promised to reverse, and an ultimate mystery which is simultaneously the ultimate mystery of genesis.

Hegel is our only thinker who has made the forward movement of advance the very center and ground of pure thinking itself, and that advance is inseparable from the dark mystery of *Trieb*. In large measure, Hegel adapted that category from the mystical thinking of Jacob Boehme, as he himself indirectly acknowledges both in the *Science of Logic* and in the exposition of Boehme in his lectures on the history of philosophy. For it was Boehme who apparently first understood the creation itself as a negative process of internal unrest or torment (*Qual*), a torment by which it establishes its own negative nature from out of an intrinsic "other." Hegel's most creative act of genius was in understanding that "other," and every true "other," as the necessary and essential "other" of itself; so that not only is "otherness" its own, but the realization of that "otherness" is the *Trieb* of all process and life. If *Trieb* is the darkest mystery in Hegel's system, it is that mystery which is the very essence of a purely Hegelian thinking, for apart from that mystery there would be no advance, and thus finally no thinking or process at all. Then nothing would, indeed, be all in all, and the primary conflict or *Qual* of Hegelian thinking may be understood as an ultimate struggle or war with a primordial nothing, a nothing which cannot become being, and cannot become being because of the ultimacy and finality of its primordial or original identity. That identity is a pure even if purely abstract identity, and even as a dialectical logic can only establish itself by reversing the primal identity of $A = A$, a dialectical movement and process can only establish itself by reversing all original or primordial identity.

So it is that the science of logic begins with the judgment that immediacy and mediation are inseparable, and the apparent opposition between them is a nullity, a nullity which is the actuality of consciousness itself. That nullity is the reversal of a primordial nothing, so that nothing itself is now inseparable from being, a nothing which has now ceased to be an abstract nothing. But that perishing is not a simple perishing or annihilation, it is far rather the preservation and transcendence of a primordial nothing in an actual nothing which is united with being. At no point is the *Science of Logic* more original than in its creation of the purely logical category of an actual nothing, a nothing which is the consequence of an original negation or sublation. Nor is this category confined to the beginning of the *Science of Logic,* it occurs throughout the movement of pure logic, as we can see in Hegel's definition of essence. Essence is the absolute negativity of being, but is the absolute negativity of being only insofar as being itself has negated itself both as immediate being and also as immediate negation, or a negation that is infested with "otherness." It is the perishing of that otherness which is the realization of essence, but that perishing is a real perishing, and is real precisely as the negativity of being. Now being itself becomes illusory being (*Schein*), and the being of illusory being consists solely in its nothingness. Yet this nothingness is its essence, for now being is the negative posited as negative (II, One, 1). Nowhere else can we see more clearly how Hegel has transformed metaphysics into a purely dialectical logic, so that both being and nothing lose every metaphysical identity which is given them, but that loss or ending is a necessary and essential realization of metaphysical thinking itself.

Thus a truly negative nothing is an affirmative or positive nothing, and if this appears to that consciousness which is rooted in the abstraction of the understanding (*Verstand*) as the acme of paradox, that is the very abstract thinking to which genesis or the beginning is incomprehensible, and incomprehensible because here being is absolutely separated from nothing. Dialectic is the higher movement of reason (*Vernunft*), in which seemingly utterly separate or opposite categories spontaneously pass over into each other; and this is a purely immanent dialectic in which opposites realize their unity, and thereby cease to be opposites as such. The Hegelian *coincidentia oppositorum* is an identity of the opposites, and a real and actual identity, unlike its Buddhist counterpart. Now being *is* nothing, even as nothing *is* being, and that "isness" is the very actuality of beginning. No such beginning is possible in Buddhism, nor in any dialectic which simply identifies "is" and "is not"; for therein an affirmative nothing is impossible, and impossible because such a dialectic forecloses the possibility of an actual negation. It was Hegel and Hegel alone who established both the logical and the philosophical possibility of an actual negation, an actual negation which initially is genesis or the beginning, and finally is that total negation which is all in all.

Yet here a deep and ultimate problem presents itself, for if ending is beginning, in what sense is it beginning? Buddhism can know beginning and ending as simply identical, just as Buddhism can know the past and the future as identical, and identical because all time is finally an empty time, even as all space is finally an empty space whose center is everywhere just as its circumference is nowhere. That is a time and space which precludes the possibility of beginning, or of an actual beginning, even as it precludes the possibility of an actual ending. Is Hegel's dialectical logic finally identical with a Buddhist dialectical logic, and is that identity made manifest in Hegel's persistent choice of the circle as the primary image of the movement of logic or pure thinking? And if this is a circle in which the end is the beginning, is it not thereby the primordial cycle of eternal return, a cycle which finally annuls the actuality of its evanescent points or moments? Is it Hegel rather than Nietzsche who is the first modern philosopher of eternal return, so that the absolute liberation which the conclusion of the *Science of Logic* proclaims is a liberation from the irreversibility of time? And is that freedom which is a constant motif of the science of logic finally a freedom in which the individual simply is the universal or a freedom which simply reveals the truth or necessity of destiny? If no thinker other than Nietzsche has so passionately struggled with a primordial nothing, does that struggle finally issue in capitulation, and a capitulation to that original nothing which is all in all?

To judge Hegel to be a pagan thinker, and finally a purely pagan thinker, is to engage in just this judgment. For this is to reach the judgment that the Biblical God is finally absent from Hegel's system, and wholly absent from a purely Hegelian thinking, and absent if only because that thinking is a purely circular thinking, and thus is finally closed to either the possibility or the actuality of a real genesis and a real apocalypse. While Christian Neoplatonic thinking has often identified genesis and apocalypse, it has not always done so, as witness Augustine, and never has that thinking realized anything approaching the purity and finality of that identification in the *Science of Logic*. Fortunately or unfortunately, however, the *Science of Logic* is not wholly clear at this point, and unclear because of the elusive identity therein of both God and *Trieb*. If the content of the science of logic is the exposition of God as He is in His eternal essence before the creation, and if that content is identical with its method, is the science of logic finally a logic of that primordial nothing before and apart from the creation? No, it must be insisted, if only because such a judgment would preclude the possibility of a truly Hegelian negation, a negation which is the very essence and center of the science of logic. So likewise, *Trieb* must be absent, and wholly absent, in a primordial nothing; and if that absence is the absence of creation, that is an absence which is the absence of the science of logic, for then there would be no possibility of an advance or forward movement.

Now if a forward movement is absolutely essential to a Hegelian science of logic, what if the advance of the science of logic is quite simply the return to the ground, and an eternal return to an original ground? And if absolute actuality is the absolute as such, and if pure reflection is the return of the absolute into itself, is not pure reflection quite simply an eternal return, and the return of the absolute to itself and to itself alone? Is the Hegelian absolute a flight of the alone to the alone? No, because the Hegelian absolute is not alone, just as the Hegelian infinite is not alone; it is only the "bad infinite" which is only itself, for the true infinite and the true finite are essentially united. The absolute Idea or Notion is everything, and its movement is the universal absolute activity, an activity which is both a consequence and an embodiment of *Trieb,* and of that *Trieb* which is the sole and absolute force of pure reason. That is a force which is present throughout all life and activity, just as that is the force which dawns in the beginning, a beginning which would be impossible apart from *Trieb,* even as beginning itself is impossible apart from the absolute Idea or Notion. Thus the necessity of that beginning is inseparable from the necessity of absolute spirit or the Hegelian absolute, and hence the return of that absolute into itself is not a return to a primordial nothing, but rather a return to absolute beginning, and to the absolute necessity of that beginning, a necessity which is inseparable from the necessity of absolute spirit itself.

If there is nothing at all, nothing in heaven or in nature or in mind, which does not equally contain both immediacy and mediation, then a primordial nothing is truly and only a nullity. So likewise a God who truly and ultimately *is* before or apart from the creation is equally a nullity, and it is precisely because Hegel is an "atheist" that he is not and cannot be judged to be a pagan. A paganism which is innocent of the Biblical God is innocent of the Creator, a once-and-for-all Creator who "is" God, and is God just because God is the Creator. Paganism, in this perspective, is a celebration and affirmation of a primordial nothing or totality, a totality which is wholly on the yonder side of the creation, and thus a totality which is not and cannot be the creation. An absolute and once-and-for-all beginning is wholly alien to paganism, and even as such a beginning is wholly absent from all non-Biblical worlds, it is wholly absent from every God or absolute which is not the Creator.

Augustine himself forbade the question of the identity of God before the creation, and this is because this is a question which is foreclosed to one who has heard the self-revelation of the Creator. For that revelation, even as the creation itself, brings an end to a primordial emptiness or totality, an ending which is the ending of an undifferentiated or original totality. The Biblical name of I AM is simply unspeakable in the horizon of that totality, and unspeakable because that totality is closed to the very possibility of a once-and-for-all creation, and is so closed because that totality could not possibly or actually begin.

The Hegel who knows the deep nullity of that God who is eternally prior to or infinitely apart from the creation is the Hegel who precisely thereby essentially knows and thereby affirms the uniquely Christian Creator, or that Creator who *is* creator only by absolute nullification of every primordial ground, so that Hegel is an "atheist" only by way of a uniquely Christian thinking. That is the very nullity which unveils the ultimate nullity of a primordial emptiness or nothingness, and if a realization of that nullity impels an apprehension of an actual nothing, that actual nothing is the consequence of the ending of an original nothingness. So it is that an actual nothing is necessarily present in the thinking of absolute beginning, an actual nothing which is a necessary consequence of that beginning, and an absolutely necessary consequence of the ending of an undifferentiated nothingness or emptiness. But that actual nothing is itself all in all, and so all in all that its very presence and actuality forecloses the possibility of a return to an undifferentiated totality or emptiness. Thus it is that the Hegelian absolute cannot return to a primordial emptiness or totality, but only to that beginning which is absolute genesis, so that an archaic or primordial return is here impossible, and impossible if only because of that *Trieb* which is the actual center of absolute spirit. Consequently, if here ending is beginning, that beginning is not an original or undifferentiated totality, not that Emptiness which is Nirvana, but rather beginning as an actual beginning, and a beginning in which the creation is fully and actually at hand.

What, then, is the Hegelian circle? It cannot be an archaic or primordial circle of return, just as it cannot be a Buddhist circle of pure emptiness, and cannot be because it cannot return to an undifferentiated totality or emptiness. The truth is that the Hegelian circle is not an empty circle, not a circle which is empty of actuality, but rather a circle which is absolute actuality itself. Therefore it is a circle which is absolute necessity, and an absolutely total necessity, a necessity which is the destiny of history itself, for it is the necessity of a fully actual consciousness, a consciousness which is the nullity of the opposition between immediacy and mediation. That "God" whose exposition is the science of logic cannot finally be identified with any form of the metaphysical God, thus that God cannot be understood in any metaphysical sense as a God wholly transcending the creation. Hence that God cannot be the God who is God and only God, but rather that God whose actuality is inseparable from and finally identical with actuality itself. The Hegelian *actus purus* is finally and wholly a non-metaphysical actuality, for it is a purely immanent actuality, and as such a non-transcendent actuality, and even a non-transcendent actuality when it is apprehended in its eternal essence "before" the beginning or the creation. That "before" cannot be a metaphysical before, not a metaphysical transcendence, even if it is a truly logical transcendence. For there is no actuality whatsoever which is truly or finally other than the actuality of world or creation, so that there is not and cannot be an eternal circle of divine activity and life which is truly or finally other than that actuality which is present and real in the full actuality of consciousness itself.

Now even if there is no direct exposition of the "death of God" in the *Science of Logic,* every movement of this exposition is an abstract embodiment of that "death." Not only does a metaphysical transcendence here disappear, but every trace of a truly and finally transcendent God has vanished, and that vanishing is the realization of a pure and total immanence. This is a purely abstract form of that total immanence that Nietzsche will enact in his proclamation of Eternal Recurrence, and even as that eternal recurrence is the very opposite of a primordial eternal return, and is so if only because of its celebration and exaltation of a present and actual moment, the Hegelian circle is the opposite of a primordial or Buddhist circle. Nor is it the opposite of that circle in a Hegelian sense, for there can be no identity of these opposites; or, if so, only in the sense that the Hegelian circle can only be the consequence of the disappearance of a primordial circle, and that disappearance is a real and actual disappearance. Here, all purely and totally abstract identity wholly vanishes, and vanishes in the very union of immediacy and mediation. But that vanishing is the vanishing of a primordial emptiness or an original and undifferentiated totality, a vanishing of an eternal now which is a wholly and finally transcendent now. That vanishing is the "death of God," but a death of God which is now pure act or pure and absolute actuality, as the eternal act or *actus* of God is now a wholly immanent and therefore a totally present actuality.

Yet this realization even deepens the problem of the identity of a Hegelian or purely logical beginning. Although Hegel can conclude the initial essay in the *Science of Logic* on "With What Must the Science Begin?" with the remark that God has the absolutely undisputed right that the beginning be made with Him, this is immediately followed by an insistence that in the science of logic the absolute or God is in the beginning "only an empty word." That empty word is realized in the very beginning of thinking, a thinking that knows "only being," and therefore the content of that thinking is only an empty or inactual word. Thus actuality "begins" with the emptiness of a being which is "only being," and even if this emptiness embodies an actual potentiality for *Dasein* or world, it nevertheless is an actual emptiness, and an actual emptiness which will resolve itself into that being which *is* nothing. Accordingly, this is a "beginning" which is the beginning of bare immediacy, and even if that is a mediated immediacy, and mediated by an empty if actual consciousness, beginning itself and even absolute beginning or genesis is the beginning of an actual emptiness.

Nevertheless, that actual emptiness is infinitely other than an inactual or primordial emptiness, and infinitely other in a strictly non-Hegelian sense, for Hegelian language cannot speak of a primordial or an inactual emptiness. A purely inactual emptiness is an absolutely silent emptiness, thus it cannot as such pass into speech, nor can it be a ground of actual consciousness or world. Creation out of nothing therefore cannot be creation out of a primordial void, but far rather creation out of an actual emptiness, an actual emptiness or an actual nothingness which is that nothingness when God is "only word." This is that nothingness when nothing *is* being, and if this is a "moment" in the life and activity of absolute spirit, that is a moment which by a purely logical necessity is a moment of immanent transition of opposites into each other. Now nothing *is* being, and even if it is "only being," and an "only being" which is an actual nothingness, that nothingness is actual, and therefore it is truly wholly other than a purely inactual or empty totality. This is the one and only pure or absolute transcendence which is present in Hegelian thinking, and even if it is an invisible and silent transcendence, and silent and invisible because it cannot pass into actual language or actual thinking, it is nevertheless a transcendence which occurs in Hegelian language and thinking, and occurs precisely because that thinking is a totally mediated thinking.

Hegelian thinking, however, is not only a logically mediated thinking, it is also and necessarily so a historically mediated thinking. Indeed, it is only Hegelian thinking which is logical and historical at once, and purely logical and purely historical at once, a thinking which is finally the full coincidence of the science of logic and the phenomenology of spirit. So it is that the Hegelian "beginning" has both a logical and a historical ground, and not only a historical ground but a historical genesis, and that genesis is the historical realization of the death of God in the modern world. Only that genesis made possible the manifestation of that God who is "only word," or the actualization of that being which *is* nothing, an actualization which is the realization of an actual nothing.

While pure thinking had never previously known or realized such an actualization, when it occurs in the *Science of Logic,* it occurs through a purely logical necessity, but a logical necessity that had never earlier been possible or real. Yet now it is so real as to be irresistible, and not only irresistible but irrevocable, an irrevocability which is an embodiment of a uniquely modern consciousness, and a uniquely modern consciousness which is an embodiment of the death of God. While that consciousness is first fully realized in the *Phenomenology of Spirit,* it only realizes a purely logical embodiment in the *Science of Logic,* a science of logic which is the logical realization of the phenomenology of spirit, and therefore a logical realization of the death of God. Hence we must inevitably ask if the birth of a uniquely Hegelian immanence is itself a consequence of the death of the transcendence of God?

Hegelian transcendence is a purely immanent transcendence, and it is a purely dialectical transcendence precisely for that reason, and a transcendence which is fully actual in the uniquely Hegelian movement of pure negation. That is the transcendence which dawns "in the beginning," and it dawns as the actual negation of a pure inactuality, an actual negation realizing an actual nothingness, and an actual nothingness which is the first "moment" of creation. While that moment is "only being," and an only being which is nothing, that is the nothingness which is the advent of world itself, and the advent of that world which is the creation of God. But it is the creation of God just because it is the absence of the pure transcendence of God, an absence which occurs when God is "only being," and only that being which is nothing. Only the abandonment or the negation of the transcendence of God makes possible the creation of the world, a creation which is the self-embodiment of God, or the self-embodiment of the pure immanence of God, an immanence which is the self-embodiment or the self-emptying of the pure transcendence of God. Not only is a metaphysically or religious transcendent God absent from the *Science of Logic*, but that absence is absolutely necessary for the very movement of the science of logic, a movement that is most clearly manifest in its initial expression. For the beginning of the science of logic is the beginning of a pure immanence, a pure immanence without even a shadow of pure transcendence, so that it can even be manifest and real as a being which is nothing. Now, an actual beginning is the beginning of an actuality in which "God" is dead, this and this alone is genesis or absolute beginning, an absolute beginning which is the beginning of an absolute immanence.

It is in the *Science of Logic* and the *Science of Logic* alone that we may discover a purely logical realization of genesis, and if that is a logical realization which is the realization of pure immanence, that is an immanence which does begin, and it begins in that actual nothing which is the first moment of the absolute Idea or Notion, just as it ends in the full actualization of absolute spirit, an actualization which is the final liberation of all and everything. That liberation is apocalypse itself, and yet it is a totally immanent apocalypse, and thus it is an apocalypse which can begin as an actual nothingness. For that actual nothingness is on the way to apocalypse, and even if this is only the initial moment of that way, it is the beginning and the absolutely necessary beginning of an irreversible and irrevocable process culminating in apocalypse. But it can culminate in a totally immanent apocalypse only because it can and does begin as an actual and immanent nothingness. Nothing is or could be more important than that nothingness, for it alone makes possible and real an absolutely immanent actualization. Now even if that beginning is an eternal beginning, it is an eternally actual beginning, and a beginning which is renewed in every actual moment. So that is a beginning which eternally recurs, and eternally recurs in that circle returning upon itself, a circle in which the end is the beginning.

But if an actual beginning and an actual ending are finally inseparable and indistinguishable, they are so only as a forward-moving beginning and ending, a forward movement which is the very reversal of the backward movement of a primordial eternal return, a reversal which is the advent of genesis or creation. That advent is the advent of *Trieb,* a *Trieb* which is a forward-moving drive and impulse, and a *Trieb* foreclosing the possibility of a pure and inactual emptiness. That *Trieb* is the very center of absolute spirit, even as it is the center of a pure and absolute negation, thus that negation is a forward-moving negation, and even forward moving when it realizes that end which is the beginning. Accordingly, that beginning cannot be only a once-and-for-all beginning, as Hegel explicitly declares in the third part of the lectures on the philosophy of religion, at the beginning of the section on "The Idea of God In and For Itself." Yet even if it is an eternally recurring beginning, it is nevertheless an actual beginning, and therefore is wholly other than the beginning of the primordial cycle of eternal return. For this is the beginning of *Trieb* itself, and the absolute beginning of that absolute which is *Trieb,* and if this is the beginning of an eternally forward circle of return, it is also and necessarily so the absolute beginning of the purely logical and totally immanent God. Is it then the genesis of God, and the genesis of the uniquely Christian God, that God who is the consequence of the "death" of God, and that God who is and only is an absolute actuality?

2

HEGEL AND
THE CHRISTIAN GOD

If Hegel is our only philosopher who has attempted, and perhaps even realized, a purely philosophical understanding of the Christian God, that was a project that was never possible in the era of Christendom, and impossible therein because that world was so profoundly grounded in the Classical world, hence its philosophical thinking was inevitably Classical and Christian at once. Only nominalism truly and finally challenged that union, but nominalism was itself a primary seed and ground of those forces which finally effected a disintegration of Christendom, a disintegration which is virtually complete with the occurrence of the French Revolution. Even if theologians as early as Tertullian challenged the union of Athens and Jerusalem, that is a challenge which is never realized until the disruption of Christendom, then occurring most decisively in Luther. For even the purest Christian philosopher of Christendom, Augustine, could not escape a Neoplatonic ground, and Aquinas could renew Christian philosophy only by embodying a new Aristotelianism, an Aristotelianism that itself was mediated to the Christian world through Judaism and Islam. While Nietzsche could judge every Western expression of thinking to be a disguised form of theological thinking, and is so if only because every Western conception of Being is finally a conception of God, Nietzsche's own proclamation of the death of God is the consummation of Western philosophical thinking as a whole, and hence at this crucial point it is in full continuity with Hegelian thinking. Thus we confront the paradox that a purely Hegelian thinking is at once a pure negation of the Christian God and yet an intended realization of what faith knows as the innermost life of God, a life which *is* death, for it is the ultimate sacrifice of an actual totality of love, and nevertheless that death or crucifixion is resurrection, and is the resurrection of a totality which is God and world or actuality at once.

Now it is vitally important to realize that Hegel was the first and perhaps only philosopher to center his thinking upon crucifixion and resurrection, the fact that this never occurred within the historical world of Christendom is itself an all too significant sign of the non-Christian ground of that world. If such thinking is possible only after the end of Christendom, it may well be that a uniquely Christian theology is possible only as a consequence of the historical realization of the death of God, a realization which is absolutely fundamental to the thinking of Hegel and Nietzsche alike. While Kierkegaard is the purest Christian thinker in the modern world, no thinking is more deeply grounded in the end of Christendom than is Kierkegaardian thinking, for that thinking is a Hegelian thinking, even if a reverse Hegelian thinking, and even as Hegelian thinking it is grounded in the Incarnation as the absolute center of thinking and history at once. Hegel's Christian thinking is simultaneously a deeply historical and a deeply logical thinking, and while his interpreters have only begun to unite the *Phenomenology of Spirit* and the *Science of Logic,* there can be no doubt that this union is fundamental to a purely Hegelian thinking, and at no other point is Hegelian thinking so unique in the history of world philosophical thinking. A uniquely Hegelian negation or sublation (*Aufhebung*) is logical and historical simultaneously, and if that is a *coincidentia oppositorum,* it is an identity of those opposites which have been most estranged and other than each other in the world of late modernity.

The *Science of Logic* presents the appearance of being a purely non-historical work, but that is an illusion, and it is an illusion first because it so clearly could only have been written in the modern world. Moreover, Hegel himself again and again in the *Science of Logic* correlates the science of logic and the phenomenology of spirit, a correlation which is an essential correlation, and an essential correlation above all because of the absolute primacy here of pure negation. Finally, the methods of the phenomenology of spirit and the science of logic are identical, differing only insofar as they occur in all too different realms or worlds. But those worlds themselves are finally identical, and identical if only because absolute spirit is one spirit, and its very life or movement is a pure negation which ultimately is one negation, a negation that is a total negation which is all and everything. Hegel was not only the first true philosopher of history, but his is a philosophy that is comprehensively historical, and not least so in the *Science of Logic,* a science of logic whose every movement and development is finally historical. For it moves from the first moment of thinking and of life until a full and final apocalypse, an apocalypse which is not only the totality of a purely logical thinking but the totality of an implicit and necessary historical consciousness as well. So it is that both the beginning and the ending of the *Science of Logic* and the *Phenomenology of Spirit* are in full correlation with each other, and that is the beginning and ending of a forward and historical evolution of consciousness, an evolution that has actually occurred historically, and yet an evolution that logically is absolutely necessary and inevitable.

But this evolutionary enactment is also and necessarily so an enactment of the evolution of God, most clearly so in the *Phenomenology of Spirit,* but no less so in the *Science of Logic,* as absolute spirit evolves from pure immediacy to total actuality, an evolution that is the movement of absolute Idea or Notion, and a movement that is the consequence of *Trieb,* a *Trieb* or primal urge that is the innermost center of absolute spirit. If only because the phenomenology of spirit is the realization of a historically manifest expression of spirit, here *Trieb* is explicitly *kenosis,* a kenosis or self-emptying which is an "externalization" of spirit itself. It is in the very depths of history itself that spirit abandons the form of substance and becomes "subject," an abandonment which is the death of God, and a death of God which is the consummation of spirit's emptying itself into time and space. That emptying is fully actual even if abstract in the *Science of Logic,* and it occurs already at the beginning of that science, where Hegel can declare that at the end of the development of absolute spirit, absolute spirit is known as freely "externalizing" itself, abandoning itself to the form of an immediate being. That abandonment or kenosis is itself the negation of negation, a negation in which the infinite becomes finite, thereby finally realizing concrete totality, and a concrete totality which is the totality of life. But the absolute is also itself in and as the objective world, here its "other" is its own objectivity, an objectivity which is realized both in nature and in spirit. For "nature" and "spirit" are simply different modes of realizing the life and activity of spirit, just as art, religion, and philosophy are simply different modes whereby spirit apprehends itself. Accordingly, at the opening of the final chapter of the *Science of Logic,* on the absolute Idea, Hegel can say that logic exhibits the self-movement of the absolute Idea only as the original *word,* a word which is an *outwardizing* or *utterance (Äusserung),* but an utterance or expression that in being so expressed immediately vanishes as something outer (*Äusseres*). That vanishing *is* the realization of kenosis or self-emptying, a *kenosis* which is *Trieb,* and thereby is absolute negativity.

Now even if the movement of the science of logic is the movement of that pure absolute which Hegel identifies as the eternal essence of God before the creation, and thus is a purely abstract movement, it is nonetheless an actual movement, and an actual movement which *is* the movement of self-emptying. Indeed, the actuality of self-emptying is actuality itself, and even if a purely logical self-emptying is not a historically manifest self-emptying, it is in full correlation with that self-emptying which is the domain of the phenomenology of spirit, and finally neither is fully real or actual apart from the other. So it is that the original *word* of the science of logic is a kenotic or self-emptying word, which in emptying itself immediately vanishes as something outer or "other," and *is* itself in that very vanishing, a vanishing which is its own life and movement, and a life which is *Trieb* or *kenosis.* This is that absolute life which the *Phenomenology of Spirit* knows as realizing itself in spirit's abandoning the form of substance and becoming "subject." But, in the *Science of Logic,* that deep destiny of spirit is present in the beginning, and not only present in the beginning, but present as the beginning, a beginning which is simultaneously the beginning and the ending of movement and life. Hence it is the beginning and ending of absolute spirit or "God," a God who is actual only insofar as God "begins," and a God whose beginning is beginning and ending at once.

There can be no doubt that Hegel intends the kenosis of the *Phenomenology of Spirit* to be a purely philosophical realization of what faith knows as crucifixion and resurrection. While in the *Science of Logic* that kenosis is realized in a purely abstract form of actuality, that actuality is an "abandonment" of itself, therein and thereby it is a self-negation, and a self-negation which is a negation of negation. Faith knows the negation of negation as the crucifixion or the death of God, and even if that negation is an abstract negation in the science of logic, it is the very center of that science, just as it is the deepest ground of a purely Hegelian thinking. If that thinking is a thinking of what the Christian faith knows as God, as Hegel again and again declares, and if Hegel can so forcefully and so continually identify the Christian religion as the absolute religion, that is because he understands Christianity as the fullest manifest expression and realization of absolute spirit itself. This is that absolute spirit which is finally the sole content and movement both of the phenomenology of spirit and of the science of logic, which is to say that this content and movement is finally and solely the Christian God. And if this is our only philosophical thinking which knows God only as the Christian God, this is that God who is *only* self-emptying or self-negation, and therefore cannot be the God who is *only* God, or the God who is and only is an absolutely transcendent impassivity, or an absolutely sovereign majesty. The God who can, indeed, be known as being "in-itself" (*an sich*), can only actually be so known by the negative movement of God's being "for-itself" (*für sich*), and that is a self-negating or self-emptying movement: a movement in which spirit realizes itself as subject only by abandoning itself as substance, and that itself is the life or movement of *Trieb* or *kenosis*.

But if the God who is "in-itself" is finally illusory and unreal apart from the God who is "for-itself," theologically that can only mean that the God who is the absolutely transcendent God is finally illusory and unreal apart from the Crucified God, just as the power and the majesty of God are finally unreal apart from the love of God. Therefore the Christian affirmation that God *is* love is inseparable from the uniquely Christian confession of the passion and the death of God. If that death is ultimately resurrection, it is so only through the final ending of the God who is God and only God, or the God who is simply and only "Being in-itself."

The *Science of Logic* knows the God who is only God as the "bad infinite," the infinite that cannot become finite, and if that is the purely and only abstract God, that abstraction is an empty or vanishing abstraction, and is so immediately in the very movement of absolute spirit. Thus there is not and cannot be a God who is only "in-itself," or a God who is *only* God, and this because God is a "living God," a God who cannot finally be solitary and alone, and cannot be so alone precisely because God is God. But God *is* God only by not being only God, only by not being pure transcendence, and that self-negation is present and real in every act or actualization of God. So it is that this ultimate self-negation is just as fully present in the creation as it is in the crucifixion, a creation which is the ending of a purely transcendent transcendence, just as the crucifixion is the ending of a purely religious transcendence. Neither a religious nor a purely metaphysical transcendence is present as such in the science of logic, and if they do become present or manifest in the phenomenology of spirit, this is a presence which is finally an absence. For here their actualization is inseparable from their negation, a negation which is a true and actual reversal of abstract spirit or the "bad infinite."

The God who is God only by not being God is a uniquely Christian identity of God, and even if that God is seemingly absent from Christian scholasticism, it is not so when that scholasticism undergoes its own reversal with the advent of nominalism and a uniquely Christian mysticism. Clearly, the Godhead of Meister Eckhart is a Godhead which is not God, or not only God, and just as Eckhart is one of Hegel's deeper sources or grounds, Hegel's absolute spirit may be understood as a purely conceptual realization of Eckhart's Godhead. Unfortunately, Hegel had little interest in or knowledge of medieval philosophy, even as he was largely ignorant of medieval culture. He was far more fascinated by the Oriental world than by the medieval Western world, for he could know the Oriental world as the antithesis of the Occidental world. That antithesis, for Hegel, is most purely present in Hinduism; for he could know the highest point of Hinduism as a detached contemplation of Brahman wholly for itself, a contemplation which comes into existence only in a deep absorption in nothing, an absorption which is the consequence of a wholly empty consciousness and intuition. Yet that absorption effects a transition wherein the subject becomes identical with Brahman, and a unity is realized which is grasped as totality itself.

While that totality wholly transcends all subjective self-consciousness, it nevertheless initiates a genuine independence, an independence realizing a separation of empirical self-consciousness from absolute self-consciousness, as Hegel declares in the section on Hinduism in the lectures on the philosophy of religion. Here, God attains true objectivity for the first time, and only now does the break between objectivity and subjectivity begin. Now God is truly and intrinsically objective, for God is "essentially object" and therefore is altogether in opposition to human beings. Our reconciliation and return from that abstract yet objective power occurs only in the Incarnation, for true incarnation is the abandonment of all intrinsic objectivity or substance, an abandonment ending the possibility of that submergence in unconsciousness which Hegel knows as a union with Brahman-Atman or Nirvana.

Hegel could know that Oriental union as the antithesis of the uniquely Christian union with God, nevertheless he could know it as a real even if abstract union, and it does initiate that break between objectivity and subjectivity which is consummated in Christianity. That consummation is the final ending of all transcendent objectivity, and now objectivity is known for the first time as the realization of subjectivity, and therefore objectivity perishes as an objectivity which is "in-itself." Such a final perishing of transcendent objectivity is the death of God, but the death of God which is the incarnation of God is historically realized only in the modern world, then it first occurs in that Unhappy Consciousness which realizes itself by losing all the essence and substance of itself, a self-consciousness that realizes itself by interiorly and individually realizing that *God Himself is dead* (*Phenomenology of Spirit* 785). This realization is the inbreathing of spirit, whereby substance becomes subject, and if thereby substance becomes actual and universal self-consciousness, that is a self-consciousness which dawns in the Incarnation, an incarnation which is the true advent of pure self-consciousness precisely because it is the ending of all objective substance. Thus true incarnation is the ending of the objective God, a God who only now can be known as the "bad infinite," an infinite which cannot become finite, and an infinite which ends and finally ends when the true infinite becomes truly finite. And if that is an incarnation effecting a reconciliation with God, it is a reconciliation which is possible and real only when God perishes as God, or perishes as that God who is only God.

The first *Zusatz* or lecture-note in the third and final part of the *Encyclopaedia of the Philosophical Sciences* insists that the aim of all genuine science is that mind shall recognize itself in everything in heaven and earth. Finally this can only be a comprehensive knowledge of mind in its absolute infinitude, an infinitude that was given the world by Christianity, for Christianity first gave to consciousness a perfectly free relationship to the infinite. Hegel can go on to declare (in the *Zusatz* to *381), that Christian theology itself conceives of God as spirit, and contemplates spirit not as something quiescent, but rather as something which necessarily enters into the process of distinguishing itself from itself, of positing its own Other, and which comes to itself only through this Other. Thus God has revealed Himself through Christ, and fully and finally only through Christ, a Christ in whom the infinite becomes finite, and it is by God's unity with the Son, "by this being-for-himself in the Other," that God is absolute spirit (*Zusatz* *383). Only Christianity knows God as absolute spirit, and thereby and therein only Christianity knows absolute freedom, an absolute freedom that is realized only by the infinite becoming finite. If Hegel was the first philosopher of religion to systematically relate Christianity to the world religions, that is a relationship in which Christianity is the absolute religion only by being the consummation of the world religions, a consummation which is the realization of absolute freedom.

There can be no doubt that Hegel's concept of absolute spirit is fully intended to be a conceptualization of the uniquely Christian God, and if such a conceptualization never previously occurred in the history of thinking, or never occurred so as to center upon the uniquely Christian God, that is a centering which is a centering upon the Incarnation, and upon that incarnation which is the death of the purely transcendent God. Here, the uniquely Christian God is fully and finally God only in that death, and even if that death is simultaneously the resurrection of God, that resurrection ends every actuality which is not at once the actuality of both the finite and the infinite, and that ending is quite simply the Hegelian apocalypse. So it is that the advent of that death and resurrection is the center of world history, and the center of consciousness as well, a consciousness which in Christianity and Christianity alone fully becomes and realizes itself as self-consciousness. That self-consciousness is finally the self-consciousness or the self-knowledge of God, for God is God insofar as God knows or realizes Himself, and that self-knowledge of God is the self-consciousness of consciousness itself, for it is our self-consciousness or self-knowledge in God (Encyclopaedia *564). Consequently, history itself is finally the history of God, a history which is theodicy, and is ultimately the theodicy of the uniquely Christian God.

Hegel may even be understood to be the first philosopher of history because he was the first philosopher to center thinking itself upon the uniquely Christian God. Therein Hegelian thinking is a rebirth of Augustinian thinking, and is so because of the primacy of self-consciousness in Hegel and Augustine alike. But Hegelian thinking is also and even thereby a fully and finally historical thinking, a historical thinking which dawns in The City of God, but is only consummated in the Phenomenology of Spirit. Then it is consummated in a pure and comprehensive thinking of kenosis, a kenosis which is the self-emptying of God, and the self-emptying of God in the Incarnation. That is the incarnation in which the finite and the infinite are fully and finally united, a union which is at once a purely essential and a purely historical union, and therefore a union releasing the totality of historical actuality. Only now does history itself dawn as a fully and finally forward-moving process, a forward-moving process inseparable from the Incarnation, and inseparable from the Incarnation if only because it is that incarnation alone which initially realizes the infinitude of finitude itself. That infinitude is the totality of history, and the totality of that history which is the evolution of God. If the forward movement of history is finally the forward movement of God, just as the forward movement of the science of logic is the forward movement of absolute spirit, that forward movement is the embodiment of the Trieb or kenosis of God. That Trieb or kenosis is God, for God is that pure or absolute negativity which is the source and ground of all life and activity, a life and activity which is finally the self-negation or the self-emptying of God. Therefore absolute spirit is the pure otherness of itself, an otherness which is most fully actual and manifest as such only in historical actuality, but that is the very actuality which Christianity and Christianity alone knows as the incarnation of God.

Again and again, and throughout his work, Hegel engages in a deep theological conflict with both pure pantheism and pure agnosticism, each of which he interprets as a simple and non-dialectical negation of the Christian God. Hegel can know pantheism, whether in Hinduism or in Spinoza, as a refusal both of the immediacy of the world and of "subject" or subjectivity itself, an immediacy and a subjectivity which perish in the One. But he could know agnosticism, or, rather, modern agnosticism, as a refusal of the deepest identity and activity of God. Perhaps his deepest wrath was directed against the theologians of his day, theologians who maintained that God Himself is finally unknowable, a dogma which Hegel insists is a refusal of the Christian God, because it is a refusal of both Christ and revelation. While Hegel always treated Kant with deep respect, and even did so at this point, he was contemptuous of theological agnosticism, just as he was contemptuous of the dominant pietism of his day, a pietism which he knew as a simple inversion of Christianity. For the very exaltation of religious feeling is a refusal of the revelation of God, just as it is a refusal of the acts of God in history; and is, indeed, a regression to a pre-Christian religious world, a world which is innocent of the Christian God. Hegel understood the theologians of his day to be engaged in just such a regression, just as he understood the Catholic Church to be a regression to paganism, and above all so because of what he knew as the scholastic God of Catholicism, a God who could not truly become incarnate.

Now even if German pietism was grounded in the Incarnation, Hegel insists that such a ground is illusory if pietism believes in the religiously transcendent God, even as he maintained that religious "belief" as such is a final barrier to pure insight, and a final barrier to pure insight into the uniquely Christian God. For it is religious belief or imaginative representation of any kind (Vorstellung) which is finally negated by the Incarnation, an incarnation which is the ending of that infinite which is only infinite, and thus finally the ending of every understanding and every consciousness which is a consciousness or understanding of the finally transcendent God. That ending is apocalypse, and an apocalypse which Hegel knows as the final ending of every infinite or beyond which is not totally present, and totally present in history or finitude itself.

Yet nothing is more elusive than the Hegel apocalypse, an apocalypse which is both the final beginning and the final ending of history itself, and an apocalypse which seemingly realizes a consummation in a purely Hegelian thinking. Hegel did not hesitate to identify his own era as the final age of the spirit, just as he reached the judgment that the absolute philosophy which now is born is the final unity of art and religion (*Encyclopaedia* *572), a unity in which the true content of art and religion is now the content of absolute philosophy. So likewise the lectures on the philosophy of history culminate with the last stage of history, a stage in which secular life is the positive and definite embodiment of the Kingdom of God, and an age which is *"our world"* and *"our own time."* Only now can it be known that world history is theodicy, and even if that theodicy realizes itself through violence and horror, that horror itself is an expression and realization of the "cunning of reason." Hegel even constructs a purely logical argument for the "cunning of reason," which is offered at the conclusion of the second section of the second volume of the *Science of Logic.* That section of the volume on subjective logic is devoted to the realized end of teleology, wherein Hegel posits the infinite progress of mediation, but that progress has a conclusion in which external purposefulness really only comes to be a means, and in the "realized end" the means vanishes, and vanishes in that concrete totality which is the absolute Idea. That absolute Idea is a purely logical conception of the Christian God, and the uniquely Christian God, a God who is declared to be "pure personality" at the conclusion of the *Science of Logic,* which solely through the absolute dialectic which is its nature embraces and holds everything whatsoever within itself.

If the conclusion of the *Science of Logic* is an apocalypse, and a Christian apocalypse, it is an apocalypse which is a circle in which the end is the beginning. But that apocalypse is also the conclusion of the *Phenomenology of Spirit,* wherein history itself is identified as spirit emptied out into time, a kenosis of itself which is that negative which is the negative of itself. History is the contingent manifestation and realization of spirit, but that contingency when known through the phenomenology of spirit can be realized as the "Calvary of absolute spirit," a crucifixion which is the full actuality of God, an actuality apart from which God would be lifeless and alone. Finally, history is apocalypse, an apocalypse which is finally crucifixion, and is that crucifixion which is the very life or resurrection of God. But if that is an apocalypse whose ending is its beginning, is that beginning the beginning of the life or resurrection of God, and therein and thereby the beginning of history itself? Indeed, are the "life" of God and the actuality of history two poles of that one absolute which is absolute negativity, a negativity which is the negation of itself, and thus a negativity which is absolute self-negation or self-emptying? History itself, by its own integral and essential identity, must have a real beginning, and an actual beginning, a beginning which is the beginning of real contingency. And that contingency must be a full or pure contingency, and therefore a contingency which is the necessary and intrinsic "other" of absolute spirit. Yet if that "other" is inseparable from absolute spirit, and apart from that "other" the Godhead itself would be lifeless and alone, then Godhead itself must begin, and contingently begin as history itself. Now even if Hegel can speak of history as the "externalization" of absolute spirit, absolute spirit would not be and could not be itself apart from that externalization, and that externalization cannot be a *maya* or *lila* as it is in Hinduism, not a mere appearance or play, but rather that "labor of the negative" apart from which God would not be God.

Hence, "God" must begin, and begin as that "other" which is the "other" of God. If Christianity alone knows that true "other" which is the "other" of God, Christianity alone knows that beginning which is the beginning of God. Thus only Christianity knows that history which is the history of God, a history with an absolute beginning and an absolute ending, and a history which is finally the history of God. But if that beginning and ending is an eternal beginning and ending, is it possible for Hegelian thinking to affirm the acts of God as real and actual acts, or as acts which are essential and contingent at once? If the pure actuality of absolute spirit is a totally immanent actuality, can or does that actuality truly begin, or is that beginning simply and only an eternally recurring or purely circular beginning? Now if absolute beginning contains mediation within itself, a crucial argument in the opening of book one of the *Science of Logic,* is it therein actually or truly other than an unmediated immediacy? For if a true negation of unmediated immediacy is absolutely necessary for absolute beginning, then that actual otherness which is a consequence of that negation is truly and essentially different from an unmediated immediacy, and that difference does reflect and even embody the vanishing shadow or echo of unmediated immediacy. So that even if Hegel can continually insist in the *Science of Logic* that there is nothing whatsoever that does not equally contain both immediacy and mediation, and that absolute immediacy is absolute mediation, that mediation cannot be actually real, even as beginning cannot be actually real, if an unmediated immediacy has so totally vanished as to be without either echo or trace. For if immediacy is always and only a mediated immediacy, then how could mediation actually begin, or how could there be an absolute beginning or genesis? Is that "other" through which beginning occurs eternally other, and eternally

35

other as the "other" of absolute spirit, so that absolute spirit always and necessarily is the otherness of itself, and therefore cannot actually begin as that otherness? Then it would follow that God "begins" only in the sense that God is eternally beginning, just as the negative movement of spirit's becoming its own "other" would be simply and only a realization of spirit's own original and eternal identity.

All of these questions are different ways of asking if the Hegelian absolute can undergo a real and actual transformation. Is a purely Hegelian negation a negation which is equally affirmation so that finally there is no real distinction between affirmation and negation? Then a Hegelian logic would be a Buddhist logic just as a Hegelian phenomenology would be an eternal as opposed to a historical phenomenology, for then there would be no real negation which is an actual negation, or an actual negation which is a real loss or perishing. There would appear to be a profound ambiguity at the very center of the Hegelian system, an ambiguity which can be given a theological formulation by asking whether or not Hegel's absolute spirit truly is the Christian God.

While Hegel clearly intended that identity, it does not follow that such an identity is actually realized in his system, or could be realized in any such system. Even more concretely, one could ask if the Hegelian death of God is truly a philosophical conceptualization of the Crucifixion, or is it a conceptualization of an eternally recurring ending which is an eternally recurring beginning? For if the ending of crucifixion is an eternally circular ending, the crucifixion would be an eternally recurring event, just as the creation would be an eternally recurring event. Then neither event would be a once-and-for-all event, or an event which is the unique act of God, and only act at all in the sense that it is an eternally recurring act. Perhaps Hegel's real distinction in a Christian perspective is that he was the first purely pagan thinker in Christendom, and so pagan that he could employ a uniquely Christian language as a primary way of realizing a purely and totally non-Christian identity. Yet that judgment also entails the judgment that Hegelian historical thinking is either pre-historical or post-historical thinking, or perhaps a thinking so purely ahistorical that it is pre-historical and post-historical at once. And if the historical as such has a profoundly ambivalent or elusive identity in Hegelian thinking, that is an elusiveness that is inseparable from the question of the Christian identity of the Hegelian absolute.

Nevertheless, Hegelian thinking, even as all truly modern thinking, is such a profound challenge to Christian theological thinking that in its wake Christian theology as such has no assured or solid ground, apart from a pre-modern orthodoxy, and that is precisely the orthodoxy which has either collapsed or been wholly transformed in the modern world. Moreover, it is Hegelian thinking and its Kierkegaardian embodiment which has initiated theology into the ultimacy of the Incarnation, an Incarnation which is Crucifixion, and a Crucifixion which is Crucifixion and Resurrection at once. Indeed, it is only in the wake of Hegelian thinking that Christian thinking has become historical thinking, or that the Bible itself became manifest and real to theological thinking as a truly or fully historical revelation. That modern theology which was born in the nineteenth century was truly revolutionary at each of these points, or, at least, potentially so. Yet the most powerful Christian theologians of the twentieth century, Barth, Bultmann, Tillich, and Rahner, are all profoundly ahistorical theologians, each of whom engaged in a deep negation of Hegelian thinking, and each of whom finally affirmed a purely non-Hegelian God. The same might well be said of the major Jewish thinkers of the twentieth century, Rosenzweig, Buber, Levinas, and Derrida; so that one could characterize modern theology as a whole as a profoundly anti-Hegelian thinking. But the truth is that it is thereby a profoundly anti-modern thinking, and if it was Hegel who gave birth to a uniquely modern theological thinking, an anti-Hegelian theological thinking is inevitably an anti-modern theological thinking.

Thus wholly absent from such anti-modern theological thinking, with the profound exception of Kierkegaard himself, is a true theological affirmation of a Hegelian *Trieb* or *kenosis*, and if that is the most distinctively Christian ground of Hegel's system, that is also the ultimate source and ground of a purely Hegelian negation. While opposites may well be identical in Hegel's system, they are identical as real opposites, and as opposites which are realizations of their own inherent otherness. Opposition itself is deeply present in the Hegelian absolute, an opposition which is an absolute opposition, and an opposition apart from which absolute spirit would be lifeless and alone. As Hinduism and Buddhism so fully demonstrate, it would be "world" itself which would be absent apart from the self-negation of absolute spirit. For if world itself is truly actual and real, its ultimate ground cannot be a pure passivity or an inactual emptiness, but rather a ground which itself is absolute "life" or activity. Nothing is a deeper mystery in the question of God than the nature and identity of that absolute activity or actuality, and while Hegel could follow Spinoza in knowing that actuality as that one substance which is finally an indivisible totality, he profoundly differed from Spinoza in knowing that substance as an absolute self-negation or self-emptying. Only thereby is that substance truly "subject," and at no other point is there a deeper difference between Hegel and Spinoza, or between Hegelian thinking itself and the philosophical thinking which preceded it. And if Spinoza and Hegel are the deepest idealistic thinkers in the West, and also those thinkers who have created the purest Western systems of thinking, they are also those thinkers who are our purest theological thinkers, and the only ones who have given us total conceptions or totally comprehensive conceptions of God.

The question of the identity of God is perhaps the deepest question posed by Hegel's system, and that question is also the question of the presence or absence in that system of the uniquely Christian God, and, more specifically, the question of the presence or absence therein of the Crucified God. Clearly, this question cannot even be asked of Spinoza, and even if Spinoza and Hegel alike deeply affirm the absolute love of God, just as each affirms the absolute providence of God, Spinoza's God can in no way be associated either with death or with evil. But Hegel's God is a God who from the beginning becomes alienated from itself, therein withdrawing into itself and becoming "self-centered"; and this "evil existence" is not in itself alien to God, but rather essential to the very identity of God as God (*Phenomenology of Spirit,* 780). This is that purely negative movement of God which realizes that God who is "being-in-itself," a negative movement which is absolutely necessary to make possible the death of God. And that is the death which reconciles absolute essence with itself, a reconciliation which is the death of the purely alienated or the purely abstract God (*Phenomenology of Spirit,* 779). The conclusion of the *Science of Logic* knows that death as absolute liberation, a death which is the Calvary of absolute spirit, and a Calvary apart from which God would be only that purely abstract spirit which Hegel can discover in Hinduism and Spinoza alike.

Only the death of God is the full realization or actualization of absolute spirit, and that death is absolutely necessary and essential to an absolute spirit which realizes itself as its own "other." That is the very otherness which is the full opposite of every non-Christian apprehension of the identity of God, so that nothing is more uniquely Christian than an affirmation of such an otherness. This is clearly present in Hegel, and more decisively present in Hegel than in any other thinker except Nietzsche, and if Nietzsche and Hegel are those thinkers who most purely know the death of God, they are also those thinkers who most decisively know the uniquely Christian God. Perhaps nothing could offer more conclusive evidence of the absolute antithesis between Christianity and philosophy itself. Yet Hegel and Nietzsche are also our only philosophers who are philosophical and historical thinkers at once, and each realized a profound historical thinking that is a consequence of the death of God. Each thinker knew that death as a historically actual death which fully inaugurated modernity itself, just as each thinker knew historical actuality itself as an absolute self-alienation or self-estrangement, and a self-estrangement which is the self-alienation of the very center or subject of consciousness itself. It is the absolute reversal of that self-alienation which Nietzsche celebrates as the eternal dance of Eternal Recurrence, just as it is also such a reversal which Hegel knows as the eternal return of absolute spirit, an eternal return which is the actual embodiment of the *Trieb* or *kenosis* of absolute spirit.

That *Trieb* or *kenosis* is the ultimate ground of actuality, including most certainly historical actuality, and it is only the realization of that ultimate ground which makes possible the apprehension of a purely historical actuality, an ultimate contingency that is impossible apart from an ultimate self-negation or self-emptying. So it is that pure contingency does not appear and become real in consciousness until the historical realization of the death of God, for pure contingency as such is impossible apart from an ultimate ground, and impossible apart from the self-emptying or self-negation of that ground. Thus it is precisely because both Hegel and Nietzsche could so deeply know the death of God that they could so profoundly know a historical contingency. While only Hegel could know that contingency as absolute necessity, that is because only Hegel could know actuality itself as the actuality of God. The Hegelian system is truly an empty system if it is empty of God, and empty if it is empty of the Crucified God. Only that death is the ground of a purely immanent consciousness and actuality, and if this is true of Hegel and Nietzsche alike, for each knew an actuality which is finally empty of all metaphysical and religious transcendence. That is an actuality which is an embodiment of the death of God. That death is absolute liberation, and is so for both Nietzsche and Hegel, but only Hegel knows that liberation as the liberation of God. For only that death reconciles the Godhead of God with its own otherness, an otherness that is a real and actual otherness, and an otherness whose very negation is an absolute liberation realizing an absolute freedom, and a freedom which Hegel could know as a freedom inaugurated by the Incarnation.

Hegel alone conceptually knows the atonement as the atonement of God with God, as the atonement of the inactive and abstract God which is "in-itself" with the totally active and embodied God which is "for-itself."

This occurs only through the death of that abstract God itself, a death which is crucifixion, yes, but which is also the resurrection of concrete totality into absolute freedom. Here, crucifixion is resurrection, an identity which is first proclaimed in Paul and the Fourth Gospel, and thus an identity which is at the very center of an original Christianity, but an identity which was not fully realized theologically until Hegel. And it was realized by Hegel only by way of a passage through the death of God, a passage which is a passage into the very depths of God, depths which are nothing less than the kenosis or self-emptying of the Godhead, and depths which release that Godhead into the "otherness" of Godhead itself. That otherness certainly comprehends historical actuality, and a totally imma-nent historical actuality; indeed, a historical actuality which truly becomes or realizes itself only as a consequence of that death. Thus the death of God is the center of history, and the center of that total history which is the evolution of freedom and of life. But that center is also the center of a purely logical or a purely conceptual thinking, a thinking which advances only by negating or emptying itself. So it is that the method of that thinking is a pure and actual negation, a pure negation or a pure negativity which is the movement and activity of absolute spirit itself. While that absolute spirit is absolute immediacy and absolute mediation at once, it is so only as an embodiment of that primal urge or *Trieb* which is its innermost nature. Now if that *Trieb* or *kenosis* is illusory, then so likewise is the Hegelian system as a whole; for then self-negation would not be an ultimate and absolute movement, and the Hegelian system would unveil itself as being a system of that purely abstract spirit which Hegel himself, and even in the *Science of Logic,* could identify as "Evil" (I, One, 3, c).

Hegel could know an ultimate affirmation of purely abstract spirit as the supreme and most stubborn error, and that is an affirmation which he knew as comprehending Brahman-Atman, Spinoza's substance, and the God of Christian scholasticism. For that is a Godhead which is absolutely inactive and quiescent, and a Godhead which Hegel knew as being realized only by way of a regressive withdrawal from life. Nietzsche could know that withdrawal as *ressentiment,* a *ressentiment* which is the source of what Nietzsche knew as the Christian God, a God who is the very deification of nothingness (*The Antichrist* 18). Hegel, too, could know that God as the Christian God, or, rather, as that God whom Luther knew as the God of judgment and Hegel knew as the "bad infinite." Yet it is precisely as such that that God is alienated from the Godhead, and even if that alienation is necessary and essential to the very life of the Godhead, that is an alienation which finally negates itself, and that negation of negation is

Hegel and the Christian God

absolute liberation. Now if Hegel could realize a pure thinking which is a negation and transcendence of Christian belief, he nevertheless continually insists that pure belief is preserved in the dialectical movement of pure negativity, and is preserved precisely by being transcended. So it is that Hegel again and again calls upon the Fourth Gospel as his primary scriptural witness, insisting that what that gospel knows as spirit is what he knows as absolute spirit, a spirit that is a purely kenotic or self-emptying spirit, and a spirit that *is* the incarnate Christ. But can we believe that the *Phenomenology of Spirit* and the *Science of Logic* are philosophical realizations of the incarnate Christ, and thus realizations of the uniquely Christian God?

Nothing is more distinctive of Hegel than his resolution to end all mystery, and above all so to end the mystery of God, a mystery that his system knows to be ended with the Incarnation, an ending which is finally the ending of all mystery whatsoever. At this point it is true that he is very close to his deepest modern philosophical counterparts, Spinoza and Nietzsche; but he is deeply unlike Spinoza and Nietzsche in knowing the ending of that mystery as an act of God, and not only as an act of God, but as that act by which the Godhead is most fully actual as itself. If that act is the pure negation of the alienated God, the alienated God who is and only is "in-itself," that act is the ending of the beyond, or the ending of that pure transcendence which cannot become incarnate, or that "bad infinite" which is simply and only the opposite of the finite. It might even be said that Hegel identifies the deepest evil with the deepest mystery, and just as he could know the ground of evil as an absolute solitude which is an absolute isolation, that absolute solitude is absolute mystery, and a mystery which is enacted with every enactment of evil. Yet like Spinoza and Nietzsche, Hegel's deepest thinking is an absolute affirmation of actuality. But not until Hegel does such a philosophical affirmation comprehend evil itself, and even the deepest evil, which Hegel can know as a means or way by which absolute spirit realizes itself. Thus Hegel, unlike Spinoza, but fully anticipating Nietzsche, could know the deepest evil as being fully embodied in the alienated God, and embodied in the absolute solitude or the absolutely solitary "I" of that God, an "I" that is wholly enclosed within itself, and that absolute self-enclosure *is* absolute evil.

Historically, it must be remarked that no such image or idea of God is present or is realized until the dawning of the modern world. For unlike its apparent Gnostic counterpart, this is an understanding of the alien God as being finally a self-expression or a self-realization of the redemptive God.

If here Hegel's historical source is the mystical thinking of Jacob Boehme, that thinking itself is the expression of a uniquely modern imagery that is as early as Bosch, an imagery which realized its supreme linguistic and poetic triumph in Milton's Satan. Milton was the first Christian visionary to apprehend a dialectical and polar unity between Christ and Satan, so that the exaltation of Satan in *Paradise Lost,* the first such exaltation in Christian language, is inseparable from Milton's apprehension of the actual and total death of Christ. That death itself is possible only through the power of a wholly fallen yet nevertheless triumphant Satan, and yet that death is the one and only source of freedom and grace in a fallen world. Not until *Paradise Lost* does Christian vision know and realize a purely dialectical identity of ultimate death, just as not until Hegel does philosophical thinking know the pure negativity of evil and death. That negativity is not historically manifest as such until the advent of the modern world, and if nothing more manifestly distinguishes the ancient from the modern world, nothing is more characteristic of a uniquely modern world than the totality of its vision of death. So it is that Hegel knew the French Revolution as the full birth of the modern world, then a universal freedom was first born, but initially that freedom is a cold and abstract universality, and the sole work and deed of that universal freedom is death, and a truly new death which has no inner or interior significance whatsoever (*Phenomenology of Spirit* 590). This is that death which is a uniquely modern death, a death which is historically realized in the uniquely modern realization of the death of God, and only with and in that realization does consciousness fully and finally become metaphysically and religiously groundless.

Consequently, it is not possible to apprehend or know an ultimate and final death until the advent of the modern world, and even if there are images of that death in Christian art and iconography, these do not occur until the ending of ancient or patristic Christianity, just as they are not fully realized in Christian painting and sculpture until the fifteenth century. Only with Luther does that death fully pass into Christian thinking, just as there is no philosophical realization of that death until Hegel. For only the modern world knows both the ultimacy and the finality of death, hence the question of the Christian identity of Hegelian thinking is inevitably a historical question, inasmuch as it can only be posed within the historical context of the modern world. Aquinas could speak for the whole ancient tradition of Christian theology in maintaining that God's nature eternally remains impassible, and therefore Christ's passion did not concern or affect his Godhead (*Summa Theologica,* III, 46,

8). Not until Milton's *De Doctrina Christiana* will a theological treatise affirm the total death of Christ, a death affecting the whole of his nature, but precisely thereby a death that is the sole source of redemption (I, xxi). Not even Luther or Calvin could break with the patristic dogmas of Christianity, dogmas foreclosing the possibility of affirming the total death of Christ, and doing so because they were wholly closed to the possibility of either the death or the transformation of eternity. Only with the Radical Reformation are those dogmas truly challenged, a reformation which was a primary source of the English Revolution, and that revolution historically initiated modern revolution, a revolution or revolutions which finally ended the ancient world.

Hegel can be understood theologically only in the context of that historical ending, and that inevitably poses the question of whether or not Christianity itself can be actual and real if it decisively breaks away from or transcends its historical origin and ground in the ancient world. Certainly Hegel negated that ground, but this is a negation which intends to be a preservation of that ground, and a preservation of that ground in a truly new and universal world. In this perspective, the question of the Christian identity of Hegelian thinking is necessarily the question of the possibility of a uniquely modern form and realization of Christianity itself. Can Christianity actually negate itself so as to truly transcend itself, and to transcend itself by moving beyond its original expressions? That is also the question of whether or not Christianity is a forward-moving form of faith, and a historically evolving faith, a faith evolving through its own deep transformation. No thinker poses this question more deeply than does Hegel, and precisely Hegel as the totally systematic thinker. So it is that this question is not confined to the philosophical arena, it equally occurs in art and literature, just as it so occurs in politics and society, and in every dimension of history and culture. Unquestionably, ancient Christianity has either collapsed or been transcended in all of these realms, and if that transformation is truly the end of Christendom, can that ending be a genuinely transcending movement of Christianity itself? Kierkegaard could know the end of Christendom as making possible the recovery of an original faith, and the recovery of that faith in an all too modern "subjectivity," a subjectivity which is a negation of objectivity, and a negation of that objectivity which has reversed an original faith. Accordingly, Kierkegaard knew the end of Christendom as the ending of a deep negation of Christianity within itself, a negation realizing itself in the triumph of Christendom, a triumph which was necessarily the negation of faith, and the negation of faith precisely in its objective realizations.

Kierkegaard's dialectical understanding of Christianity is a reverse Hegelian understanding, and is so in understanding the history of Christianity as a backward movement reversing an original faith, but it is deeply Hegelian in apprehending the profound historical transformation of Christianity, a transformation wherein and whereby modern Christianity has become exactly the opposite of New Testament Christianity. While Hegel could know the history of Christianity as the third and final age of world history, he therein knew that history as a universal history, and a universal history which becomes manifest as such in the modern world. Thus, for Hegel, the very estrangement of the modern world from its historical seed and origin in primitive Christianity, is a decisive sign of the profound transformation of Christianity itself, a historical transformation which is an embodiment of the forward movement of absolute spirit. That forward movement is realized more fully and more finally in Christianity and in Christendom than it is in any other historical world, and at no other point is Christianity more distinct from the world religions, so that it is of Christianity and Christianity alone that one could ask if a profound historical transformation could be the realization of an original faith and praxis.

Hegel understood this transformation to be centered in the death of God, a death of God originally occurring in incarnation, crucifixion, and resurrection, but a death of God which is realized universally with the full historical advent of the modern world. Yet the very symbol of the death of God is historically unique in the history of religions, and historically unique both as a real and actual death, and as a final and ultimate death, and as that one death which is the sole source of liberation and redemption. Nevertheless, this symbol has historically evolved in Christianity, and at no other point has Christianity manifestly undergone such a deep and comprehensive historical transformation. For even if the enactment of the death of God may be understood to be at the very center of the New Testament, that enactment almost immediately but nonetheless comprehensively disappears in ancient Christianity, except insofar as it is present in a uniquely Christian liturgy and worship. The death of God as a comprehensive symbol is only reborn in early medieval art, and not triumphing in medieval art until the fifteenth century, and not until the seventeenth century does the death of God become embodied in Christian poetry, and it is not comprehensively realized in poetic vision until the prophetic and apocalyptic poetry of Blake, just as it does not become embodied in philosophical thinking until Hegel.

Therefore the death of God is not a dominant or commanding symbol in historical Christianity until the advent of the modern world, and if that advent begins with Luther, as Hegel so deeply believed, it only gradually evolved in a uniquely modern consciousness and sensibility. Not until the end of the eighteenth century does the death of God become fully manifest historically, and then it does so decisively only through the violence and the terror of the French Revolution, a revolution which both Blake and Hegel know as the historical realization of the death of God. That is the very point at which the Christian Church decisively passes into the periphery of history, a history which now and for the first time is a fully secular history, and the advent of that secular history embodies the end of Christendom. But that advent is also and even thereby a full historical actualization of the death of God, an actualization ending all traditional or given grounds of morality and judgment, just as it ended the established grounds of politics and society. Now, the death of God is not only an interior event, but a publicly actual event, and so actual as to be a universal event. Accordingly, Hegel could know the French Revolution as the first universal event in world history, for it was that event which inaugurated a new and universal history, a universal history which is a universal process of secularization, and a secularization that Hegel could know as the positive embodiment of the Kingdom of God.

Here, we are very close to the deep "offense" of Hegel's system, and offense even in a Pauline sense, for it was recreated as such by Kierkegaard, who did so by employing a Hegelian language and dialectic. While it is true that Kierkegaard knew the offense of Hegel's system more deeply than has any other thinker, it is also true that Kierkegaard employed a Hegelian language both in his understanding of faith and in his understanding of the Incarnation. Only now is the Incarnation manifest as the absolute paradox, and an absolute paradox not only to an objective understanding but also to the believing consciousness of faith, so that the Incarnation is a profound and ultimate offense to even the deepest faith in the pre-incarnate God. So likewise is the Incarnation an absolute paradox and an absolute offense to a pre-modern Christianity, so that Kierkegaard called for a contemporaneity with Christ that is a leap over two millenia of Christian history, a leap that itself is possible only with the end of Christendom. That is the end which is an apocalyptic ending for both Kierkegaard and Hegel, even as it might well have been for Luther himself, and if Kierkegaard and Hegel are descendents of Luther, at no point is this so true as it is in their realization of faith as an ultimate offense. While a Kierkegaardian passion of faith is alien to Hegelian thinking, that thinking is no less centered upon a pure subjectivity, but a pure subjectivity which is logical and historical at once.

That is the very subjectivity which ends all objective expressions of thinking and consciousness, an ending which is the ending of ancient Christianity, and therein and thereby is the realization of a universal consciousness and world.

Now even if such a realization is what Kierkegaard could know as a pure objectification both of consciousness and of faith, an objectification which is the pure antithesis both of the individual and of "faith," such an objectification has manifestly occurred, and not only in Christendom, but in the world as a whole. Both Kierkegaard and Nietzsche could understand an original Christianity as becoming exactly the opposite of itself in Christendom, and if this has occurred in no other religious tradition, no other religious tradition has generated a universal historical world, or a universal historical world which is actually dominant throughout the world. Both Hegel and Kierkegaard could know modern secularism as a secularization of Christianity itself, a process finally realizing a universal world, and even if that world is the very opposite of an original Christianity, it arose within Christianity, or within the disintegration or transformation of Christianity. Yet for Hegel that disintegration is an *Aufhebung* of Christianity itself, a self-negation which is a self-transcendence, and a self-transcendence preserving even if moving far beyond an original Christianity. Hegelian thinking offers no greater theological challenge, and just as Hegel understands full modernity as the essential and historical consummation of the history of Christianity, that is a universal consummation which is realized in no other religious world, and precisely because no other religious world has so profoundly transformed its own original beginning. A uniquely Christian beginning is surely a radically sectarian beginning, and no other religious beginning has so wholly transformed itself in its own initial expressions, a transformation continuing in Christian history as it does in no other religious tradition, until Christianity has finally either returned to a purely sectarian ground or has realized a new religious world which is simultaneously a secular or atheistic world.

Perhaps the question of whether or not Hegel is a Christian thinker is finally the question of whether or not Christianity is and only can be a pre-modern form of faith. While it is true that this is a historical question, it is simultaneously a theological question as well, and is most clearly and most forcefully a theological question in posing the question of whether or not Christianity is grounded, and deeply and ultimately grounded, in the death or self-negation of God. Paradoxically, and not so paradoxically, this is also the question of whether Christianity is a universal faith or a particular and historically individual faith and movement. For, if Christianity is realized in the death of God, it can pass into or even realize a universal historical movement, a movement which has perhaps occurred in full modernity; whereas, if Christianity is alien to that death, it is now inevitably destined to be a sectarian or historically isolated faith. No thinker so deeply and so comprehensively understands and enacts Christianity as a universal faith and movement as does Hegel. Indeed, it is just that universality of faith which is manifestly the center of his system, and if this is a system which can enter or comprehend every realm, it is the only Western system since Aristotle which has such a potentiality. And just as the discovery of Aristotle revolutionized medieval theology, the discovery of Hegel has revolutionized modern theology, and perhaps most so when that theology has given itself to a reversal of Hegelian thinking, a process already beginning with Kierkegaard.

Our time as well as the late Middle Ages may well be a time of profound transformation, and if that late medieval world gave birth to modernity, and a modernity which both to the non-sectarian Protestant and to the modern Catholic is a Christian modernity, then our time may well be giving birth to a universal faith, and a universal faith which will both negate and transcend everything which we have actually and historically known as Christianity. Now even if that is an apocalyptic ending, it could precisely for that reason be a transcendental ending, an ending transcendentally ending that transcendence which we have known and realized in our past, but thereby opening us to a true transcendence of that transcendence, and therefore a true transcendence of everything which we have known and realized as God. Hegel conceptually gave birth to that possibility, and that is a possibility which is a Christian possibility, but a universal possibility as well. Perhaps only thereby can Christianity be a universal Christianity, and if that is the historical destiny of Christianity, such a destiny is surely at hand.

3

THE NECESSITY
OF BEGINNING

Nothing is more unthinkable, and more purely unthinkable, than the once-and-for-all and absolutely unique event of genesis. Aquinas himself, who metaphysically and theologically discovered the *novitas mundi* or the newness of the world, affirmed that the *novitas mundi* is known only by way of revelation (*Summa Theologica* I, 46, 2), so that the once-and-for-all event of genesis cannot be known by even the deepest and purest thinking as such, but only by the equally unique event of revelation. If nothing more deeply distinguishes Aquinas' Aristotelianism from that Islamic Aristotelianism which was its historical source, nothing more deeply distinguishes the uniquely Biblical symbol of genesis from its counterparts in an archaic mythology and ritual, and it is precisely the prophetic proclamation of the absolute sovereignty of Yahweh which is the final Biblical negation of the archaic cycle or circle of eternal return. Judaism, Christianity, and Islam are all profoundly grounded in that negation, and so, too, is a post-Classical Western history and consciousness, and nothing could be a deeper reversal of that consciousness and history than would be a return to an archaic cycle of eternal return. Yet the question must be confronted as to whether or not such a return is actually possible. Or actually possible for that consciousness which originated in an absolute negation of eternal return, an origin which is the origin of that subject or subjectivity which is the inevitable consequence of that negation, and inevitable consequence if only because it is the absolute negation of eternal return which calls forth, and necessarily calls forth, that subject or center of consciousness which is uniquely itself.

Only an absolute negation and transcendence of eternal return makes possible a subject or an "I" which can only be itself, an "I" which is a once-and-for-all and unique "I," and therefore an "I" embodying the once-and-for-all and absolutely unique event of genesis. That "I" itself is unthinkable, or unthinkable in pure thinking, and even if it is overwhelmingly present in the *Phenomenology of Spirit,* it is wholly absent in the *Science of Logic,* and must be absent to make possible pure thinking as such. So likewise is that "I" absent in all truly post-Hegelian or post-Kierkegaardian thinking, just as it is absent from the ancient world as a whole. Nothing more deeply unites a pre-Christian and a post-Christian thinking and consciousness than does the absence of that "I," an absence which is the absence of unique and once-and-for-all events, events which have never been manifest or actual in consciousness apart from the impact of a once-and-for-all and absolute genesis. That impact is the impact of a fully unique revelation, a revelation wholly closed to pure thinking itself, and a revelation that is the realization of the unique and absolute event of genesis. If Augustine was the first philosophical thinker to know that "I" which is the unique center of consciousness, he knew it by way of his discovery of Paul, and therefore knew it as an "I" that is sin and grace at once: sin by way of its will to be and only be itself, and grace by way of its very existence itself, an existence that is possible and real only by way of the grace of God.

That grace is the grace of absolute genesis, a genesis that is the sole source of our existence, and thus that existence is wholly and only good. Yet that very existence in its interior presence to us is turned against itself by virtue of our rebellious will, a perverse and fallen will which in its ownmost center rebels against its Creator. That rebellion is original sin, but nothing causes original sin, just as nothing causes an evil will, for an evil choice proceeds not from nature or being, but rather from a deficiency of being deriving from our having been created from nothing (*City of God,* XII, 6). That deficiency is an actual nothingness, therefore it can actually be realized in sin, and even if sin is possible only for that one creature who was created in the image of God, it is possible in the freedom which is embodied in that image, and that is a uniquely individual and personal freedom which was philosophically discovered by Augustine.

That freedom is unrealized apart from the realization of absolute genesis, and silent and unmanifest to that consciousness which is innocent of an absolute genesis. Thus there is no consciousness of such freedom in either the archaic, the Oriental, or the Classical worlds, for those worlds are closed to an absolute genesis, and are so closed if only because they are bound to an eternal cycle of return. So likewise are those worlds closed to an actual nothingness, an actual nothingness which can become realized and embodied in sin, and embodied in that evil will which is a wholly solitary will. This is that unique will which wills to be and only be itself, and thereby wills to be that "I" which is only itself, an "I" which is the unique "I" of self-consciousness, even if it is possible and real only by way of the grace of an absolute genesis. So it is that Augustine could know original sin and the sinful will only by knowing the absolute grace of genesis, and even if that genesis is unknowable to pure thinking itself, it is inevitably present in the realization of the sinful will, and thence will be present in that thinking which embodies the sinful will. That thinking first occurs philosophically in Augustine, and that occurrence was a philo-sophical revolution, a revolution realizing for the first time the primacy of the subject of consciousness, a subject which is self-consciousness, and a self-consciousness which is free and enslaved at once. For this is a freedom which is inseparable from the slavery of sin, or which cannot be known or realized apart from the realization of the sinful or solitary will, a will whose very sinfulness derives only and wholly from itself.

If a pure and genuine thinking of freedom is last present in Hegel, or last present in the deepest philosophical consequences of Hegelian thinking, Marx, Kierkegaard, and Nietzsche, that is a thinking which knows pure evil as an absolute isolation or solitude. That is a solitude which is a truly inverse freedom, a solitude which is wholly free and wholly enslaved at once, and a solitude embodied in that unique "I" which is only itself. Now even if such solitude is an illusion, it is the illusion of sin, and that sin is an actual nothingness, and an actual nothingness which is unveiled only by the absolute event of genesis.

Augustine could know the "I" of God as that one pure or unitary "I" wherein there is a unity of will and being or act and will. Therein it is wholly other than our dichotomous "I," for whereas God's will is one with His being, our will is turned against our being, our true and essential being, because we will to be the sole source and author of our own individual existence. That is the pride which is the source of original sin, but that self-centered will does not as such "exist," it is rather an actual or embodied nothingness. That embodied nothingness is interiorly real to us, and most real to us in the fullest moments of our self-consciousness, moments which are moments of self-will, and therefore moments in which we are aware of the power of our interior depths. But those depths are ultimately empty depths, and empty if only because they are embodiments of an actual nothingness, an actual nothingness which is the actuality of sin. As a Neoplatonist, Augustine could know evil as an illusion, but as a Pauline Christian he knows sin as the totally fallen will, and even if that will is metaphysically a privation or absence of being, interiorly it is a total presence, and a total presence of sin.

But once metaphysics comes to an end, as it does with the full realization of the modern world, then a metaphysical absence or privation is realized as a total emptiness. This occurs in Nietzsche's proclamation of Eternal Recurrence, even as it occurs in the purest expressions of the late modern imagination, as a metaphysically groundless emptiness thereby and therein becomes all in all. While Augustine could only have responded to such a totality by identifying it as a totality of sin, he could surely know such a totality as having its seed in the sinful will. That is the will which is the historical origin of the City of Man, a City of Man which is the very antithesis of the City of God, and just as we truly know sin only by knowing the grace of God, we know the grace of God as the absolute negation of sin or emptiness.

That is the grace which is enacted in genesis, and therein enacted as a creation out of nothingness, therefore it is an absolute act of grace, and is the absolute act of that "I" which is absolute power and absolute love at once. But for Augustine, as opposed to Aquinas, the creation is not a new act, and there is no "new" will in the creation: for God wills all that He wills simultaneously, in one act, and eternally (*Confessions* XII, 15). Accordingly, the creation is an eternal act, and is the eternal act of the eternal will of God, a will which is absolute power and love. But Augustine, even as the Christian scholastic tradition which was inspired by him, could know an absolute unity of love and being, a unity which is lost with the end of Christendom. That loss is the loss not only of a unitary God, a loss first philosophically occurring in nominalism, but also the loss of a universe of love, as most ecstatically and comprehensively celebrated by Dante. For even if the world or the creation is known in Christendom as a contingent world, and thus a world absolutely dependent upon the Creator, it is a world which is solely created by God, and thus is totally good, a unitary goodness or grace which is lost with the advent of the modern world. Then and only then an actual nothing is manifest as "being," a being which Hegel could know as "being-in-itself," and which Milton epically embodied as Satan, a Satan whom Blake could epically enact as the Creator, and whom Melville could epically enact as Moby Dick. And that Satan is real in the modern world, and real as it never was in the ancient world; for if Augustine could maintain that a belief in the ultimate liberation of Satan is a belief whose error would manifestly surpass all errors in its perversity (*City of God*, XXI, 18), that is because the will of Satan is a will of pure nothingness, a will which Dante could envision as a wholly silent and imprisoned giant who is incrusted in ice. Milton's Satan is the very inversion of that ancient Satan, an inversion which is the consequence of the birth of a new world, and a new world which could know an absolute energy of evil which has no real precedent in the ancient world.

Aristotle's *energia* or pure actuality is the very identity of God as the Unmoved Mover, an *energia* that Aquinas conceives as the "act of being." If Aquinas therein embodied a truly new Aristotelianism, that is an Aristotelianism that is a philosophical realization of a new Gothic celebration of the world, a celebration that is absent from the ancient Christian world, and most clearly absent in Augustine. Augustine could celebrate God and God alone, and above all so God the Creator, the sole source of the goodness of existence, an existence which of itself and in itself is nothing. Aquinas could know such a contingency, but he did not know it as Augustine knew it, and this because he could know an *analogia entis* that Augustine could never know, and Augustine could not know such an analogical relationship between the creature and the Creator because he could never know a world which in its own actuality is an embodiment of the goodness of the Creator. But Aquinas' *analogia entis* did not and could not truly survive in Christian thinking beyond the ending of the Gothic world, an ending which is the ending of a uniquely Gothic integration of nature and grace and of reason and revelation. This ending is the advent of a new and radical contingency, a radical contingency which can and will be imaginatively envisioned as a truly new nothingness, and a new nothingness which will triumph with the closure of the modern world, as epically enacted in *Finnegans Wake*. Now that is a nothingness which neither Augustine nor Aquinas could know, and if it could be apprehended by an Augustinian thinking it would no doubt be recognized as an ultimate liberation of Satan, a liberation which is simply an illusory identity of Hell.

Yet nothing so clearly distinguishes a Christian and Western thinking from all other thinking than does the primacy and centrality which it inevitably gives to the ultimate question of origin. We can find no such deep and comprehensive concern for ultimate origin in the ancient world apart from Israel, and if what most decisively distinguishes the people of

Israel from all other peoples in the ancient world is the ultimacy with which their own traditions focus upon origin, that is because Israel alone knew genesis as a once-and-for-all and total event. At no other point is Israel a deeper source or ground of Christianity, and even a source of Christian thinking itself, a thinking which would be inconceivable apart from the genesis of the Hebrew Bible, and thus inconceivable apart from the category of absolute beginning. Simply to recognize that such a beginning is wholly absent from all primordial and all ancient worlds is to recognize the uniqueness of our thinking, and nowhere else is our thinking more absurd to the non-Western mind, or more inconceivable to a thinking and a consciousness that is innocent of what we have known as revelation. Now if Hegel could refuse creation or genesis as a once-and-for-all and absolutely unique event, a refusal that is a repetition of Spinoza, that is a decisive sign of Hegel's and Spinoza's distance from Christendom. But Hegel, even as Nietzsche, was totally given to the question of origin, and that question has not abated even in the twentieth century, perhaps being most manifestly present in our most openly revolutionary traditions, Marxism and Freudianism, but being no less present in even our most empirical science.

At no point does the ultimate question and the ultimate category of origin become more manifest than in a consciousness that can only know the forward movement of time. That is the point at which there is the deepest gulf between an ancient and a post-ancient consciousness, and if an ancient consciousness is inevitably grounded in a cycle or circle of eternal return, a post-ancient consciousness is grounded in a forward and irreversible movement of time. While our laws of physics are time symmetric, which is to say that they are equally real and meaningful in either a backward or a forward movement of time, our actual physics, and above all a new astrophysics, are seemingly inevitably given to a forward and only forward movement of time, just as modern biology is inconceivable apart from the forward movement of evolution. Even if the deep ground of this apprehension is inconceivable, there can be no doubt of its overwhelming presence in modern scientific thinking, or of its comprehensive power in modern technology. Nietzsche's Madman, in proclaiming the death of God, unveils therein a disappearance of our entire horizon, so that we are now continually plunging backward, sideward, forward, in all directions, straying thereby through an "infinite nothing." Even though the Madman falls silent and recognizes that he has come too early, for the death of God is more distant from us than the most distant stars, this is nevertheless a death that we have effected ourselves. Certainly, so long as we can know, and only fully and truly know, a forward movement of time, we will not yet have fully embodied the death of God; for we will not yet have escaped or transcended our origin in a forward movement of revelation, a forward movement that is the necessary and inevitable consequence of an absolute beginning or genesis.

Our astrophysics is manifestly grounded in a full and essential correlation between an absolute beginning and an irreversibly forward movement of time, and if that absolute beginning would now appear to be scientifically undeniable, so likewise the forward movement of time is inescapable for us. And it is inescapable even if it is interiorly and humanly meaningless to us, and no doubt most humanly meaningless in our deepest scientific apprehensions of time. But those apprehensions are real, and not simply because of their technological and social consequences, but are real as pure thinking itself. Just as scientific thinking is the most comprehensive thinking of the twentieth century, that is a thinking which knows, at least in its actual even if not in its formal or abstract expressions, the forward movement of time, and such an actually forward movement of time is unthinkable and inconceivable apart from an absolute beginning. Now even if that absolute beginning is unthinkable as such, and unthinkable as a once-and-for-all and unique event, it is nevertheless inescapable, and inescapable for that thinking which is the dominant thinking of the twentieth century. If only at this crucial and ultimate point, it is clearly impossible for us to recover an eternal cycle of return, and thus impossible for us actually to know a pure or real reversibility of time, or even to know a pure and actual backward movement of time, or a movement of time which is ultimately forward and backward at once.

Nietzsche's Zarathustra identifies "it was" as the will's most secret melancholy, for the deepest source of the bondage of the will is the brute fact that we cannot will backwards, and thus we are wholly powerless against everything that has occurred and has been done (Zarathustra, II, "On Redemption"). Indeed, everything that we have known as will is a will that can only will forward and not backward, and if that will does not become interiorly manifest until Paul, or philosophically manifest until Augustine, it nevertheless has subsequently dominated our Western consciousness, and even becomes absolute in Nietzsche's Will to Power. But that is a will which breaks itself in its desperate attempt to recreate all "it was" into "thus I willed it" and "thus I shall will it," a breakage that is a shattering and perhaps final disappearance of that unique "I" which was born with the advent of the will. Yet that disappearance is not a disappearance of an irreversibly forward movement of time, a movement which becomes even more ultimately manifest and overwhelming in the twentieth century, and does so precisely in those expressions of thinking, consciousness, and society which are most distant from and most other than the unique and irreducibly individual "I." Now even if that "I" which is a uniquely individual and forward-moving will is a consequence of the historical ending of the ancient world, a world that in its deepest ground ends with the advent of Israel, and finally ends with the advent of Christianity and Islam, that ending which is the beginning of self-consciousness or the unique and individual "I" is simultaneously the beginning of the realization of an ultimate and finally forward movement of time itself.

But a finally and ultimately forward movement of time is unimaginable and inconceivable apart from a once-and-for-all and absolute beginning, an absolute beginning which itself is irreversible, and that is an irreversibility foreclosing the possibility of an eternally backward movement of return. Hence, if we cannot know, or truly or purely know, an absolute and once-and-for-all beginning, we nevertheless know an absolutely forward movement of time which is its necessary and inescapable consequence, a forward movement of time which we cannot escape or annul, and cannot do so even in the wake of a disappearance of our "I." While that unique "I" was born with an absolute negation of the cycle of eternal return, it seemingly will not wholly perish so long as it is impossible to recover an eternal return. Nor can that "I" fully perish so long as the deep question of its ultimate origin is inescapable, an inescapability which is inevitably present in the actual presence of the symbol or the category of absolute beginning. And if we cannot escape that ultimate beginning, a beginning which dominates our thinking and consciousness as it has never done so before, then we cannot escape the question of absolute origin, an origin which is an absolutely unique and once-and-for-all event.

At no other point are we so distant and estranged from Hegel's *Science of Logic,* a logic that can only know a beginning which is an eternal beginning, and an eternal beginning releasing and eternally releasing an eternal circle of time. That time can now be real only as a wholly unmanifest time, and thus a wholly abstract time, and an abstract time that for us is inevitably a pure and inactual abstraction, that very abstraction that Hegel himself identifies as the deepest and most stubborn error. Now even if Hegel was the first thinker to understand the universality of the forward movement of history, he was wholly innocent of a prophetic sense of that catastrophic history which was to follow his own time, and this despite the fact that such a prophetic vision was almost immediately to become so profoundly embodied in Marx and Kierkegaard, and at no other point are Marx and Kierkegaard more distant from Hegel.

While the late Hegel could declare in the Preface to the *Philosophy of Right* that the philosophical Owl of Minerva takes flight only as the dusk begins to fall, dusk itself was unknown to Hegel, or known only as the ancient and pre-modern world. If Hegel's very apprehension of absolute time as a forward but circular time closed his thinking to the possibility of a cataclysmic and apocalyptic ending, that is the very apprehension which most distances Hegelian thinking from the twentieth century, just as it equally effected a deep fissure between Hegelian and post-Hegelian thinking. While nothing so characterizes the truly twentieth century world as does an apprehension of cataclysmic ending, that is an ending that is not only unknown to Hegel, but equally unknown to all of those modern philosophers who preceded him. *Faust* II was published almost immediately after Hegel's death, an all too symbolic event, for here the modern mind and imagination fully embodies an eschatological and comprehensive ending, even if here that ending is the full epiphany of a primordial ground and consciousness. Just as every full and profound expression of the imagination in late modernity has embodied such an ending, that is an ending that even now is proving to be socially and politically inescapable, and far more so for us if only because of the ultimate impossibility of a true historical movement of return.

But that is an impossibility which is the inevitable consequence of a once-and-for-all and irreversible beginning, and if it is only in the world of late modernity that pure irreversibility has become universally real, that is an irreversibility that is now comprehensibly embodied in consciousness and society, an embodiment that is finally inseparable from a new and apocalyptic ending. Yet that ending has drawn forth and made finally actual a beginning that is an irreversible beginning, and an irreversible beginning releasing a forward movement of time, an ultimately forward movement of time that is finally inseparable from an apocalyptic ending. Indeed, it is the realization of that ending which makes universally manifest an irreversible beginning, and if that beginning is logically and essentially unknown to the philosophical traditions of both East and West, it is overwhelming in that thinking and in those worlds which are a consequence of the terminus of those traditions.

Consequently, we face the paradox that while an absolute and once-and-for-all beginning is unthinkable, and purely unthinkable, it nevertheless dominates our thinking and consciousness, and does so if only because we so deeply and inescapably know both the forward and the final movement of time. A Buddhist apprehension of the impossibility of a real and actual beginning, just as a Buddhist apprehension of a time and history which is simultaneously a forward-moving and a backward-moving time, is inconceivable to us. And inconceivable because we inevitably know a forward movement of time which is irreversible, and irreversible not only in cosmic and biological time but also in interior and historical time. Nothing has been more revolutionary in modernity than the triumph of a new historical consciousness that realized the impossibility of a historically backward movement of return. The realization of that impossibility occurred in the very context of a truly new realization of the forward movement of history and consciousness, an ultimately forward movement foreclosing the possibility of a return to what only now is fully manifest as the historically past. Therein the Enlightenment is manifest as a revolutionary breakthrough, and a breakthrough immediately posing an ultimate threat to our religious traditions, for it precluded the possibility of a historical return to either the Bible or to an original and apostolic faith. Inevitably, the Enlightenment engendered a profound religious reaction, and the most profound reaction which our religious traditions have ever known, and one which even now dominates not only our religious institutions but our theological thinking as well.

Yet the full birth of modernity was not only the triumph of a new historical and scientific consciousness, it was the triumph of a new self-consciousness as well, an autonomous consciousness that is liberated from either a cosmic or an ontological ground, and therein a self-consciousness that is grounded only in itself. That is a self-consciousness which Augustine knew as the sinful will, and a sinful will that is an ontological nothingness, and an ontological nothingness precisely because it is only itself. Augustine could know that will as a willing of eternal death or nothingness, a will that is born with original sin, a birth which is a realization of that nothingness out of which the world was created. The actual nothingness of the sinful will is realized in the interior depths of self-consciousness, and even if those depths become manifest only through the presence of God, that is a negative presence which issues in an absolute self-negation and guilt. But Augustine knew that self-negation as issuing in justification, a justification by grace alone, and by the grace of that Creator who is absolute love and absolute power at once. While an Augustinian self-consciousness is inseparable from the presence of God, a truly modern self-consciousness is an ultimately autonomous consciousness, hence it is first fully embodied in Milton's Satan. What Goethe and Nietzsche could know as a Faustian consciousness, is, indeed, a truly modern self-consciousness, a self-consciousness that is deeply and only itself, and therefore a consciousness that *is* a consciousness of death. Therefore we know death as it has never been known before, because our selfhood is a selfhood which was never known before, and never so known because never previously did consciousness realize itself as that subject which *is* only itself.

If death has realized an overwhelmingly interior presence in modernity which was never so present before, that is a consequence both of a long historical movement and of a distinctively if not uniquely modern interior quest and voyage. That voyage begins with Dante's *Inferno,* which is nowhere more Augustinian than at this point, and it reaches its purest poetic and dramatic expression in Shakespeare; but it does not become dominant or all comprehensive until the nineteenth century, when it realizes a truly new actuality of death, a death which is the very fulfillment and consummation of a uniquely modern interior voyage, and a death which therein and thereafter becomes a total presence. Hegel could know that death as the interior realization of the death of God, a realization which is the actualization of a total self-consciousness, and a total self-consciousness which is inseparable from the actualization of a total death. No such actual and total death has apparently ever been present in consciousness before, perhaps its deepest analogue is a Buddhist emptiness, but that emptiness is the emptiness of an illusory actuality of consciousness or selfhood, whereas the death which has dominated our consciousness and imagination is the very realization of consciousness or self-consciousness itself. That realization has ended every true or actual image of immortality, a process already beginning in the seventeenth century, but one which is only fully realized in the twentieth century when all images of immortality either disappear or become inverted into images of eternal death.

Hinduism may well be our most ancient and primordial religious tradition, and also that tradition which has engendered the most multiple and seemingly contradictory religious movements; but all of these movements are grounded in karma or reincarnation, and nothing is more impossible in these traditions than the very possibility of death. Now if Hinduism and Buddhism are those traditions which most totally and most comprehensively embody an eternal circle of return, they are thereby those traditions in which the actuality of death is most illusory and unreal, and not simply because of the pervasive role of reincarnation in these traditions, but also because here there can be no final movement which is not a movement of return, and death can be an actual ending only insofar as it is an actual beginning. Nothing could be further distant from that death which dominates the modern consciousness and sensibility, and not least because we so deeply know and realize a forward movement of time which is irreversible, and such a pure irreversibility of time precludes the possibility of an ending which is a beginning, or of an actual ending which is an actual beginning.

But this, too, is the consequence of a once-and-for-all and irreversible beginning, and if this is not realized in our history and consciousness until the advent of modernity, that very immortality which was such a deep ground of Christendom is an embodiment of the archaic movement of eternal return. And it is so because the eternal life which it knew was a return to either an unfallen heaven or an eternal nothingness, an eternal return which is inseparable from the very belief in immortality. That is the belief which most immediately comes into crisis with the dawn of modernity, and a crisis which is already at hand in the purest metaphysical and religious thinker of early modernity, Spinoza. While that crisis does not become publicly and historically manifest until the French Revolution, then it occurs with an irresistible finality, and one which even impelled Robespierre to a final and fatal attempt to arrest the chaotic consequences of that revolution. Robespierre's failure to succeed in establishing a public religion of immortality and the Supreme Being is not a sign of the failure of Dechristianization in the French Revolution, it is far rather a sign of that newly and uniquely modern antithesis between objectivity and subjectivity, an antithesis foreclosing the possibility of an objective realization of a new interior and solitary subjectivity. Now there is an absolute opposition between objective and subjective identity, an opposition which both Marx and Kierkegaard knew so deeply, and an opposition which is finally the consequence of the loss or reversal of that very symbol of eternity which had once been the deepest ground of Western consciousness and society.

For now eternity disappears as an eternity which is only eternity, a disappearance which is not only a disappearance of the immortality of the soul, but a disappearance of all life which is not life and death at once, and actually life and death at once. That disappearance is the final disappearance of an eternal return, or of an eternal return that is a return to an eternity that is other than time, or to an eternity that is an individual and interior eternity. All such eternal return is finally ended with the triumph of modernity, and nowhere more so than in the realization of a movement of time that is only a forward movement, and as such a movement that interiorly ends any images or ideas of either an immortality or a resurrection which is life and life alone. Now if that ending is a final realization of a once-and-for-all beginning, and is so if only because of the newly realized impossibility of returning to an eternity that is prior to that beginning, that ending is the consequence of a unique and absolute beginning. That beginning can only be the ending of a primordial and circular eternity, and is so in its very realization of an absolutely forward movement of time. The advent of that forward movement of time is the ending of an eternity that is truly other than time, a timeless or purely quiescent eternity, or an eternity that is an unmoved mover or an eternally impassible actuality. Indeed, it is precisely the ending of such a timeless eternity that is the actualization of an absolutely forward movement of time. So it is that beginning *is* ending, or the beginning of a truly and finally forward movement of time is the ending of a time that is an eternal now, or a time that is present, past, and future simultaneously, or a time that is timeless insofar as it is not an irreversible time, or not a time that is and only is a forward movement of time. And that beginning can only be a unique and once-and-for-all event, and can only be so because it is truly the ending of an inactive or inactual eternity or totality, a totality whose very perishing could only be a once-and-for-all event, and must be so if only because of the totality of an inactual eternity.

No such perishing is manifest upon horizons of consciousness which are distant from the Western and the Christian world or worlds, but those worlds are also innocent of an absolutely forward movement of time. So likewise are they innocent of an absolute negation of a return to an original or primordial eternity, a return which is a return to an original paradise or primordial bliss. Thus those horizons of consciousness cannot truly know a paradise lost, a paradise which is wholly and finally lost, and lost by the very advent of a forward and irreversible time, a time that can never return to its original source or ground and not even return by way of an apocalyptic restoration if apocalypse is the realization of a truly new eternity. That is the origin which is truly lost with the advent of a purely irreversible time, and that irreversible time is necessarily a forward moving time, and therefore it cannot return to a purely empty or inactual or passive eternity. Indeed, it is precisely the impossibility of that return which is realized by the full actualization of a unique and once-and-for-all event, an event which is an absolute beginning only insofar as it is not an eternal beginning, and is a unique beginning insofar as it is the ending of eternal return. Eternal return is as such and by necessity a return to an eternal now, an eternal return which is finally everywhere, and is everywhere as an absolutely inactual or inactive totality. That is a totality which a non-Christian vision can know as paradise, but that is a paradise which is alien to Christian vision, even being absent

60

from the *Paradiso,* whose final verse celebrates that ultimate love which moves the sun and the stars, sun and stars which did not exist in an original eternity, and whose very motion and movement is alien to that eternity, an eternity which is absolutely quiescent. But that is the very quiescence which our consciousness and sensibility have come to know as death, and as an ultimate and irreversible death.

If the modern consciousness is nowhere more manifestly unique than in that ultimacy with which it is centered upon death, that is an ultimacy which is already present in Bosch and Luther, just as it is so present in Rabelais and Shakespeare, and even in the full dawning of the modern world as a whole. Even the discovery of the infinity of the universe which gave birth to modern science in the seventeenth century is the full realization of the death of a celestial sphere which is other than our terrestrial sphere, only that death made possible the comprehension of universal mathematical and physical laws, just as that comprehension is inconceivable in a world or horizon which is open to a return to a quiescent and inactual eternity. The very mind which comprehends those radically new mathematical and physical laws is a mind that is a truly new subject or center, a center of consciousness now liberated from the encompassing presence of all primordial images, and only that liberation made possible a purely autonomous thinking. That is the thinking which is the thinking of a new mind or subject, and a new subject which is not only finally free of all archaic presence, but that is the very freedom which is inseparable from a dissolution of every integral or interior relationship of the subject to the cosmos itself. Only that dissolution made possible the purely autonomous subject, but that dissolution is the dissolutions of eternal life, or the dissolution of that life for this new subject of consciousness. Eternal life can only interiorly be real in the subject of consciousness, but now that subject is a purely autonomous and therefore purely isolated subject, thus it can never know an eternity which is other than itself, or an eternity which is beyond its own horizon of thinking.

All too naturally the Faust myth arose at just this time in our history, and even as Goethe was the thinker and poet who understood this myth most profoundly, Goethe was the one major thinker who deeply attempted a reversal of modern science. But clearly such a reversal is impossible, and that impossibility is also the impossibility of a true reversal of our history, and only such a reversal could make possible for us an interior recovery of eternal life or immortality. No other time or history has known such anguish at the loss of immortality as has full modernity, but that loss is necessary and essential to a full modernity, a modernity that is

61

inconceivable apart from the dissolution of all ancient worlds. Yet that dissolution can be understood to be an inevitable consequence of absolute genesis. That genesis is a unique and once-and-for-all beginning, and a once-and-for-all beginning which is absolute beginning. Therefore it finally ends every beginning which is an eternal beginning, or every beginning which is the beginning of eternal return, and thus the beginning of eternal life.

Israel was the site of the historical inauguration of that beginning, and Israel was the arena in which there first occurred an absolute negation of eternal return, a negation foreclosing the possibility of a longing for immortality, which now can be identified as apostasy from Yahweh. Now even if immortality was resurrected in a new Judaism, and far more deeply resurrected in Christendom, that is nevertheless a resurrection of eternal return, and a resurrection which was reversed in the very advent of modernity. While only Spinoza truly and purely knew that reversal in early modernity, that reversal is surely present in the new physics and the new philosophy of the seventeenth century, just as it is implicitly but nevertheless profoundly present in the new painting and new poetry of that century. For that reversal is inseparable from the advent of the pure subject of consciousness, a subject which is the beginning of a pure subjectivity, and therefore the ending of every subject which can return from that subjectivity.

That is the subjectivity which for the first time knows the totality of death, and that made possible a deep turning from the past, a past that only now is known to be irrevocably past, and therefore irrevocably dead. Only now does a deep and comprehensive turn toward the future occur in our history, and that is a turn inseparable from the dissolution of the past, a dissolution which itself is an epiphany of death, as most violently enacted by the French Revolution itself. Certainly Christendom died in the course of this ultimate turn toward the future, and, ironically, only that death made historically possible a Christian initiation into the ultimacy of the Crucifixion, an ultimacy that is manifest in Christian art only with the waning of the Middle Ages. That it is unknown to Dante and Aquinas is a decisive sign that it is alien to Christendom, and it only becomes fully known in a purely Christian thinking in Kierkegaard's reversal of Christendom, but even that reversal is a birth of the pure subjectivity of faith itself. That is a subjectivity which is alien to every objective presence, an alienation which is the alienation of a pure self-consciousness, and a pure self-consciousness which is even alienated and estranged from itself. So it is that a pure self-consciousness is an absolutely precarious self-consciousness, it is absolutely groundless in its own center, a center which is now interiorly manifest and real as death or dissolution itself.

But that death itself can be known as a realization of absolute beginning, an absolute beginning which is the death of a quiescent and inactive totality, and therefore the death of every ground in that primordial totality. Absolute beginning is the beginning of that death, and even if absolute beginning cannot be known by pure thinking itself, that death is realized in the pure subject of that thinking, a pure subject which can only fully enact itself by enacting or actualizing its own death. That is the subject which is the subject of every full expression of the modern imagination, and even as the subject of a pure objectivity is an absolutely self-alienated and self-emptied subject, the subject of a pure subjectivity is no less self-emptied and self-alienated, so that finally it can know itself as death and as death alone. Already that death is known to Marx, and nothing is a deeper ground of Marxism, and if Marxism is the most purely revolutionary thinking which the world has ever known, that thinking is inseparable from the dissolution of a pure subject, which here can be known only as an absolutely alien subject. But the realization of that alterity is absolutely essential to the absolute negation of Marxism, a negation of every history which is grounded in the past, and therefore a negation which is a repetition of absolute beginning. And it is a repetition of absolute beginning by actually realizing a death or ending of an old totality, a totality that only now is actual as an empty totality, an emptiness which is the emptiness of a total death.

Yet that total death is an embodiment of the absolutely forward movement of time itself, and thus an embodiment of an absolute genesis. Thus that embodiment embodies the absolute necessity of beginning, and of a unique and once-and-for-all beginning, a necessity apart from which a total death would be inconceivable and impossible. If such a total death, and such a comprehensibly total death, is inescapable in full or late modernity, that death can be a beginning as well as an ending, a beginning that is nowhere more fully manifest than in Marxism itself. Now even if history is that "cunning of reason" which reverses every conscious will and intention, and thus a cunning that now has reversed even Marxism itself, that would not annul that forward movement of history which Marxism knows so absolutely, just as it would not annul absolute beginning itself. Absolute beginning is absolute origin, and if absolute origin looms before us now as it has never done so before, clearly that can occur even in the absence of the pure subject of consciousness, an absence in which that subject becomes invisible and inaudible. But that absence occurred precisely when a forward-moving actuality became overwhelming, and perhaps most overwhelming to the pure subject of consciousness, which is now disappearing in a horizon in which there are neither limits nor grounds. And that is a horizon released by an absolute genesis, an absolute genesis which is absolute beginning, and therefore the beginning of the absolute ending of an inactual or impassive ground.

Within this perspective or horizon of consciousness, absolute origin is a necessity of destiny or of actuality itself, a necessity which is an absolute necessity, and therefore an absolute necessity of beginning, and of a once-and-for-all and irreversible beginning. Only that absolutely unique beginning could make possible an absolutely forward movement of time, and if Hegel could know *Trieb* or *kenosis* as the deep and ultimate ground of that beginning, that is because he could only finally know an eternity which is united with time, or an infinite that is united with the finite. Therefore he could not finally or purely know an infinity or an eternity that is only itself, or a God or Creator that is only itself, or a pure transcendence that is not finally a pure immanence. For a real and actual disappearance of a religious, a metaphysical, and a celestial transcendence is the inevitable consequence of the triumph of modernity. Yet that disappearance is itself the necessary and inevitable consequence of a unique and once-and-for-all beginning, a beginning that can be an absolute beginning only insofar as it can realize itself as being all in all. Thus it must inevitably negate and transcend an eternity that is an eternal now, or an eternity that is a primordial eternity, or an eternity that is an eternal return. An absolute genesis is an absolute negation of that eternity, a negation that is finally the consummation of a pure transcendence, or a consummation of every transcendence which is not and cannot be a pure and total immanence.

That consummation is actually realized in history itself, and in that history and that consciousness which we most deeply know to be our own, a history which in modernity itself has been a progressive dissolution of a pure and actual transcendence. That disappearance is not yet complete in Spinoza and Hegel, and is so conceptually only in Marx and Nietzsche, who realize a pure immanence of thinking as a whole that Hegel and Spinoza could know only logically or abstractly. If that logic bound both Spinoza and Hegel to an abstract beginning that is an eternal beginning, and an eternally circular beginning, that abstract beginning breaks asunder when it is fully realized interiorly and historically, an ultimate breakage which occurs in Marx and Nietzsche alike, and then is comprehensively enacted in the full and final realization of modernity. So it is that we are now long distant from Spinoza and Hegel, just as we are distant from Blake and Goethe, but Nietzsche and even Marx maintain their historical and interior presence, and do so if only because they so profoundly understood and embodied a chaos that we so deeply know to be our own. That chaos is not an eternally recurring chaos, but rather a chaos that is actually and totally present, and totally and actually present in an irreversible history or destiny, a destiny which is a cosmic and historical destiny simultaneously, and a destiny which is a consequence of a unique and absolute beginning if only because it is so deeply and so purely irreversible. Marx and Nietzsche knew that beginning as Spinoza and Hegel did not, for they know it as a finally irreversible beginning, a purely irreversible beginning that cannot be annulled by either consciousness or history. Therefore that beginning itself is chaos, a chaos that is the full and pure reversal of all pure reversibility, and a chaos that is the center of actuality itself. A uniquely modern chaos is a totality of chaos, or a chaos that is an "infinite nothing," therefore it is not only an inevitable and inescapable chaos, but also an absolutely necessary chaos.

That absolute necessity is the absolute necessity of beginning, and not the necessity of an eternal beginning, but far rather the necessity of a unique and once-and-for-all beginning. Only such a beginning could actually realize the absolute necessity of an absolute chaos, for only such a beginning could be the actual and final ending of an original totality that is an eternal now, or an original totality in which the center is everywhere. That is the origin which is now inescapable for us, and if both our thinking and our imagination are obsessed with origin, that is an obsession that is inseparable from the very activity of our consciousness, or from its real and full activity. For now we know a consciousness that is an absolutely groundless consciousness, and that very groundlessness is our origin, an origin which is our destiny, and a destiny which we can know only by knowing that very origin. Indeed, it is precisely beginninglessness that we cannot know, and even if our consciousness is now ever more distant from a real and actual historical beginning, that very distance is simultaneously a distance from an eternal beginning, and is so if only because we can neither imagine nor conceive a true or actual absence of beginning, and cannot do so because we cannot realize or conceive an absence of time, and the absence of that time which is embodied in an irreversible beginning. Accordingly, if we cannot think a unique and absolute beginning, or purely think it, we nevertheless cannot think apart from it. Thus we cannot know either a thinking or a consciousness which does not embody absolute beginning, and embody it as an absolute necessity, and an absolute necessity which now and for the first time is wholly inescapable. While that necessity can interiorly be realized as chaos, and even cosmically and historically known as chaos, such a comprehensive chaos does not lessen or abate the absolute necessity of that chaos, it far rather deepens it, and deepens it because now and for the first time we know the absolute and total necessity of that chaos itself.

But to know that necessity is to know the absolute necessity of a unique and absolute beginning, and it is truly and absolutely necessary precisely in that uniqueness, a uniqueness which is the uniqueness of a once-and-for-all and purely irreversible event. If that very irreversibility is a pure contingency, it is a pure contingency which is a pure necessity, and is the absolute necessity of the beginning of an absolute chaos. So as opposed to an archaic myth of origin, which inevitably knows origin as an origin out of a primordial chaos or void, and precisely thereby a chaos that eternally returns to its primordial opposite or contrary, a unique and absolute beginning knows origin itself as an absolute and irreversible chaos. As an irreversible and absolute chaos, that chaos voids or empties an original totality or plenum, and voids it so as to realize a chaos or centerlessness which is only itself, and is only itself as the absolute necessity of itself. Nothing but such an absolute necessity could foreclose the possibility of the repetition of beginning, and of the eternal repetition of beginning, a repetition that finally and actually ends with the ultimate enactment of a pure and total irreversibility, an irreversibility which is the irreversibility of absolute chaos or pure contingency. That is the origin which is overwhelmingly present in our world, and even if it is absent as such in every other world, that is an absence which is the absence of an absolute chaos.

Absolute chaos can only be for us both an actual and an ultimate death, and if our world is that one world which comprehensively embodies an ultimate loss of paradise, that loss is the loss of an eternal beginning, and an eternal beginning which can eternally be repeated as beginning. That is precisely the beginning which we have lost, and therefore we have lost every beginning which is not a once-and-for-all beginning, or every beginning that can eternally be repeated as beginning. The simple truth is that the only beginning which we can actually think and know is a unique and once-and-for-all beginning, and if we cannot truly think that beginning, we cannot think beginning at all. Yet we inescapably think beginning, and inescapably think of beginning as absolute beginning, and if such thinking is not pure thinking, it is the only thinking which we can know, and it is just by evading that thinking that we evade thinking itself.

Inevitably, our thinking is obsessed by origin, and by a unique and absolute origin, and so obsessed as has been no other thinking, with the all too significant exception of that rabbinic thinking which is absolutely bound to the genesis of Torah. Rabbinic thinking itself, however, is the consequence of a loss of the archaic world, a loss which first occurs in Israel. Modern thinking is the consequence of the final loss of the archaic world, and thus the final loss of a primordial eternal return, and thereby the loss of an eternal beginning, or of any beginning that can eternally be repeated or renewed. That loss is the realization of an absolute and unique beginning, for the impossibility of eternal return is finally identical with the necessity of a once-and-for-all beginning, and the absolute necessity of a unique and absolute beginning is the absolute impossibility of eternal return.

4

THE NECESSITY
OF GOD

If a unique and once-and-for-all beginning is an absolute necessity for us, a necessity inseparable from our thinking and consciousness, that necessity is finally the necessity of God. Not until the full disruption of the modern world did our thinking know a pure necessity which is not the necessity of God, and if that disruption most decisively occurs in Marx and Nietzsche, that is a disruption which is the advent of a pure atheism, and a pure atheism which had never been known or manifest before. Yet our all too modern atheism is an atheism that knows the necessity of a unique and absolute beginning, and must know that necessity if only to sustain a pure atheism that would be impossible and unreal if beginning is an eternal beginning. For then beginning could be repeated and renewed by way of a backward movement of return, a movement that inevitably would be a return from that atheism which is so uniquely our own. While modern atheism is a comprehensive atheism, it nowhere is more total than in its apprehension of the final ultimacy of its own time and world, a time that could be a final or apocalyptic time only if it could not return to an earlier moment of time. But that impossibility of return is the necessary and inevitable consequence of a once-and-for-all and irreversible beginning, and an impossibility of return which is unreal apart from that beginning. So it is that a pure and final atheism is impossible apart from a unique and absolute beginning, and that impossibility is the impossibility of a simple or literal atheism, or an atheism that does not know the death of God. Only the death of God could make manifest or real the ending of every eternity which is not the eternity of time itself, and thus the ultimate ending of every consciousness which is not a fully embodied consciousness, or of every consciousness which is not an eternally groundless consciousness.

If that is a consciousness whose only ultimate ground is the full actuality of world and time, that is a consciousness which is impossible apart from the full realization of the absolute groundlessness of an inactual, or passive, or undifferentiated totality. That realization can only be the consequence of an absolute act, an absolute act of negating or emptying an original totality, which is to say that very totality which is manifest as the primordial origin and ground of consciousness itself. Not until the full advent of the modern world did a consciousness appear and become real which was free of the encompassing presence of that primordial ground, for even if that presence was suspended or abated in the purest moments of the classical Greek consciousness, that suspension was only a brief suspension, just as the pure presence realized by that consciousness was only a purely immediate and instantaneous presence. Only with the full loss of every ancient form of eternity does a primordial horizon fully disappear from view, and that disappearance brought with it a truly new and total affirmation of God and of God alone, as conceptually realized by Descartes and Spinoza. That very affirmation is inseparable from a new and all pervasive doubt, a pure and radical doubt never known before, and a radical doubt impelling a new and all too solitary affirmation of God. Now a consciousness is fully born which is a primordially groundless consciousness, and thus a radically solitary consciousness, or a consciousness which is finally pure subject and subject alone.

We sense all too clearly and all too decisively the final power of such a subject in becoming open to either an interior or a historical regression. Indeed, regression as such was only discovered with the full realization of the modern world, and the deepest power and profundity of both Marx and Nietzsche was expressed in their continual unveiling of such regression, a regression expressing itself in every dimension of our consciousness and society. That is a regression which is a compulsive return to a primordial quiescence, and it is precisely because this is an impossible return for us that our regression is by necessity a pathological movement, and a pathological movement which becomes total as such only with the full advent of a uniquely modern consciousness and society. Only in the modern world does either an interior or a historical return become manifest and real as a pathological return, and if this has given us a truly new nostalgia for innocence, that is because we can only know innocence as an innocence lost, and finally lost. That loss is the loss of a primordially grounded consciousness, or an integral consciousness that is subject and object at once, or subjective and objective at once. Therein and thereby an ultimate rift or gulf is established in consciousness itself, a gulf between a subjective center and an objective horizon or world, and an uncrossable gulf foreclosing the possibility of a return of that center to a consciousness that is objective and subjective simultaneously. Just as such an ultimate impossibility of return was never present in consciousness before, regression was never previously manifest as regression itself, a regression or compulsive return that is an absolutely impossible act, an impossibility that itself is a necessary even if final consequence of a unique and irreversible beginning.

That irreversibility can only be a deep and ultimate irreversibility, and a pure and total irreversibility, an irreversibility that is the necessary consequence of a total and all comprehensive act, and an act that is itself the real and total opposite of an undifferentiated and quiescent totality. Only the negation or emptying of such a totality could realize an ultimate and total irreversibility, and even if that negation is a self-negation or an emptying that is a self-emptying, such negation or emptying could only be realized in a real and actual act. And therefore in a unique and absolute act, an act which is an ultimate and final enactment of a pure actuality which is the very opposite of a passive and quiescent totality. Now an original or primordial totality truly disappears, and that disappearance is a real and actual disappearance. For even if it only gradually disappears in the course of the evolution of that consciousness which embodies it, that disappearance occurs, and occurs with an irrevocable finality. Such irrevocability is a necessary irrevocability, and an absolutely necessary irrevocability, one which is fully manifest in our consciousness and history, and overwhelmingly so in that history and consciousness which has lost every ground in a primordial eternity. If nothing is more clearly manifest in a uniquely modern consciousness and society than a deep and ultimate groundlessness, that groundlessness is a necessary consequence of the loss of an eternity that is eternally the same, or an eternity that is an eternally unmoving ground, or an eternity that is "in-itself" eternity, or "in-itself" Godhead or God.

Spinoza was the first pure thinker to know the actuality of an eternity that is inseparable from the actuality of the world, or an eternity that is at once a *natura naturans* that is the substance of God and a *natura naturata* that is the worldly mode of God's attributes (*Ethics* I, Proposition XXIX), and this profound revision of scholastic terminology is the very reversal of the thinking of Christendom. This crucial distinction between *natura naturans* and *natura naturata* was probably taken over by Spinoza from Aquinas, but he revolutionized it by defining *natura naturans* as including substance and its attributes and *natura naturata* as including all the modes of substance whatsoever, both finite and infinite, so that *natura* itself is an integral and essential totality comprehending everything whatsoever. Spinoza thereby knew a totality of God that was never upon the horizon of medieval thinking as such, and that is a totality that fully and irreversibly dawned with the advent of the modern world. That advent is the advent of a totality that is "all in all," but it is only all in all by not being that God who is only God, or that eternity which is only a primordial and transcendent eternity. At this crucial point Spinoza and Hegel are united, and this unity of our purest and most comprehensive modern philosophers is a unity reflecting a truly new actuality of the world. That actuality is a consequence of a realization of the ultimate actuality of the world, an ultimate actuality that is itself the disappearance of a potency or potentiality that is not itself a pure actuality. That disappearance is the final disappearance of a purely abstract or inactual or passive totality, and therefore the disappearance of a purely transcendent Godhead, or a Godhead which is truly other than the actuality of the world.

Hegel and Spinoza are also united in so purely knowing the impossibility of returning to or actually realizing an eternity that is prior to time, or an eternity preceding an absolute beginning, or an eternity that is not in-itself and for-itself the Creator. Now, it is fully manifest that there is simply nothing whatsoever which is prior to an absolute beginning, and this disappearance of every given metaphysical and religious transcendence is the realization of the totality of creation, and the totality of the act of creation. That act is an act enacting the ending of a primordial totality, or an original and undifferentiated totality, and therefore the ending of a totality that is not a purely immanent and totally present totality. But the pure apprehension of that ending is itself a repetition or renewal of a once-and-for-all beginning, but now a conceptual renewal making conceptually manifest the totality of that beginning, and the totality of that act which is the act of creation. For that act is the absolute negation or the absolute emptying of a purely quiescent eternity, and only that emptying or that negation could wholly and finally shatter and dissolve an original and total quiescence. Already in Spinoza that quiescence is totally silent and invisible, and silent and invisible as it had never been in pure thinking before, and if only at this point Spinoza is a revolutionary thinker, and a revolutionary thinker going far beyond even Aristotle and Descartes. Yet Spinoza's "atheism," which is an inversion of every possible theism, is at bottom a pure and total affirmation of "God," and an affirmation of that God who is purely and only the Creator, and therefore an affirmation of that God who is not and cannot be a purely transcendent Creator.

Spinoza knew that God only by knowing a "nature" which is God, a nature which is an inevitable necessity from the nature of God (*Epistola* 43), and an inevitable necessity by which things cannot be other than what they are. Nature or the world is an absolutely necessary realization of God Himself, and if nature therein is a modality of God, that is a modality apart from which God would not be God. Spinoza differed most clearly from the medieval philosophers who preceded him by denying the freedom of the will of God, that is a denial necessitated by his apprehension of the absolute necessity of God's causality, a necessity which for Spinoza is inseparable from the absolute necessity of the world. Thus Spinoza identifies power as the very essence of God, a power transcending intellect, will, and love, for these are only attributes of God, and must be referred to the *natura naturata* and not to the *natura naturans* (*Ethics* I, Prop. XXXI). So it is that Spinoza reduces every final cause to an efficient cause (I, XXXVI), and even the creation itself negates or excludes all causes except the efficient cause, an efficient cause which is the absolute power of God. Such a power of God had only been known in Christendom in nominalism, a nominalism in which the God of reason and the God of revelation broke asunder. But now that power of God is known not only as absolute power, but as an absolute power transcending every other identity or activity of God.

The epiphany of that power in Spinoza's thinking is accompanied by a reason that can perceive things only as they are in themselves. Therein it knows all things whatsoever not as contingent but as necessary, for only the imagination looks upon things as contingent (*Ethics* II, Prop. XLIV). But this means that for Spinoza the will and the intellect are one and the same, and if this is a truly new philosophical understanding of the will, it is thereby a new understanding of the will of God. Now we can understand that we do everything whatsoever by the will of God alone, and if our highest blessedness is in the knowledge of God alone, therein we know that all things follow from the eternal decree of God, and therefore there is no absolute or free will (*Ethics* II, Prop. XVIII). God Himself is free only in the sense that He alone acts only from the laws of His own nature, but there is no design in God just as there is no freedom in man, for our freedom just as freedom itself is the freedom to enact an absolute necessity. And if only God is a free cause, that is because only God is the first cause, and human freedom is simply that firm reality which our understanding acquires through immediate union with God, as Spinoza declares at the conclusion of his short treatise on God, man, and beatitude. Accordingly, everything has been predestined by God, and not by the will or design of God, but rather by the absolute nature or the infinite power of God. While Spinoza can affirm that virtue and power are identical (*Ethics* IV, Definition VIII), the power of God by which God Himself and all things are and act is the very essence of God (I, Prop. XXXIV). That essence is and only is absolute power, an absolute power which is the "actual power of God or Nature" (IV, Prop. IV), and all power whatsoever is part of the infinite power of God or Nature, which is to say part of the very essence of God Himself.

The absolute power of God *is* the power of God the Creator, that is the power which not only enacts the world, but is, indeed, the very actuality of the world itself. That actuality is absolutely necessary, and is absolutely necessary because it *is* the actuality of God. That actuality may be understood as the actualization of God, or what Spinoza conceives as *natura naturata,* which he defines as everything which follows from the necessity of the nature of God. These are all the modes of God's attributes, and without which God can neither be nor be conceived (I, Prop. XXIX). But if God cannot be conceived apart from His modes, neither can these modes be conceived apart from God, just as existence itself cannot be conceived apart from God, and cannot be because it cannot be conceived apart from absolute power. Now even if existence itself has never been so conceived before, absolute power had never been so manifest before, or conceptually manifest, an absolute power which is absolutely inseparable from all existence whatsoever. So it is that Spinoza conceptually created a wholly new identity of "substance," a substance that radically transformed the medieval conception of substance, and did so by denying every distinction between an infinite and a finite substance. Spinoza followed the medieval philosophers by maintaining that only that which is really and absolutely "in-itself" can truly be called substance, and therefore only God is truly substance. But now that substance is inseparable from the power of the world, and is so inseparable because that power is an infinite power, and therefore is finally only a mode of God Himself. Only an understanding of that power makes possible a true understanding of God, a God how is absolute power, and therefore is the absolute power of the world. Thus it is that that which is absolutely "in-itself" is in-itself only insofar as it is "for-itself," or only insofar as it is the actualization or realization of itself, an actualization which *is* the very embodiment of God.

All too naturally Hegel profoundly struggled with Spinoza as his deepest modern precursor, even as Spinoza so struggled with his medieval forebears, and if all of these philosophers are united in knowing the absolute necessity of God, that is a necessity which is not known as the absolute necessity of the world until Spinoza. But that is a necessity which can be an absolute necessity only by being the necessity of God, and if that is a necessity which is only manifest with the dawning of the modern world, that is a necessity which can only be conceptually apprehended by a uniquely modern philosophy. Inevitably, this occasioned a new understanding of creation, an understanding which first appears in Spinoza, for now the act of creation is not only inseparable from the act of God, but is inseparable from all actuality whatsoever. And unlike an Aristotelian understanding of actuality, this is an understanding of the infinity of actuality, an infinity which is the infinity of the creation itself, and therefore an infinity which is Creator and creation at once. Hegel and Spinoza are united in maintaining that God only knows Himself through His creation, just as God *is* God only through the creation. But God is fully and wholly God in the creation, and there is no God which is "in-itself" apart from the creation, just as there is no creation which is "in-itself" apart from God.

This deep "atheism" of Spinoza and Hegel alike is a response to the absolute actuality of the world, an actuality that is unmanifest until the closure of the Middle Ages. If that actuality is triumphant in the scientific revolution of the seventeenth century, that is a revolution that ended the finitude of the world or the universe, thereby ending the very possibility of finitude in the medieval sense, an ending which is also the ending of a purely celestial or heavenly transcendence. Now transcendence itself can be manifest and real only as absolute immanence, an immanence which Spinoza knows as substance, and Hegel as absolute negativity. But that substance or that negativity is an infinite power, an infinite power never known in the ancient world, a world that was conceptually innocent of an absolute beginning. If medieval philosophy did know that beginning, it could not conceptually know it, or know it purely conceptually, and therefore it could not know a power of the world that is an infinite power. Spinoza is the first philosopher to know that power, or to purely know it, and thus he was the first philosopher to conceive a transcendent power that is and only is an immanent power, or a power which is the full and total union of infinity and finitude.

The very idea of infinity is alien to the ancient and pre-Christian world, for when it seemingly occurs in the Greek philosophical tradition, the infinite or *to apeiron* has wholly pejorative connotations, representing a substratum which is formless, characterless, and indeterminate, and even the uniquely positive occurrence of *to apeiron* in Anaximander refers to an infinite which is not spatially unlimited. Yet in medieval philosophy God is "absolutely infinite," and that is God's highest perfection, a perfection necessarily distinguishing the Creator from the creature, infinity being the unique privilege of God's perfection, and finitude the unavoidable *defectum* of the necessarily imperfect creature. That is the traditional ontology which is decisively and finally shattered in the seventeenth century, and even if Descartes himself could adhere to that ontology, it is effectively ended in Newton's astrophysics, a revolutionary new science consuming that metaphysics which was its historical source, and therefore ending an infinity that is only a heavenly infinity, even as it ended the finitude of space and time. Spinoza was the first philosophical thinker to understand that infinity, and when Spinoza understands the infinity of extension or infinite quantity as *natura naturata,* that is equivalent to Newton's naming of absolute space as God's *Sensorium* in his *Opticks.* For now, and for the first time, infinity is fully realized as the infinity of the world.

If Newton's thought was formed and developed in opposition to that of Descartes, it certainly was so in its apprehension of infinite or absolute space, a space that in all directions is extended to infinity, whereas for Descartes space or the world is only indefinite, in contradistinction to God's infinity. Newton's absolute space, even as Spinoza's infinity of extension, is the realized space of God, and if Newton could know the Cartesian God as being absent from the world, in the General Scholium which concludes the *Principia* he affirms that God who "constitutes duration and space." And God constitutes duration and space because finally time and space are an absolute time and space, and hence are the duration and space of God. Deeply heretical as he was, Newton was nevertheless a profoundly Christian believer, and not least so in the creation of his newly comprehensive mathematical physics, a physics which he believed had destroyed what he judged to be the atheistic materialism of Descartes, and destroyed it by unveiling an infinite or absolute time and space which is inseparable from God. For Newton, even as Spinoza, understood God's presence as a *substantial* presence in the world, and just as God exists necessarily, "by the same necessity He exists *always* and *everywhere*" (*Scholium Generale*). But that always and everywhere is an infinite time and an infinite space, an infinite time and space which is time and space itself, and the only time and space which can be mathematically and physically comprehended at once. That is the very comprehension which gave birth to modern science, a birth which is an embodiment of the absolute actuality of the world, an actuality which is the actuality of an infinite universe.

While that actuality only gradually dawned in our history and consciousness, it is definitively realized with the full birth of the modern world in the seventeenth century, a birth that finally issues in an ending of every previous idea and understanding of God. Accordingly, every medieval conception of God simply but inevitably disappears in all genuinely modern thinking, there is no modern thinker of real stature who is a theist in the medieval sense, just as there has never been a genuine synthesis of medieval and modern thinking. Nor is this disappearance confined to pure thinking, it ever more decisively occurs in the modern imagination as well, an imagination that initially becomes sundered from that God who is God and only God, but which in late modernity envisions that God as an empty or alien void or nothingness. Nevertheless, neither our thinking nor our imagination has been able to escape or to wholly transcend the necessity of God, and the absolute necessity of God. For even if that necessity is identical with the necessity of the world, it is nonetheless an absolute necessity, and an absolute necessity apart from which the world could not be known or envisioned as an absolute actuality. Nietzsche knew this more purely than did any other thinker, which is precisely why the "death of God" is so absolutely fundamental in his thinking, and at no other point is Nietzsche so deeply the philosophical precursor of the twentieth century. Neither our thinking nor our consciousness can truly and finally escape God, so that even a "Godless" consciousness must name God, and name God even if only proclaiming the death of God, a proclamation apart from which a fully and finally modern consciousness would be simply and literally groundless.

Yet Nietzsche's proclamation of the death of God can be understood as a reenactment or renewal of a unique and absolute beginning, and it is precisely as such that it has wiped away our whole horizon. And that disappearance is not and cannot be an eternally repeated disappearance, but a once-and-for-all disappearance, and Nietzsche himself could understand it as the most important event in history. So it is that with that disappearance there has finally and wholly disappeared an eternity that is only eternity, or an eternity that is not time, or an infinity that is not the infinity of the universe. Already Spinoza knew that disappearance, just as Newton did in a far more elusive and yet far more comprehensive way, but both Newton and Spinoza knew that disappearance as the epiphany of the totality of God, and knew that totality by knowing the totality of the world. Both Hegel and Nietzsche renewed that totality, and renewed it by carrying it forward into the totality of history and consciousness, a new history which is a new infinitude, and a new infinitude which is an interior but nevertheless totally comprehensive infinitude. That infinitude is in full continuity with the infinitude discovered in the seventeenth century, just as it, too, is a dissolution of the medieval and metaphysical God, a dissolution which is the dissolution of all medieval and ancient worlds. But that dissolution is also and even thereby a realization of absolute beginning, an absolute beginning which is the beginning of an absolute time and space, an absolute time and space that could never be apprehended in pre-modern thinking, and could not be if only because that thinking could not transcend an unmoving or pre-temporal eternity. That eternity has never been recovered in the modern world, and certainly not in twentieth century science, a science which has lost even the shadow of a metaphysical or religious transcendence, and even lost everything that is not the consequence of a once-and-for-all and irreversible beginning.

That loss could be for us, even as it was for Nietzsche, a decisive way of knowing and realizing that "Being begins in every now" (*Zarathustra* III, "*The Convalescent*"). But that now is not an eternal now, or not the eternal now of transcendent Godhead, but rather an immediate and actual now, and a totally actual now. And that is a now which *is* only insofar as it is not a transcendent now, or not an eternal and undifferentiated now. Nietzsche knew *ressentiment* as a flight from that actual now, a flight engendered by an inability or refusal to bear the pain of an absolutely groundless moment, and an absolute irreversible moment. This is a flight which is embodied in all of those eternities which are celebrated in our ancient and primordial traditions, and a flight which is fully and totally embodied in the uniquely Christian God, that one God which is the will to nothingness pronounced holy. That is a holiness which is reversed in Nietzsche's proclamation of Eternal Recurrence, a reversal which is a reversal of *ressentiment,* and a reversal that is possible and real only because "Being begins in every Now." This is that actual now which is celebrated and enacted in the realization of Eternal Recurrence, a realization that is the realization of the totality of an immediate and actual now, and that is a totality which is and only can be an absolute reversal of the Christian God. Nietzsche could know that totality as a Godhead of absolute immanence, and while the late Nietzsche could name that Godhead as Dionysus, he certainly did not thereby name the Greek, god, Dionysus, nor any other ancient deity or moment. Historically, a pure and total immanence dawns only with the closure of the medieval world, for that is an immanence that is possible and real only with the ending of a purely transcendent eternity, or only with the real and actual dissolution of a celestial or heavenly transcendence that is truly other than the pure immediacy of an actual earth and time.

Just as Nietzsche could proclaim Eternal Recurrence only by proclaiming the death of God, Spinoza could think *natura naturans* only by thinking *natura naturata*. If Spinoza and Nietzsche have been our most God-obsessed thinkers, and far more obsessed by God than Aquinas or any other scholastic thinker, that is an obsession that is interiorly necessary to fully apprehend either the eternity of time or the infinity of finitude. We can even find such an obsession, although in a far different form, in Hegel himself, who could declare in the Preface to the *Phenomenology of Spirit* that: "The True is thus the Baccanalian revel in which no member is not drunk." No thinkers in history have so centered their thinking upon God as have Spinoza, Hegel, and Nietzsche, but no other thinkers have known such a pure and absolute necessity. If that necessity is finally identical with a pure and absolute contingency, or a contingency which has lost even a shadow or an echo of a transcendent necessity, only a deep and ultimate realization of that loss can call forth or embody a pure immanence that is eternity itself. There is a full continuity in our modern history and thinking that moves from the initial loss or ending of a purely transcendent infinity and eternity in the seventeenth century to a final loss of that infinity or eternity in the nineteenth century. Therein there is a genuine continuity between Spinoza, Hegel, and Nietzsche, which is not a continuity of pure thinking alone, but also a continuity in the very fullness of our history. And if that history undergoes an apocalyptic realization in Hegel, Marx, and Nietzsche, that is the realization of an irreversible beginning, and of an irreversible beginning that can only be consummated in an apocalyptic ending. That is the ending which is celebrated and exalted in Nietzsche's vision of Eternal Recurrence, even as it is fully drawn forth and fully affirmed in Hegel's philosophy of history and in Marx's dialectical materialism, for Hegel and Marx are also apocalyptic thinkers, and apocalyptic thinkers in knowing the absolute ending of an absolute beginning.

Now it is precisely because a truly apocalyptic ending is a once-and-for-all ending that it is the final realization of a unique and irreversible beginning. So that even as an apocalyptic ending can only be an absolute ending, an irreversible beginning can only be an absolute beginning. Each is the embodiment of an absolute act, an absolute act that is nameable in our language only as the eternal act of God, or only as the eternal act of absolute actuality itself. That is the act which Spinoza knows as the absolute power of God, a power transcending everything that Spinoza can know as intellect, will, and love, even as *natura naturans* transcends *natura naturata*. Spinoza could know a nature in which there is only one substance, the infinite substance of God, a substance that is *natura naturans,* even as its modal extension is *natura naturata.* That modal extension is both the body of God and finally all body or extension whatsoever, and if this was the primary way by which Spinoza apprehended the unity of nature, that is a unity which is not realized in pure thinking until Spinoza. But that is a unity which is scientifically realized by Newton, and neither Newton nor Spinoza could conceive the unity of nature apart from the full and final union of God and nature. That is a polar or dipolar union which has only truly or fully been realized by Newton and Spinoza, and if that union has subsequently perished in our history and thinking, it has only so perished as a purely conceptual unity, even while thereby releasing or realizing the absolute actuality of nature or the universe.

If the seventeenth century is the most revolutionary of our centuries, the revolution which it embodied is not a unitary revolution, as can most clearly be seen in the deep discord between its scientific and philosophical expressions and its purely interior and imaginative expressions. Nowhere is that profound dissonance more fully manifest than in *Paradise Lost,* for while our supreme modern epic gives us our purest and most total poetic vision of the unity of nature, that unity is here a wholly pre-fallen unity, and a pre-fallen unity which is lost with the fall and subsequent triumph of Satan. Now nature or world itself is a dichotomous world, and a dichotomous world in its deepest center, a center which is finally an absolute dichotomy between Satan and the Son of God. Milton's Satan is unique if only because of his cosmic and majestic power, and so likewise is Milton's Son of God unique, and not simply because that Son is not the fullness of the Godhead (an Arianism that Milton shared with Newton and many others), but rather because Milton's Son or Messiah is the polar opposite of Satan, and that is the opposition which is the driving energy of the poem. Raphael's account of the creation in Book VII conjoins the creation itself with the original rebellion of Satan and the fallen angels, a creation that the Father affirms will "repair" the detriment done by that rebellion. Then the Father declares that the creation will be by His Word or His "begotten Son," for even though the Father is uncircumscribed and fills infinitude, He will "retire" in the act of creation, and therein "put not forth my goodness" (VII, 160). For that is a goodness that cannot be fully present or real in a universe created in response to the rebellion of Satan, and even if that universe or world is destined to be "changed to heaven" (VII, 154), it can be so transformed only by the sacrificial and atoning death of the Son. That ultimate death is now made necessary by the dark power of Satan, a dark and purely negative power, but nevertheless a power embodying the "High permission of all-ruling Heaven" (I, 212). So it is that the energy or power of *Paradise Lost* itself is a dichotomous power, for even if this epic is a celebration of the integral and harmonious order of a pre-fallen universe, that is an order which is lost with the triumph of Satan over an originally innocent humanity, so that *Paradise Lost* is a "wake" for a unity of nature that has disappeared, and disappeared in a universal and cosmic movement of fall.

Not until Hegel will pure thinking realize such a dichotomy, and if that is a dialectical dichotomy which most clearly distinguishes Hegel from Spinoza, it is Spinoza's God or absolute power itself which Hegelian thinking realizes as a dichotomous power. While this is clearly an inversion or reversal of Spinoza, and an inversion of Spinoza's God or infinite Substance, that very substance is now apprehended as a self-alienated substance, and realized as such in a newly self-alienated and self-estranged consciousness. That is the very consciousness which is epically inaugurated in *Paradise Lost,* an inauguration which is a celebra-tion of a new interior energy, and an interior energy which is ultimately divided in its innermost center. While that center is unknown to Newton and Spinoza alike, it is perhaps most deeply alien to Spinoza, who could only know a pure necessity which is a pure harmony or coherence, and even a pure harmony between body and mind which has only been known by Spinoza. That is a harmony which disappears with the French Revolution, a disappearance even effecting the pure harmony of Haydn and Mozart, and even if the late Mozart and Beethoven transcended that disappearance by creating a truly new and dichotomous harmony, that is the very harmony which is known by Hegel, but only so known by way of the new portal of a wholly self-alienated and self-estranged consciousness.

Just as Hegel effected a conceptual realization of that new consciousness which is embodied in *Paradise Lost,* so likewise did he create a conceptual embodiment of that fall which is the center of *Paradise Lost,* a fall which is a fortunate fall, and fortunate in its ultimate realization of a uniquely apocalyptic redemption. While neither Milton nor any other poet before Blake could fully or decisively envision that redemption, that is a redemption which is ecstatically celebrated in Blake's apocalyptic vision, just as it is philosophically enacted in Hegel's system. And in both Blake and Hegel that is a redemption which is the consequence of the death of God, indeed, its deepest consequence, for only that death makes possible an ultimately new and pure and total immanence. So it is that "Self-Annihilation" plays the same role in Blake's system as does self-negation or self-emptying in Hegel's system. Each is finally the self-emptying of the uniquely Christian God, a self-emptying which is realized in crucifixion, and realized in that crucifixion which is crucifixion and resurrection or apocalypse at once. Even as Blake was the first poet who was or became a fully and purely apocalyptic poet, Hegel was the first thinker who was a fully apocalyptic thinker, and the apocalypticism of Hegel and Blake alike is inseparable from an ultimate realization of the death of God, and the death of that God who is "Being-in-itself" or Satan. Not until Blake and Hegel is absolute evil given an ultimate and divine identity, and a divine identity which is ultimately a redemptive identity, for only the crucifixion or self-negation of that pure and total otherness releases apocalypse. Indeed, that self-annihilation is apocalypse, and is that apocalypse which is the inevitable consummation of the very birth or advent of a pure and total otherness.

But that consummation is the consummation of a unique and irreversible beginning, a beginning that only now can be known as the inauguration of absolute otherness, for even if such vision is apparently the rebirth of an ancient Gnosticism, it is certainly not so insofar as it knows that otherness as an essential and intrinsic otherness, or an otherness that is inseparable from actuality itself. Blake's naming of the Creator as Urizen or Satan has no true parallel in ancient Gnosticism, for Gnosticism could never know Godhead itself as an alien Godhead, just as it could not know an alien deity or power as a finally redemptive power. Blake's purest epics, *Milton* and *Jerusalem,* envision the "Self-Annihilation" of Satan, a self-annihilation which is an apocalyptic redemption, and an apocalyptic redemption which is the total realization of the apocalyptic Christ. That Christ *is* the total reversal of Satan or the Creator, and the total reversal of the original act of creation, but thereby and therein it is the apocalyptic consummation of that eternal act. Apocalypticism itself is wholly illusory and unreal apart from that act, so that while the original act of creation is reversed in apocalypticism, it is not thereby annulled, but rather renewed and transcended in its own absolute reversal. Nothing more deeply gives witness to the original and absolute act of creation than does an apocalyptic enactment, for even Nietzsche's vision of Eternal Recurrence is a visionary enactment of an absolute act and actuality, an actuality that is the very act of creation itself. So it is that Nietzsche could know the will as the Creator, but that will is the Will to Power, a power that is absolute power itself, or that very power which Spinoza knew as Godhead itself.

If Marx and Nietzsche are our purest atheistic thinkers, they are so only as apocalyptic thinkers, and apocalyptic thinkers who are united in thinking an absolute reversal. That reversal itself is apocalypse, but an apocalypse that could be real only if it is the reversal of the absolute act of creation, for apart from that reversal, reversal itself could not be an absolute act. But only such an absolute enactment makes a truly modern atheism possible, but if that atheism is not only possible but real, then so likewise is an apocalyptic enactment real.

Paradoxically, and not so paradoxically, it is the very atheism of Marx and Nietzsche which most clearly makes manifest for us the totality of a once-and-for-all act. That act itself is absolutely new, and if it was Nietzsche and Marx who most decisively embodied an absolute novum, that novum could only be the renewal of the act of creation itself. Marx could not or would not know that obsession with God that Nietzsche embodied, but he realized an absolute negation of religion which is its counterpart, and if such a negation is absolutely necessary to realize a truly new and apocalyptic world, that is a negation inseparable from a negation of the Creator, a negation which is most purely realized by Nietzsche. Yet that is a negation which is possible only by way of an absolute act, an act which our history and consciousness have known as the eternal act of God. True or full atheism is a reversal of that eternal act, and a reversal therein bearing witness to that act itself, for apart from that act and its renewal genuine atheism would be illusory and unreal. Pure atheism itself is the most forceful witness to God in late modernity, and even if pure atheists are very rare if not non-existent, an atheistic vision is now our deepest and most comprehensive vision, and a uniquely twentieth century vision is simply inconceivable without it.

Yet that vision is finally a vision of the necessity of God, a necessity apart from which there could be no pure atheism, or no pure or actual act of negating the act or actuality of God. And if that act is an apocalyptic act, it is precisely as such that Blake and Nietzsche embodied it, even as a comparable act is present in that materialism and positivism which is so comprehensively present in the modern world. Nothing truly comparable to modern secularism has ever been present in the world before, and if that secularism has so fully and finally become an inescapable secularism, that is a secularism which is the consequence of a transformation of the world, and a transformation which our vision has ever known as an apocalyptic transformation.

An apocalyptic enactment is the embodiment of an absolute novum, a novum which was the deepest goal of Nietzsche and Blake alike, and a novum which in its uniquely modern embodiment is an absolute negation of the Creator. But that novum is therein and thereby fully coincident with the novum of a once-and-for-all beginning, each is an absolute act or actuality, and each is an absolute novum, a novum effecting and embodying an absolute emptying or negation of that totality which is absolutely other than itself. If this coincidence is a *coincidentia oppositorum,* the coincidence of the opposites of absolute beginning and absolute ending, so that alpha *is* omega, even as omega *is* alpha, that coincidence is a coincidence of real opposites, and a coincidence that is impossible apart from absolute opposition. That is an opposition that is known and realized only with the advent of modernity, for not only is it absent from the non-Western world, but even from the pre-modern Western world. While that opposition was certainly present in an original Christian apocalypticism, it is wholly transformed with the advent of Christendom, a transformation most purely and most deeply occurring in Augustine's revolutionary understanding of the purely internal and interior opposition of sin and grace. But that opposition comprehensively and historically explodes with the closure of the Middle Ages, an explosion which is the birth of a truly new apocalyptic transformation, as a purely internal opposition becomes a cosmic and a universal opposition, and a universal opposition eventually transforming the totality of history and consciousness alike. While it is true that Newton and Spinoza could know a harmonious and unitary totality, no such totality has been imaginatively realized since Dante, just as it disappears from thinking itself with the full realization of the modern world. And even if Hegel could realize such a totality, he could only do so by way of a purely and totally negative thinking, a negative thinking embodying a pure and total self-negation, and a self-negation realizing itself through a purely dichotomous center or subject of thinking. Then and only then could thinking itself know the absolute self-negation or self-emptying of God, a self-emptying or *kenosis* which is the death of God, and the death of that God who is "Being-in-itself" or a pure passivity or aseity.

Hegel has been our only thinker who purely and truly knew that self-negation, thereby that self-negation is realized as totality itself, but that totality is necessarily in-itself and for-itself a pure opposition. But Hegel could know that opposition as a unitary and harmonious opposition only in its purely logical mode, a logical mode which is an abstract mode, and one which has subsequently been realized by no other thinker. Abstract thinking itself is annulled and reversed by Marx and Nietzsche, even as it was so by Kierkegaard, and that annulment is the very opposite of an abstract negation, and is realized as such in the great body of the modern imagination. Now a true nihilism is released in the world, a full and total nihilism, and even if nihilism is alien to a purely Hegelian thinking, it is inevitably a consequence of a deep disruption of that thinking, a disruption which becomes overwhelming and universal in the time following Hegel's death. Nietzsche knew this nihilism as has no other thinker, and he knew it as an inevitable consequence of the historical realization of the death of God, and only in the wake of that death has an absolute groundlessness come to dominate our consciousness and history. That groundlessness was unknown to Hegel, and unknown to philosophical thinking itself until Nietzsche, except insofar as it was present in a profoundly anti-philosophical form in Kierkegaard and Marx. But its realization in Nietzsche is now commonly identified as the end of philosophy, and not simply the end of metaphysics, which already occurs in Kant and Hegel, but rather the ending of a purely conceptual thinking, or the ending of all such thinking which has any point of contact with actuality.

Yet that groundlessness which has dominated our century has issued in overwhelming even if inexplicable systems of order, as witness not only our science and technology but our art, literature, and music as well. While such symmetry may well be inseparable from dissymmetry, or such coherence from incoherence, or such order from disorder and chaos, it nevertheless is an order embodying an extraordinary and inescapable power, and an inescapable power of order itself. If Spinoza could know a pure order and coherence more clearly and more comprehensively than any other thinker, and Newton's *Principia* could realize a pure and total order of the universe which has never been so manifest since, each of these revolutionary embodiments of early modernity was the consequence of the dissolution of Christendom, and therewith the dissolution of that religious and metaphysical order which had previously dominated the West. Ironically, Newton and Spinoza knew a pure order and coherence that was alien to medieval tradition, and alien because that tradition could not know a pure order that is a unitary and comprehensive order, and could not know such order precisely because it could and did know a purely transcendent God or Being. So that if the dissolution or disappearance of that Being issued in a truly new and truly unitary order, just as it issued in a truly new infinity, those embodiments of an absolute order are nonetheless realizations of the dissolution of an absolute ground. And if that dissolution has become total in full or late modernity, it has no less so generated full and total systems of order.

The crisis or chaos of the twentieth century may well be no deeper or no graver than that of the seventeenth century, and if the most revolutionary of our centuries embodied the ending of the ancient world, that ending is realizing itself as a total ending in the twentieth century. Therefore it can be and has been named as an *apocalyptic* ending, and so named and realized in many if not most of the deepest expressions of our thinking and imagination. Just as the seventeenth century gave birth to both conceptions and realizations of the totality of God, and a totality of God that had never previously been present or actual in consciousness or history, the twentieth century, too, has realized a new totality or new totalities. Yet our totalities are absolute ground and absolute groundlessness at once, or totalities that are cosmos and chaos simultaneously, and most fully and actually cosmos when chaos is their deepest and most integral ground. While it is clear that such chaos and such cosmos have fully arisen out of a nineteenth century source, a continuity which is most clearly manifest in our literature and music, it is no less clear that ours are truly new systems of order, and systems of order which now and for the first time are free of any true or actual relationship to an internal and interior center or subject. That freedom is a reversal of the new freedom of the seventeenth century, and is so precisely because it is a dissolution of any possible subject or center. And if that dissolution is a nihilistic dissolution, it is nevertheless a realization of order, and of a total order that was never previously manifest upon our horizon.

An absolute and total necessity is now universally manifest as it was never so manifest before, a necessity which once was manifest as the necessity of God, and now is manifest as a purely anonymous necessity. Only in our century has there occurred a full dissolution of the name of God, a dissolution inseparable from the epiphany of a "chaos" that is "cosmos" itself, and a namelessness and anonymity which itself is a new totality. But that totality is manifest and real as an absolute necessity, and an absolute necessity which is an absolutely dichotomous necessity, or a necessity in which cosmos and chaos are not only inseparable, but even indistinguishable from each other. Thus we can know *Finnegans Wake* as the supreme epic of our century, an epic in which there is a pure coincidence of total chaos and total order, an order which itself is a purely chaotic order, and yet the very chaos of its language embodies a totality of cosmos which had never so fully passed into language itself, or not done so since Dante's *Commedia*. Creation is the dominant epic action of *Finnegans Wake,* a creation which is fall and creation at once, and death and resurrection at once, and if its very ending is the beginning of that epic, that is a beginning which is the beginning of absolute chaos. Nevertheless, that chaos embodies an absolute order, an order here realized in language itself, and if this is a truly new language, it is also an ancient and primordial language, and now nothing whatsoever distinguishes either ancient and contemporary or sacred and profane.

Finnegans Wake is a rebirth of our epic tradition, and most specifically and powerfully so of Dante and Blake, and the enactment of creation in our contemporary epic is a full resolution of that enactment as it occurs in the *Commedia, Paradise Lost,* and *Jerusalem*. But now the creation is the realization of absolute chaos itself, a chaos that is the very order of the cosmos, and a cosmos that is God and nature at once, or Blake's "Eternal Great Humanity Divine." And now absolute chaos itself is the original and the eternal act of creation, every page of *Finnegans Wake* is a celebration of that chaos, and it is precisely as such that it is a celebration of the eternal act of God, and an act whose absolute necessity is again and again enacted in this epic, an enactment which is the very plot or action of our final epic.

Now we have come full circle from the *Commedia,* and full circle from the very beginning of consciousness and history, and if we know a chaos that was never so fully or so universally embodied before, that is a chaos that we are realizing as an absolute necessity, and an absolute necessity that is absolutely inescapable. That is a necessity which Hegel could fully realize only in a logical and abstract mode, but a necessity which Nietzsche could realize at the very center of consciousness, a center which is absolutely centerless, but is thereby an absolute necessity. That is the actuality which is Eternal Recurrence, but it is precisely thereby not an eternal return, not a return to a pre-cosmic or pre-temporal eternity, but rather a total realization of the impossibility of that return. Nietzsche knew that impossibility more purely than did any other thinker, and so knew it in his proclamation of the death of God, a death of God going far beyond a Hegelian death of God by knowing that death as absolute origin itself. That is the origin which is epically enacted in *Finnegans Wake,* and enacted as the enactment of creation itself, a creation which is the eternal fall of God Himself. But that fall is a fortunate fall, for it is an apocalyptic fall, an apocalyptic fall embodying a reversal of that pure actuality which Hegel so purely and so comprehensively knew, and a reversal of that infinite substance which Spinoza so clearly and so purely knew. Now alpha is omega only when an absolute beginning is absolute disruption, an absolute disruption of eternity itself, which is to say an actual disruption of God Himself, and if that disruption is absolute chaos, it is a chaos which is totality itself.

Now, existence *is* an absolute contingency, and an absolute contingency which is simply a real and actual existence, and thus is that existence which is most actually our own. But that existence is unreal apart from an absolute enactment, an absolute enactment which is an absolute disenactment, and is so as the absolute disenactment of a wholly undifferentiated inactuality. That inactuality is now manifest as a pure passivity, that very passivity or aseity which scholasticism could know as the Being of God, and only the absolute disruption of that passivity can now be known and envisioned as the eternal act of creation. For only a realization of that disruption makes manifest an absolute contingency, and just as ours is a unique time and world which has so deeply known that contingency, so likewise is ours that unique world which has known absolute origin itself as absolute disruption. Such disruption is now manifest in every dimension of our thinking and imagination, just as it is implicitly but nevertheless all too deeply present in a newly groundless society and consciousness, and even manifest in our religious life itself. No such horizon of consciousness has ever been manifest before, but never previously has an absolute irreversibility been so totally actual in consciousness, an irreversibility that is reversed in every movement of eternal return, and such a dissolution or veiling of the irreversibility of time is a perpetual dissolution of a full and actual contingency. Not even Aristotle could know such a contingency, and he could not know it because he could not know the necessity of contingency, and the absolute necessity of a pure contingency.

When Spinoza could know everything whatsoever as being absolutely necessary, he knew the necessity of what both Classical and medieval thinking had known as contingency, thereby he knew that contingency as the model extension of God, and if that is an apprehension of the infinity of finitude, it is also an apprehension of the absolute necessity of creation. That is a necessity which dawns in Christendom only with the advent of nominalism, and if that nominalism is a primary seed of the dissolution of Christendom, that dissolution is a realization of the absolute necessity of the Creator, and if such a realization impelled Spinoza to dissolve the freedom of God, that is a dissolution which is a realization of absolute necessity. That God whom Spinoza knew as infinite power, is that God who is absolute necessity, an absolute necessity which is finally indistinguishable from existence itself, or indistinguishable from that existence which is an absolutely necessary existence, and even an absolutely necessary existence in its very perishing or finitude. So that if Spinoza refused the very possibility of contingency, that is a refusal which is an affirmation of an absolute necessity. That is the very affirmation which Nietzsche could totally enact as a celebration of Eternal Recurrence, a celebration which is an affirmation of the absolute contingency of existence itself. And that is a contingency which is an absolutely necessary contingency, a necessity which is the necessity of actuality itself, or of a full and total actuality. Thus this is that very necessity which is known to Spinoza, Hegel, and Nietzsche alike, and is, indeed, that necessity which gave birth to modern science, and even inaugurated the modern world as a whole.

Nowhere is that absolute contingency more clearly manifest to us than in what we can now know or apprehend as the advent of an original moment of time, and if that advent is for us an absolutely necessary moment or event, that necessity is the absolute necessity of creation. For even if creation is the enactment of an absolute contingency, and the irreversible enactment of that contingency, that enactment is an absolutely necessary enactment. Only a realization of that enactment makes possible an apprehension of absolute contingency, so that absolute contingency is inseparable from absolute necessity, an inseparability at the very center of that consciousness which is so uniquely our own. Now, and only now, an affirmation of the world can only be an affirmation of chaos, and if Nietzsche was the first thinker to realize this uniquely modern truth, that is a truth which has become a comprehensive truth in our own time and world. Thus our cosmos is "cosmos" and "chaos" at once, and even absolute cosmos and absolute chaos at once, and if that is an infinitude which is a true infinitude, it is simultaneously a finitude which is a true finitude. Now nothing whatsoever distinguishes finitude and infinitude, and if Spinoza and Hegel could abstractly know that identity, that is now an identity which is a fully realized or embodied identity, a realization which is the realization of the apocalyptic identity of the Creator. Therefore it is a realization of God, and of the absolute necessity of God, a necessity which has never been more fully manifest than it is in our immersion in an absolute chaos. For if that chaos is an absolute necessity, and is truly and fully and finally absolute necessity itself, then it can only be that necessity which is the necessity of God.

5

GENESIS
AND GOD

Nothing is more deeply alien to everything which we have known as genesis than the genesis of God, or an actual as opposed to an eternal genesis of God, a genesis which is the beginning of God, and the absolute beginning of God. Yet that uniquely modern mysticism which is inaugurated by Meister Eckhart is a mysticism which knows a real distinction between God and the Godhead, thereby knowing a Godhead which is deeper than God, and deeper thereby than God the Creator. That does open the possibility if not the necessity of the genesis of the Creator, but that is a possibility wholly closed to all metaphysical thinking, and even closed to the radical metaphysical thinking of Spinoza, just as it was not openly or systematically realized by Hegel. Hegel's *Science of Logic* cannot know a truly unique and once-and-for-all act of genesis, and therefore cannot know the genesis of God as a once-and-for-all act, or as an act that is not the eternal genesis of God. A Hegelian self-negation of God is an eternal self-negation, and precisely thereby an eternal affirmation or realization of God. While that realization is negation, and an absolute negation, it is thereby an eternal resurrection or apocalypse. Now even if that resurrection is crucifixion, a Hegelian crucifixion or self-emptying is finally resurrection, and the resurrection of Godhead or absolute spirit itself. This is just the point at which there is an overwhelming gulf between the enactments of the death of God in Hegel and Nietzsche, but a gulf which is thereby a gulf between our world and Hegel's world, or between a nihilistic atheism and a pantheistic atheism.

Yet there is a comparable tension and perhaps even a gulf between the Calvary of absolute spirit in the *Phenomenology of Spirit* and the purely abstract self-negation of absolute spirit in the *Science of Logic*. Just as an actual self-consciousness is absent from the *Science of Logic,* a self-alienation and a self-estrangement of consciousness itself is absent from that logic, an absence which is the absence of an actually interior activity and life. But an interior realization is the driving power of the *Phenomenology of Spirit,* one that occurs through self-alienation and self-estrangement, a self-alienation and self-estrangement which is the very destiny of the interior subject of consciousness. That destiny is an epic destiny, and an epic destiny because it is a fully and finally historical destiny, and a historical destiny which is essentially necessary and inevitable for the truly self-alienated subject. Such self-alienation and self-estrangement is wholly inseparable from the purely interior subject of consciousness, a subject which is the center of the *Phenomenology of Spirit,* a center which is an epic center, and thereby a center ever more fully realizing itself as self-consciousness. If only at this crucial point, Hegel is a profoundly Augustinian thinker, but so likewise is Nietzsche an Augustinian thinker, and most clearly so in knowing not only the ultimate depths but the ultimate necessity of guilt and revenge. Nietzsche is never more decisively a pure thinker than in knowing the genesis of an ultimate guilt, a genesis that is the genesis of an interior consciousness, and precisely thereby a purely negative consciousness. But the genesis of that consciousness is the genesis of an absolutely alien and total judgment, a judgment that has only truly and actually been named in the naming of the Christian God.

Hegel and Nietzsche are united in knowing a full self-alienation and self-estrangement as the very center of self-consciousness, a self-alienation which is the center of all interior or subjective consciousness, and a self-alienation which is finally and ultimately an absolute self-alienation. Thereby Hegel and Nietzsche are more Augustinian than Augustine himself, or more so than Augustine could be as a philosophical thinker. But a conceptual understanding of the depths of self-estrangement is not historically possible until the historical realization of the pure autonomy of the interior subject or center of consciousness, and this does not comprehensively occur until the French Revolution. Then it occurs with such decisiveness as to end an interiority of consciousness which is not a self-alienated interiority, an ending which is also the ending of the actual possibility of knowing a "Being-in-itself" which is not a dichotomous and self-estranged ground. That ending occurs in the interior subject of consciousness, a perishing which is the genesis of an absolutely self-negating interior subject, and a subject or interior center of consciousness which Hegel and Nietzsche alike could know only by knowing the death of God. Only now is a wholly solitary "I" internally manifest and real, and an "I" whose very autonomy is inseparable from self-estrangement and self-negation. Therefore that autonomy is a dichotomous autonomy, an autonomy whose deepest ground is a dichotomous ground, and thus that very ground which Milton could envision as the absolute dichotomy between Satan and the Son of God.

Only with the full birth of modernity is the creation itself manifest and real as a purely and fully dichotomous act. Thus *Paradise Lost* knows the creation as a divine response to an original fall, the fall of Satan and the rebellious angels, just as Blake's prophetic poetry and designs could know creation as fall, a fall which is the fall of Urizen or the Creator. And unlike the Creator of ancient Gnosticism, Blake's Urizen or Satan is absolutely self-alienated at his very center, and that is a center which only in the nineteenth century is manifest as the center of Godhead itself. Yet this all too modern epic enactment of our destiny is simultaneously realized in our purest philosophical thinking, a thinking occurring between Spinoza and Nietzsche, and a thinking which is a conceptual realization of a progressive reversal of a pure infinity or a pure transcendence. But that reversal is a progressive totalization of finitude itself, a finitude which is infinite in its actuality, and infinite as the pure otherness of an originally empty or inactual or undifferentiated plenitude or totality. If that is the very plenum which is known both by ancient Gnosticism and by ancient Neoplatonism as Godhead itself, that is a plenum which is wholly reversed by the full actualization of modernity. Now the act of creation is actually manifest as being wholly other than any possible inactual or undifferentiated totality, and is so by the very actuality of its absolute act, an act which could have only a purely dichotomous relationship to a primordial emptiness or calm. Gnosticism could know the creation as a dichotomous act, but not as a purely and totally dichotomous act, not as an act which could affect Godhead itself. Indeed, it is only by knowing the plenitude of the Godhead that Gnosticism could know creation as fall, whereas modernity has known the infinity of the universe as the transformation or dissolution or reversal of an absolutely transcendent Godhead.

Augustine, in knowing the infinite goodness of the Creator, thereby knows the pure goodness of the creation itself, a goodness which is enacted in the eternal act of God. But Augustine finally came to know the eternal act of creation as being identical with the eternal act of predestination, a predestination which like the creation is an act of absolute grace, and therefore an enactment of that God who *is* love. For predestination is the ultimate source of redemption, but thereby it is simultaneously the source of all life and existence, and is so if only because it can finally be known as the creation itself. God *is* God in the eternal act of creation and predestination, just as God *is* love in that act, an enactment which is both the free and the necessary act of God. Apart from that act or enactment, there could and would be no God who is pure act or pure actuality, or no God who *is* at all. Thus the "isness" of God is the very opposite of an original quiescence or passivity which "is" and "is not" at once, as most purely apprehended by Mahayana Buddhism, so that the "isness" of God in its very essence "is not" a wholly passive or inactive totality, that very totality which Gnosticism and Neoplatonism can know as Godhead, and advaita Hinduism can know as Brahman-Atman. For it was the Christian, even if Neoplatonic, Augustine, who is the most anti-Gnostic thinker in the ancient world, and precisely so in knowing God the Creator, and thereby knowing Godhead itself as eternal *act*.

By decisively coming to know predestination itself as the eternal act of grace, Augustine could know the wholly other God as the God who *is* love, so that the very act which is most alien to our interior consciousness, the act of predestination, is identical with the eternal act of God. That is the act which we can only know by way of justification, a justification by grace alone, and therefore a justification by the eternal act of God alone. That act is predestination and creation at once, so that the act of creation is finally indistinguishable from the act of redemption, and thus the goodness of the creation is finally indistinguishable from the beatitude of eternal life. No one has ever known that goodness more purely than does Augustine, but that is a goodness inseparable from predestination, and therefore inseparable from a predestination to eternal life *and* to eternal death. That very goodness which Augustine knows as existence itself, is a goodness that is nevertheless inseparable from the absolute necessity of eternal death or Hell, a Hell that is the necessary and inevitable consequence of sin and fall, and therefore a Hell that is eternally willed by God. Or, if Augustine cannot and will not affirm that evil and death are willed by God, he can and does speak of the divine "permission of what is evil" (*The Enchiridion* XCVI). But that permission is a real and actual permission, a permission inevitably willed by God, and willed in that one act which is the eternal act and will of God. That is the very permission which is inseparable from the freedom of the human will, a freedom which is the consequence of our having been created in the image of God, and a freedom that is finally a freedom to will either eternal life or eternal death. And it is precisely because God eternally knows that fall and eternal death are our destiny that God wills predestination, a predestination which is an act of eternal love, but simultaneously an eternal act of justice which eternally consumes evil and sin in an eternal death of Hell.

So it is that the very love which embodies our redemption is inseparable from that judgment which embodies our damnation, and if predestination is an infinite act of love that loves even a sinner who rebels against the will of God, it is simultaneously an infinite judgment which eternally consumes all unredeemed sinners, or all sinners who are not predestined to redemption. At no point is Dante more Augustinian than in so fully correlating and integrating the *Inferno* and the *Paradiso,* but that integration is made possible by the *Purgatorio,* and the *Purgatorio* is the celebration of a purgatory unknown to Augustine, and unknown to the ancient Christian world as a whole. Dante is our only magisterial poet who is wholly innocent of a dichotomous center, thus he could imaginatively enact an integral and harmonious totality which has imaginatively been enacted in no other historical world. Dante could even know our freedom itself as an integral and harmonious freedom, a freedom embodying a human act that is decisive for all eternity, but that act is wholly integrated with the totality of both cosmos and history. Thus this freedom is a cosmic destiny, and therefore it is the freedom of predestination, a predestination which evoked even Dante's resistance, but nevertheless a predestination which is cosmically embodied in the *Commedia.* That embodiment is a unique embodiment, for the *Commedia* is wholly alone is so fully integrating both history and eternity and thinking and the imagination. But that world did inaugurate a new and even autonomous freedom, and a freedom which even speaks in the *"io sol uno,"* the "I myself alone" of Dante (*Inferno* II, 3). If that speech is the first full and decisive poetic actualization of self-consciousness, this is an actualization which is destined to become all in all in full modernity, but only by being the self-embodiment of a purely dichotomous center.

That dichotomous center is the self-realization of a new freedom, a freedom it is true inaugurated by Dante, but now a freedom which is a fully dichotomous freedom, and dichotomous most clearly in its very ground in self-estrangement. Accordingly, it is the renewal of an Augustinian freedom, a freedom which is known only by knowing the bondage of the will, just as Augustine discovered true freedom only by realizing the chains that interiorly bound his own will (*Confessions* VIII, 5). Once those chains were realized by Augustine as internal and interior chains, he could then know his bondage as his own, and therefore know his own freedom, for his very bondage is now manifest as a consequence of his own will. Augustine's discovery of freedom was a discovery of the will, a will unknown to the ancient world, just as an interior freedom is unknown to that world. So likewise is an interior bondage unknown to the ancient world, and if that is a bondage philosophically discovered by Augustine, that is a bondage which is inseparable from the freedom of the will. This is a bondage and a freedom which Augustine eventually came to understand as a consequence of predestination, and almost immediately thereafter it was dogmatically affirmed by the Catholic Church. While predestination was affirmed by all known medieval Christian thinkers, it only became an overwhelming reality in our history with the closure of the Middle Ages, and above all so in the Reformation. No thinker resisted and opposed the dogma of predestination more deeply than did Spinoza, yet he could do so only by realizing freedom as an absolute necessity, and a necessity which is embodied in Substance or Godhead itself. Nevertheless, Spinoza could dissolve a dichotomous center, a center which is the center of predestination, only by dissolving the freedom of the will of God. That is a dissolution which dissolves the very possibility of a real and actual contingency, thereby the infinite power of absolute necessity is manifest and called forth, but that is a necessity which dissolves every freedom which is not the freedom of necessity.

Thus if Spinoza reversed the dogma of predestination, he did so only by affirming an absolute necessity which is its counterpart, and that necessity is the very substance of the Godhead. Yet the truth is that Spinoza knew a deep freedom, a freedom unknown in the ancient world, and did so by way of what he affirmed to be an immediate union with God, and thus a union with that absolute necessity which is a free necessity. This is a union which is possible only in our understanding, an understanding or "intellect" which is identical with the will, and an understanding which can freely will only by willing necessity. But neither our deepest thinking nor our deepest imagination has ever known a freedom which is not the freedom of necessity, and if a new freedom does realize itself in modernity, that is a freedom which is fully and actually a dichotomous freedom, and is so most clearly in its own self-alienation and self-estrangement. Therein a distinctively modern freedom and a distinctively Augustinian freedom coincide, and that coincidence is the realization of a deep and ultimate dichotomy, and of a deeply interior dichotomy, but a dichotomy which is most openly manifest in the very dogma of predestination. Here, and only fully here in Christian doctrine, God is openly manifest as the God of life and the God of death, and that God of life who is the God of death. Yet only here is there openly manifest a deep ground for human freedom, a freedom inseparable from predestination, and inseparable from predestination because only predestination makes possible that deep freedom which is an ultimate act of the will. That is an act which is an eternal act, an eternal act which is released by the eternal act of God, and an eternal act which is willed in the eternal will of God. Thus it is an act which can only culminate eschatologically in either redemption or damnation, and if that redemption and that damnation are willed by God, they are so willed through the free will of humanity, for that is the will which is either justified by grace or damned by judgment, and that grace and that judgment are one in the eternal will of God.

Indeed, it is only the realization of the actuality of damnation that makes possible an interior realization of freedom, or an internal realization of the freedom of the will, a freedom of the will which is necessarily known by realizing the actuality of damnation, for only that freedom makes damnation interiorly actual and real. Thus an interior realization of the freedom of the will is an interior realization of fall, a fall which is the fall of the will itself, and a fall which is freely willed by that will. No thinker has known the fall more deeply than did Nietzsche, and he knew it by knowing consciousness itself as a wholly broken or fallen consciousness, a consciousness which in being the "labor of the negative" is the labor of repression. That repression is the consequence of an original fall, a fall which is the origin of the "bad conscience" (*Genealogy of Morals* II), but a bad conscience or *ressentiment* or No-saying whose pure reversal is the total grace or Yes-saying of Eternal Recurrence. In Nietzsche and Hegel alike, just as in Blake and Milton alike, the negative is finally positive, and the purely negative finally realizes a total grace, a total grace which is the total reversal of an original fall, and a grace which would be wholly unreal and unrealized apart from that fall. Thus that fall is finally a fortunate fall, a fall apart from which no real or ultimate opposition would be possible, yet apart from which no ultimate reconciliation or apocalypse would be possible. So it is that the very dichotomy which is a consequence of the fall is a dichotomy which is unknown apart from a realization of the fall, but that realization *is* the realization of freedom, and a realization of that freedom which is embodied in the fall.

A true dichotomy only actually enters consciousness with Paul, then it realizes a dichotomous consciousness which is the very birth of the dichotomous "I" or a fully actual self-consciousness, a birth which is a fully interior realization of that fallen will which is wholly a guilty will. This is the very will which was philosophically discovered by Augustine, a will which is a purely negative will, yes, but therein and thereby a free will which is the source of its own negativity. That interior consciousness and will which Augustine so deeply knows, is a wholly fallen will, but precisely thereby is the arena of that one freedom which we can fully and actually know. Augustine is the conceptual father of an internal and interior freedom, but that is a dichotomous freedom, and a dichotomous freedom because it is free and enslaved at once and altogether. We can know our interior freedom only by knowing the impotence of our will, but that is an impotence which we know to be fully and wholly our own, an impotence which is the impotence of the fallen will. Yet that is the very will which is the center of the Christian epic tradition, an organic and evolving tradition wherein the will ever more fully and decisively realizes its own deep negativity, evolving from the new "I" of Dante to the totally negative will of Milton's Satan to the totality of the fallen will in Blake's *Milton* and *Jerusalem*. That evolution is a historical evolution embodying the deeper currents of our history, currents finally giving birth to the totality of the purely negative "I," an "I" which is the "I" of a totally fallen Godhead. The *Commedia* knows that "I" as a totally gracious Godhead, whereas *Paradise Lost* knows it as the absolutely sovereign power of the absolutely solitary Creator, a power that must "retire" to make possible the creation, because the creation can now be realized only as the consequence of fall.

Not until the mature Blake is God Himself named as Satan, and a Miltonic Satan, a Satan who is the self-embodiment of a purely and totally negative will, but that will is finally realized as the actual will of every fully individual and interior will. Accordingly, this is the very will which Nietzsche knows as the Will to Power, even as Hegel knows it as that self-alienated God who is "Being-in-itself" or the "Bad Infinite," a will that is unreal and unmanifest apart from an absolute self-alienation, or that very self-alienation which is the center and the ground of a purely dichotomous consciousness. Nietzsche could affirm the Will to Power as the ecstatic dance of Eternal Recurrence, but he could do so only by fully realizing the death of God, a realization which is a realization of a Blakean "Self Annihilation." Now that self-annihilation is the self-annihilation of God, and a self-annihilation of the totally dichotomous God, but a God who is not known or realized as such until the full realization of modernity. Only then does the fallen will realize itself as being all in all, a total fallenness which an earlier modernity could know as being wholly realized only in Satan and Hell, but a Miltonic Satan is the lord of a fallen world, and that is a world which is totality itself in a fully realized modernity. Yet this is the very world which is the sole arena of a fully actual freedom, a freedom that is a fallen freedom, yes, and thereby a dichotomous freedom, but precisely thereby a totally responsible freedom.

All of the true soliloquies of *Paradise Lost* occur within Satan's domain, therein they embody that self-estrangement which is the self-alienation of the dichotomous consciousness, just as it is the self-realization of a purely interior and solitary consciousness. This is the very "I" which embodies our epic destiny, a destiny first interiorly enacted in Eve's temptation and fall, as Eve is tempted by a purely negative freedom, a negative freedom which is a purely autonomous freedom, and which can be realized only by an ultimate transgression, an ultimate transgression which can be enacted only in the purely negative will. That is the will which is realized in the fall, and even if it is first realized in Lucifer's rebellion, it is not interiorly realized until Eve's transgression, a transgression which is the inauguration of a purely interior dichotomy.

Just as Eve is tempted by that ecstatic delight induced by a purely negative and thus purely forbidden consciousness, a delight consummated in that ecstasy which she knew in tasting the forbidden fruit, that is a delight occasioned by the actual realization of a fully interior consciousness, but an interior consciousness which is a negative consciousness in that assault which it conducts upon itself. So it is that Milton could know such assault as a Satanic assault, an assault realizing a purely Satanic negativity, a negativity wherein "myself am Hell" (IV 75), but that is the very negativity which is the full actuality of a wholly fallen world. This is why a uniquely modern consciousness is so deeply an Augustinian consciousness, but it goes beyond that origin in knowing a total self-alienation and self-estrangement, a total doubling of consciousness wherein consciousness purely and totally negates itself. And that is the only consciousness which can actually know the dichotomy of God, a dichotomy that is initially envisioned by Milton as being realized in a solitary and alien Creator, but is fully envisioned in Blake's epic enactment of Urizen and Satan, for Blake's Satan is that Creator who is the totally dichotomous God, and a totally dichotomous God who can only be known and realized by a totally dichotomous consciousness. Nothing is more revolutionary in Blake than his naming of God as Satan, a naming which is the realization of the totality of fall, and the totality of that fall which is the eternal act of creation. Absolute beginning can now be known only as fall, a fall from the pure calm of an original and undifferentiated totality, and therefore a fall which is a pure disruption of that totality. But that disruption is the act of the Creator, a Creator who is an absolutely dichotomous Creator, and is so in that very act of disruption.

If nothing more manifestly distinguishes Christianity from all the religions of the world than does the ultimacy with which it apprehends the fall, this is an apprehension which is enacted in Christian history and the Christian consciousness, and one that ever more fully and more finally evolves as it occurs. While both the symbol and the realization of fall are primary in Paul and the Fourth Gospel, and are certainly so in Augustine, they are deeply muted in high medieval or Gothic Christianity, only to burst forth with an irresistible power with the full dawning of modernity, a dawning which is the realization of a purely negative but now universal consciousness. Now a negative or fallen consciousness realizes itself as a full and final actuality, and now the creation itself is unmanifest or inactual apart from the fall, so that even *Paradise Lost* can only envision the original goodness of the creation as a paradise lost, just as modern science can only know an infinite universe by knowing it as an absolutely naked or empty reality wholly devoid of any possible ultimate purpose or cause. That loss is the loss of everything which Christianity had once known as genesis or absolute beginning, or, at the very least, a loss of a creation which is only creation, as opposed to a creation which is fall. Now the very act of the creation is actually manifest as fall, and is so manifest in that consciousness which can actually know the world, so that now knowledge itself, and above all so an interior knowledge, is a knowledge or realization of fall.

A consciousness and a knowledge so fully embodying the fall is a primal witness to the dichotomy of the Creator, a newly realized dichotomy, and one actualizing a truly new realization of God the Creator. Ancient Gnosticism could mythically name the dichotomy of the Creator, but it could do so only by knowing the Creator as an alien God who is wholly dissociated from Godhead or pure Spirit, so that then the creation is a fall from that absolutely inactual and purely primordial Spirit. That is the very Spirit or Heaven which wholly disappears with the full advent of modernity, and if the disappearance of such a primordial plenum is already manifest in the *Purgatorio* and the *Paradiso,* it is fully manifest in *Paradise Lost,* and then is realized as the actual "otherness" of itself in *Milton* and *Jerusalem.* Now it can only be evoked as an innocence that is wholly other than experience, or a dream that is wholly other than reality, or a "noumenon" that is absolutely invisible and silent in consciousness and the world. And that invisibility and silence is not an actual invisibility or silence, not a silence or invisibility which can actually be evoked or imagined, for its actual ending is now the full and final ending of a primordial plenum or totality. But only now does fall itself become all in all, and all in all in a new history and a new consciousness, and a truly new history and consciousness which is the total embodiment of fall.

Yet that embodiment is a self-embodiment, and most clearly and most decisively so in a new interior consciousness, a consciousness which is an "unhappy consciousness," and precisely thereby a totally fallen consciousness. While this new consciousness is a rebirth or renewal of a Pauline and Augustinian consciousness, it goes far beyond that origin by losing or dissolving every integral or essential relationship to its own polar opposite. For now there wholly disappears a self-consciousness which is a consciousness of grace, or a self-consciousness which is a consciousness of a redemptive ground or source, or a self-consciousness which can know or realize itself as an arena or avenue of a redemptive transfiguration.

That dissolution is the dissolution of the very possibility of actually knowing or realizing a non-dichotomous ground, as is most decisively manifest in our distinctively if not uniquely modern images and ideas of God, for even when these are non-dichotomous, as in Spinoza, they are wholly dissociated from everything which we can actually know or name as God, and even when they are wholly empty and vacuous, as in the Enlightenment, they can only evoke a vacuous or empty God. But when they are most fully themselves as an unveiling or realization of God, as in Blake and Hegel, they are realizations of a pure and absolute dichotomy, and a dichotomy which is only deepened in their subsequent expressions, as in Nietzsche and Joyce.

Now the truth is that such images and ideas are never abated or reversed throughout the history of modernity, but only loosened, numbed, or disguised, and this manifestly occurs in our lesser artists and thinkers, for nowhere in the higher expressions of modern art and thinking have we been given a truly positive or affirmative vision or understanding of God. Nothing else is so manifestly unique in our world, not even ancient Gnosticism could know a Creator who is the embodiment of a total alienation, an alienation which is the alienation of Godhead itself. An Augustinian apprehension of the sheer goodness of existence itself has been impossible for us since the seventeenth century, if not much earlier, just as a comprehensive or epic enactment or a harmonious totality has been impossible since Dante, and impossible in even the most exalted expressions of our imagination. So it is that the existence which we can actually know is a dichotomous existence, and even a purely dichotomous existence, an existence which is the very opposite of a purely quiescent calm, or a primordial undifferentiated totality. Only in the modern world has the creation itself been manifest and real as a purely dichotomous act, an act of absolutely disenacting the pure calm of an original plenitude, and an act which could only be the absolute disruption of that plenitude.

Nothing could more fully witness to the deep bondage of ancient or patristic Christianity to a pre-Christian or pagan world than does its inability or refusal to understand or to call forth the creation as a new creation rather than an eternal creation, and if it was not until Aquinas that Christian thinking became open to the *novitas mundi* or the "newness" of the world, this alone is a decisive sign of a genuine transformation of Christianity. Now a new gulf is realized between Eastern and Western Christianity, but an even deeper gulf between ancient and high medieval Christianity, as most clearly embodied in Dante's *Commedia*. Philosophically, Christian medieval philosophy culminates in nominalism, a nominalism which is a truly new opening to an empirical or actually contingent world, and a new actuality embodying a dichotomous relationship to a purely essential realm, or to a realm in which "essence" and "existence" are unified and coordinated. If this made possible the birth of a new logical and scientific thinking, it also ushered in a new dichotomy of thinking and consciousness, a dichotomy ending that synthesis or unity established by a Dante or an Aquinas. Nominalism made possible both modern science and the Reformation, thereby realizing a truly new apprehension of God, a new apprehension of God inseparable from the birth of a new historical world. Now God can be known as being at once both fully present in the world and yet even thereby being wholly distant or absent from the world. The simultaneity of that presence and absence is not only a paradoxical relationship between God and the world, but a truly dichotomous relationship, and one which explodes in the full birth of modernity.

The Lutheran dichotomy between Law and Gospel or the righteous God and the crucified God is one embodiment of that dichotomy, just as a new mathematical and scientific realization of an infinite universe is another. While that is a universe in which the *physica coelestis* and the *physica terrestris* are unified if not identified, it is also a universe in which every formal and final cause has disappeared, a disappearance which is a disappearance of both the "will" and the "act" of God, and thereby the disappearance or the expulsion of an interior apprehension of a teleological destiny or order. As Nietzsche remarked, ever since Copernicus we have been falling into a mysterious unknown, an unknown progressively erasing or nullifying our deepest center, and therefore a vacuous unknown which is an all consuming void. And that void is not a dualistic void, not a Gnostic or Manichaean otherness, but far rather a dichotomous void, and thus a total void, or a void voiding every interior center. But that void is inseparable from the realization of our center, a new center if only because it is a new interiority, and a new interiority voiding itself in its own self-realization, hence the power of the new myth of the Faustian wager. That wager is a universal wager, one now enacted in the self-lacerations of a new solitary consciousness, a self-consciousness knowing its own damnation or eternal death in those very lacerations, so that these lacerations are a rebirth and a renewal of that dichotomous consciousness which was born in the very advent of Christianity. An internally divided and doubled consciousness is first recorded in the letters of Paul, a consciousness simultaneously knowing the glory of redemption and the terror of damnation, and the internal power of each is inseparable from the internal power of the other, even as the exaltation of a Hamlet or a Lear is inseparable from his degradation and destruction.

While in his lectures on the history of philosophy, Hegel could demonstrate a full and deep continuity between the philosophical think-ing of Augustine and Descartes, neither Hegel nor any other thinker has apprehended a genuine historical continuity between the birth of Chris-tianity and the birth of the modern world, a birth which in each is a birth of a deep and interior dichotomy. But if each is an origin of a true dichotomy, and a full dichotomy which may be apprehended nowhere else in world history, then it is inconceivable that there is not a deep historical relationship between them. Nietzsche, in understanding Chris-tianity as the origin of our nihilism, did understand such a continuity, and he understood it by knowing the Christian God as the will to nothingness pronounced holy (*The Antichrist* 18). But not even Nietzsche could or would understand our scientific consciousness or our interior sensibility as historical consequences of the uniquely Christian God, except insofar as he understood our guilt and bad conscience as such a consequence. But the deepest realizations of a true dichotomy in early modernity are Christian realizations, as witness Boehme's apprehension of a deep dichotomy at the very center of the Godhead, or Milton's epic enactment of a pure dichotomy between sin and grace or Satan and the Messiah, a dichotomy certainly known by Luther, and one which was a deep foundation of the Reformation itself. Indeed, such a dichotomy historically explodes in that revolutionary history occurring between the English and the French revolutions, and the English Revolution unquestionably had a deep Christian ground, even if that ground becomes reversed in the French Revolution, and reversed so as finally to usher in a uniquely modern nihilism.

If that is a nihilism only made possible by the uniquely Christian God, that is a nihilism which is a historical realization of that God, and a historical realization of what full modernity had known as the deep dichotomy of God. Only now is Godhead itself manifest and real as being in full opposition to itself, an opposition which is a dichotomous opposition, and dichotomous in its very opposition to itself. And only now can genesis or absolute beginning be manifest and real as a dichotomous beginning, a dichotomous beginning which is the very opposite of an undifferentiated plenum or totality, and therefore the opposite of an eternity which is an "eternal now." That is the very origin which is inseparable from a purely dichotomous "existence," an existence which we so fully know to be our own, and an existence which is the true opposite of a primordial silence and calm. But such an existence is nevertheless fully manifest in an original Christian apocalypticism, even as it is so in an Augustinian dichotomy between nature and grace, a Lutheran dichotomy between Law and Gospel, and a Miltonic and Blakean dichotomy between Satan and Christ. Hegel could know such a dichotomy as the very source and ground of all actual movement and life, an ultimate and absolute ground which Hegel knows as the self-negation or self-emptying of absolute spirit. Even in his early theological writings, Hegel knew that ground as an atoning sacrifice, a deep sacrifice which is a recurrent motif in the *Phenomenology of Spirit,* and a sacrifice which Hegel knew to be embodied in the death of God. That is the death of God which is the Calvary of absolute spirit, a Calvary which is the total embodiment of God, and a self-embodiment of the sacrifice of God.

But that crucifixion can also be known as a repetition of the creation, and of a once-and-for-all creation, a creation which is a creation out of "nothing," and therefore a creation negating that "nothingness" which is an original plenum. Such a negation could only be a dichotomous act, even as the crucifixion is a dichotomous act, each is an irreversible and ultimate event, just as each is an absolutely unique event. Both that ultimacy and that uniqueness embody dichotomy, and a pure dichotomy, a dichotomy which is a pure and ultimate opposition, and an opposition embodied in the finality of each negation. Nothing is so precarious in Christianity as is the preservation of these negations, or even their memory or recall, and if *anamnesis* or re-presentation is the very center of Christian worship, that is an *anamnesis* of an absolutely unique and final negation, and a negation occurring in genesis and crucifixion alike. Yet perhaps only a realization of the full unity of genesis and crucifixion can make manifest the purely dichotomous identity of genesis itself, a genesis which is an ultimate negation of nothingness, but an ultimate and final negation can only be a self-negation, and hence a self-negation of the Creator. The Christian can know that self-negation as being realized in the crucifixion, a crucifixion which is a self-negation of the uniquely Christian God, thus opening the possibility of understanding the creation itself as the self-negation of a primordial totality. Only thereby does a primordial totality or "nothingness" become an alien nothingness, just as only through the crucifixion does the transcendent God become the alien God, an actual emptying of transcendence which is the death of God. Just as Blake and Hegel can know crucifixion as the self-annihilation or self-negation of the alien God, that God who is Satan or "Being-in-itself," so genesis could be known as the self-emptying or the self-negation of an original nothingness, but a nothingness realizing itself as an actual or alien nothingness only in that self-negation or self-emptying.

The uniquely Christian symbol of the cross is a symbol of the ultimate enactment of an actual nothingness, a nothingness which is a full and actual death, and not only an actual death but a total death, a death which is the crucifixion of God. Now even if it was not until the advent of the modern world that Christianity could know the crucifixion as the death of God, that knowledge is inseparable from a recovery of the Bible, a scripture that had ever more deeply been lost with the very historical evolution of Christianity, and a scripture whose historical recovery effected a revolutionary transformation of Christianity. Nothing is more revolutionary in an original Protestantism than an apprehension of a pure dichotomy between the Bible and the Catholic Church, or between the Biblical God and the scholastic God, or between Christ and the Papacy. But the realization of these dichotomies made possible the realization of dichotomies between the righteous God and the crucified God, between human reason and a divine revelation, between human freedom and a divine predestination, and between a fallen creation and the triumph of grace. All of these dichotomies are genuine dichotomies, and all of them are assaults upon over fifteen hundred years of Christendom, which the original reformers deeply believed had realized the triumph of Antichrist, but which through God's grace and the blood of Christ they were determined to reverse. This was the historical context in which they could know the crucifixion as the crucifixion of God, but that is the very crucifixion which is the sole source of redemption, and is, indeed, the absolute grace of God. While such a Protestantism is inseparable from these dichotomies, it gradually evaporated with the dissolution of those dichotomies, a dissolution which is either the secularization of Protestantism or its reversal into an inverted and frozen orthodoxy, but even as these dichotomies were disappearing from an overt Protestantism, they realized a metamorphosis into far more universal expressions, until they were embodied in the fullness of modernity itself.

So it is that a new and actual nothingness which is called forth by the symbol of the cross has finally passed into a universal nothingness in our world, and a nothingness that is the very opposite of a Buddhist nothingness, and is so precisely by way of its purely dichotomous actuality. Even if it is true that our nothingness is only manifest as such in the deepest and purest acts of our imagination and thinking, and even if a new anonymous consciousness is deeply veiling every actual identity in our midst, the disintegration of our world as a Christian world is manifest for all to see, and now world itself would appear to be at a virtually infinite distance from anything which can be remembered or recalled as that world which Christianity once knew as the creation. But if our world is a truly dichotomous world, and perhaps the most purely dichotomous world which has ever been historically actual and real, then we can understand our world as the creation if we can understand creation itself as an absolutely dichotomous act. Just as a deep and comprehensive scientific understanding of the world is inseparable for us from a virtually universal nihilism, so, too, the calling forth of the brute facticity of the world in the deepest expressions of our imagination has been a realization of nihilism, and just as the greatest poets of the twentieth century have all been nihilistic poets, so likewise have our purest thinkers been nihilistic thinkers, and most clearly nihilistic in their pure and decisive dissolutions of everything whatsoever which has been given to us as either God or Being. Nowhere in either our deepest imaginative creations or in our deepest thinking may one today discover a positive or affirmative realization of the Creator, indeed, nothing is more manifestly absent from our world than everything which Christendom knew as the Creator, thereby we have certainly lost the deepest ground of world itself, or lost the ultimate ground of everything which was once manifest and real in Christendom as the creation.

Yet if we would seem to have lost everything which was once given us as the Creator, this does open the possibility for the realization of a radically new image or apprehension of the Creator, a Creator who is truly a dichotomous Creator, just as the creation itself can now be manifest only as a dichotomous creation. A Creator who is the Crucified God is certainly a dichotomous image of the Creator, and perhaps the most dichotomous image which is possible for us, and even if no such image has systematically or comprehensively been realized in our theological thinking, both

Christian thinking and the modern Christian imagination have known the Crucified God as the fullness of Godhead itself, and that does pose the possibility if not the necessity of understanding the Crucified God as the Creator. While only Blake has given us a symbolic language which openly and fully identifies the Crucified God and the Creator, a language which is the deepest and most paradoxical language of *Milton* and *Jerusalem,* that language itself can be understood as a rebirth of the Bible. It was the visionary Blake who discovered the apocalyptic identity of Jesus, and did so long before such an identity was known by Biblical scholarship, just as it was Blake who first and most fully called forth the purely dichotomous identity of the uniquely Christian God. This most clearly occurs in Blake's naming of God as Satan, but that Satan is the Creator, and not a Gnostic Creator who is the source of matter or evil alone, but a Creator who is the actual source of the totality of experience. This is the Creator who perishes or is reversed in the "Self Annihilation of God," a self-annihilation which is the crucifixion of God, and a self-annihilation which is an apocalyptic transfiguration. Hegel could know such transfiguration as a consequence of the *kenosis* or self-emptying of absolute spirit, a kenosis certainly comprehending the eternal act of genesis, so that genesis itself can now be manifest as an eternal act of self-negation.

But once genesis can be understood as an absolute act of self-negation, then genesis can be envisioned as a total act of sacrifice, and the total sacrifice of that God who *is* love. If that sacrifice is creation and predestination at once, that dichotomous actuality which is its embodiment is a kenotic or self-emptying actuality. This could only be an actuality which at its very center embodies a pure opposition, a pure opposition between its positive and its negative poles, and a pure opposition realizing absolute act, and that absolute act which is creation and predestination simultaneously. But such an act could only be an absolutely dichotomous act, and manifestly so in a predestination to eternal life and to eternal death, and even more manifestly so if the eternal act of the creation is inseparable from the eternal act of the crucifixion. So it is that when crucifixion is conjoined with creation, the creation itself can be understood as a purely and totally dichotomous act, and an act which is a self-negating or self-emptying enactment. Thereby the creation is the realization of an absolute opposition at the very center of the actuality which it enacts, an actuality which is a dichotomous actuality, and a dichotomous actuality which is embodied in the pure act of the Creator. That pure act is a purely dichotomous act, an act which is in absolute opposition to itself, and in absolute opposition to that primordial Godhead which is an inactual plenum or totality. If that opposition is the very "life" of the actuality of the Godhead, that "life" is in profound opposition to itself, and in profound opposition to itself as primordial or quiescent Godhead. Consequently, that "life" *is* "death," and finally actually realizes itself in death, that absolute death which Christianity knows as crucifixion. The symbol of the crucifixion has always been a paradox, and even an absolute paradox, just as it has been an absolute offense, an offense most deeply resisted by Christianity itself, yet an offense which has again and again released the deepest expressions of Christianity. Is such an offense now offering us the possibility of truly understanding the Crucified God as the Creator?

Theologically, nothing more deeply opposes such a possibility than does the Christian dogma of the Trinity, but even as that dogma evolved in opposition to ancient Christian heresy, one of the heresies which it most deeply opposed was the heresy of Sabellianism, a Sabellianism which is resurrected in the first great epic of our century, Joyce's *Ulysses.* The Son of God appears mythically or dogmatically in *Ulysses* only in a heretical form, and most clearly so in Sabellian Trinitarianism: "Sabellius, the African, the subtlest heresiarch of all the beasts of the field, held that the Father was Himself His Own Son" (208). Nowhere else does Joyce speak theologically with greater clarity, and if he gave us our final epics, these are epics occurring in a world in which the Father is wholly invisible as father, but this is an invisibility resurrecting a uniquely Christian mystery, the mystery of the crucifixion of God. If Sabellianism most fully makes that mystery dogmatically manifest, a Sabellianism in which the Father quite simply *is* the Son, that is a mystery which is only publicly manifest in the mass, and most particularly so in the very consumption of the broken Host. In *Ulysses,* the Creator is only a noise or a voice in the street, even if He is thereby a "hangman God" who is doubtless all in all in all of us (213), but this does make possible a new or perhaps renewed prayer to "Our Father who are not in Heaven" (227). But this is an apocalyptic prayer which is prayed to prepare the way for the final return of Elijah, a return ushering in the triumph of the New Jerusalem, which is named in the night language of Circe as the "new Bloomusalem" (484). "Bloomusalem" is finally the resurrected body of Anna Livia Plurabelle in *Finnegans Wake,* that is a body which is the apocalyptic body of the Crucified God, and therein a totally reversed body of the creation itself.

If Here Comes Everybody is our apocalyptic destiny, a destiny even now being born, that is a destiny realized by crucifixion, and realized by the crucifixion of God. Now the wheel has come full circle, as the crucifixion itself is universalized, and apocalyptically universalized in a reversed or inverted cosmos or world, an inverted world reversing everything which an orthodox Christianity has known as crucifixion and resurrection. Hence the inevitable necessity of transgression, one even realizing itself in *Finnegans Wake* in a cosmic and apocalyptic eucharist or mass, and thus a purely transgressive mass. Just as the *Paradiso* culminates in a visionary voyage into the depths of the "Infinite Goodness," depths wherein an interiorly resurrected Dante sees the scattered limbs or leaves of the universe bound by love "in one single volume" (XXXIII, 86), so *Finnegans Wake* culminates in a resurrected Anna Livia Plurabelle's final soliloquy with the cosmic dispersal of her body or leaves:

> So. Avelaval. My leaves have drifted from me. All. But one clings still. I'll bear it on me. To remind me of. Lff! So soft this morning ours. Yes. (628.6–9)

While the epic action of the *Wake* proceeds out of the dark abyss of primordial sacrifice, a primordial sacrifice which apocalyptically is creation, that sacrifice culminates in an apocalyptic repetition of "God said." Yet an apocalyptic repetition reverses primordial repetition, so that "Let there be Light" becomes "Let there be Darkness," an apocalyptic darkness reversing but nevertheless renewing a primordial abyss and light. For the night language or "not language" of the *Wake* embodies the brute and formless matter of the primordial "water," now that "water" finally speaks, and it speaks with an immediacy never sounded before, or never sounded since the original act of creation.

Accordingly, a resurrected Anna can now proclaim: "Rise up now and aruse! Norvena's over" (619.28). "Norvena" or Nirvana is over when night totally falls, but that night is an apocalyptic resurrection, and an apocalyptic resurrection of crucifixion itself. Blake, too, could know such resurrection in his vision of "The Eternal Great Humanity Divine," but that is a resurrection which is real only through a violent reversal, and a reversal of that Satan who is now our only actual name for the primordial and transcendent Creator, yet it is the death of that Satan which *is* resurrection, and a death which is finally and apocalyptically a universal death, and thereby a crucifixion which *is* creation itself. If it is impossible for the Christian to know a God who is not the Creator, now it has overwhelmingly become impossible for the Christian to know a God who is not the Crucified God, this is just a crucial point at which a modern orthodox Trinitarianism has become a sheer impossibility. While Hegel is the most trinitarian of all our thinkers, his is a deeply modern Sabellian Trinitarian-ism, and precisely so in refusing all ultimate or final distinctions within that absolute spirit who is the Godhead. Historically, orthodox Trinitari-anism has always embodied a profoundly reactionary movement, as may be observed in Augustine himself, whose *De Trinitate* is his most deeply Neoplatonic work. It was Christian heresy which generated Trinitarian-ism, and just as the Trinity is absent from the New Testament, except for those few passages which most clearly reflect a ground in the cultic life of the early church, so likewise is Trinitarianism absent from Christian apocalypticism, with the possible exception of that radical tradition initiated by Joachim of Flora, which was perhaps the most powerful heresy in the Middle Ages. However, the three images in that tradition are not orthodox images of the Trinity, since each so fully and so totally passes into the other. So likewise the three moments of the Hegelian dialectic are not orthodox Trinitarian moments, and for precisely the same reason. Indeed, anti-Trinitarianism has commonly been at the forefront of Chris-tian heresy, and just as it is an essential ground of the radical Reformation, so, too, is it fundamental in Milton and Newton, to say nothing of Blake and Joyce. So that if Barth could become an orthodox theologian only by becoming a Trinitarian theologian, thereby refusing his early radical and Kierkegaardian ground, theology can now be a Trinitarian theology only by being a reactionary theology, and not only a reactionary theology but a sectarian theology, a theology refusing every ground in our world itself.

Orthodox Christianity has always profoundly resisted the symbol of the cross, so that the cross does not truly enter Christian iconography until the closure of the patristic age, even as it does not become a full presence in medieval iconography until the end of the Gothic age. Only with the end of Christendom does the cross become fully embodied in the Christian consciousness, so that just as the crucified Christ is virtually absent from the *Commedia*, the Christ of passion is the sole source of redemption in *Paradise Lost*. All too significantly, the orthodox Christian affirmation of the absolute mystery of God, a mystery that is nowhere more fully visible than in the dogma of the Trinity, is an absolute opposition to the very possibility of the death of God, a death which is the center of the symbol of the cross. Just as we may discover no real theological understanding of crucifixion until Luther, Boehme, and Milton, it is precisely in Milton, Boehme, and Luther that there occurs the first theological realization of a purely dichotomous theological thinking and vision, and certainly dichot-omous in its inability truly to dissociate the Creator God and the Crucified God. Or, if Milton is impelled to attempt this, he can do so only by envisioning the Creator as retiring in the act of creation, so that now the Son of God is the real if not the sole agent of creation. Yet Milton knew the total death of Christ as it had never been known theologically before, a knowledge forcing him to deny the full deity of the Son of God, but also inevitably impelling him to know an absolutely sovereign and solitary Creator as a non-Trinitarian Godhead, or that very Godhead which Hegel could know as the "Bad Infinite" and Blake could envision as Satan.

If nothing is a deeper mystery to the pagan world than the mystery of creation, nothing is a deeper mystery in the Christian world than that very creation, and above all so if creation is finally inseparable from crucifixion. Then not only is the creation an absolutely dichotomous act, but a dichotomous act which is in profound opposition to itself, and in profound opposition to itself either as the "Bad Infinite" or as an absolutely solitary Godhead. But as Hegel knew so deeply, the "Bad Infinite" or purely abstract Spirit is itself the consequence of an original self-negation, an original self-negation which is the eternal act of creation, and that eternal act of creation which is the origin of a pure negativity. A purely dichotomous creation could only be an absolute self-negation and self-emptying of the Godhead, and therein and thereby can be repeated and renewed in the crucifixion. Such a repetition could only be a repetition of an absolute sacrifice, and an absolute sacrifice which now and only now makes actually manifest and real that absolute self-negation which is the *act* of creation. At no point are Blake and Hegel more deeply united than in unveiling the crucifixion as the very realization of the emptying of the Creator, only now is the Creator actual and real as a self-negated or self-emptied Creator, and self-emptied originally in the very act of crucifixion. Accordingly, it is only through the crucifixion that the Creator is finally actualized as that "Bad Infinite" which is the very opposite of finitude, only through the crucifixion that the Creator is truly actual and real as Satan. So it is that it is Christianity, alone among the religions of the world, which actually knows Satan, and actually knows Satan because it is Christianity alone which knows the crucifixion of God.

If that Satan is reborn with the full advent of modernity, as epically enacted in *Paradise Lost,* so, too, is reborn a new realization of creation as fall, then the Creator is inevitably known as an alien Creator, and the pure transcendence of the Creator is inevitably dissolved or reversed in all truly modern vision and thinking. And only now does a wholly new meaning of evil and negativity become manifest and actual, an evil and negativity inseparable from the creation itself, and inevitably inseparable from everything which can now truly be envisioned or known as the Creator. So it is that a distinctively modern philosophical thinking can only know a pure and absolute transcendence as a truly empty or negative transcendence, just as the modern imagination has never given us a truly positive or affirmative image of the Creator, and when it has most fully enacted the Creator, as in Blake and Melville, has only given us images of a purely negative Creator. Clearly the ancient world could know nothing of an ultimate evil in this sense, and certainly not if it was innocent of the very possibility of infinity, and if it is only a post-Classical thinking and vision which can know or unveil the infinity of God, that is the very infinity which is progressively realized in modernity as a truly alien or empty infinity, and empty and alien above all in its pure and absolute transcendence.

No such infinity is present in ancient thinking and vision, unless it is present in Neoplatonism, but Neoplatonism is born only with and in the dissolution of the Classical world, and even if Christian philosophy for well over a thousand years was a Neoplatonic philosophy, it could be so only by being in deep tension with its Greek philosophical ground. Nothing could be further from Greek philosophical thinking than the very idea of the pure infinity of God or Being, and if that is an idea which is not truly transcended in our thinking until Spinoza, then it is transcended with such finality as to foreclose its occurrence in all subsequent thinking which is a pure thinking, a foreclosure which is the ending of a truly metaphysical transcendence. But that ending simultaneously occurs in the deeper religious consciousness of the West, and most clearly so in the Reformation, a Reformation that is the birth or renewal of a purely interior and individual faith, but a faith that precisely thereby is liberated from either an essential or a necessary relationship to a primordial ground that otherwise would wholly enclose it.

Hegel could know the Reformation as the full advent of the free individual, a freedom which is the necessary consummation of the birth of Christianity itself, and a freedom realizing itself in a truly new and wholly interior self-consciousness. Yet that self-consciousness can only be a pure self-consciousness by way of its own negation and transcendence of a primordial and "objective" ground, a ground that is finally nothing less than that infinite Being which is and only is "Being-in-itself." If "Being-in-itself" is a Hegelian identity of the purely alien God, that is the God whom Luther knew as the God of Judgment and "Law," but that is the God who is crucified through a free and total grace, and a grace which is finally the grace of God the Creator.

Thus both Luther and Hegel could know the alien God as not only being negated and transcended but also as being fulfilled and consummated in crucifixion and resurrection. This is just the point at which a uniquely Hegelian negation and self-negation is most clearly unveiled, for that negation *is* affirmation, just as crucifixion *is* resurrection, but *is* resurrection only insofar as it *is* crucifixion, just as negation *is* affirmation only insofar as it *is* negation. Consequently, the Creator is all in all in an eternal self-negation, but that is a self-negation which is finally the self-emptying of the crucifixion, and therefore an eternal act which is an eternal act only insofar as it is a self-negating act, or only so far as it is absolute sacrifice or crucifixion. If the Creator becomes all in all in an absolute self-negation or self-emptying, that is the negation which is embodied in the unique event of crucifixion, which is precisely why the crucifixion is the consummation of the creation. Moreover, if the crucifixion is the repetition of the creation, it is a repetition of the original act of the creation, but now a repetition actually and totally realizing that original act as being all in all. Now and only now is it an act totally comprehending Godhead itself, thereby realizing the totality of Godhead itself, a realization which is the realization of the total self-emptying of the Creator.

In this perspective, we can see that Christianity's affirmation of the absolute infinity of God is a reversal both of crucifixion and of creation, but a reversal which is only actually possible as a purely negative reaction to the crucifixion. Just as no movement in history has so radically reversed and transformed itself as did Christianity in the first century of its existence, so no other historical movement has undergone such a comprehensive and far-reaching historical evolution. At no point is that evolutionary transformation so decisive as is the gulf which we now know to lie between the Kingdom of God which Jesus embodied and proclaimed and that absolutely passive *aseity* of the Godhead which is the center of a fully mature Christian orthodoxy. No other religious tradition has known such an infinitely "other" deity or sacrality, and at no other point is there a greater distance between Christianity and Judaism and Islam. But a fully comparable distance lies between orthodox Christianity and primitive Christianity, so that renewals of primitive Christianity have inevitably been assaults upon orthodox Christianity, just as actual renewals of Jesus have inevitably been assaults upon the orthodoxy of the Church. And if Christianity has known deeper heresies and deeper heretical movements than any other religious tradition, at no point have these heresies been deeper and of greater historical consequence than in "heretical" assaults upon the absolute *aseity* of the Godhead, assaults which begin at least as early as Paul's proclamation of the ultimacy of the crucifixion, and assaults which we can now apprehend as inaugurating the full birth of the modern world. But in full modernity, Christian "heresy" passes into a total historical actuality, an actuality culminating in the death of God, and in the death of that God who is the pure *aseity* of the Godhead.

Orthodox Christianity knows that *aseity* as the Creator, but just as that *aseity* is wholly negated and reversed in crucifixion, that is a reversal calling forth and making manifest and actual a pure reversal of an absolutely sovereign and transcendent Creator, so it is a reversal of that reversal which calls forth and realizes the pure *aseity* of the Creator, an *aseity* which is an absolutely self-enclosed and infinite Being. If Hegel could know such Being as "pure evil," just as Blake could know it as Satan, no such apprehension has ever arisen beyond the Christian world, because only Christianity has known the Crucified God, and thus only Christianity has known the intrinsic opposite of that God. Yet to know that God is to know the Creator as the Crucified God, and is to know the creation as the absolute sacrifice or the absolute self-emptying of that God. That is the creation which is the original self-negation of God, an original self-negation which is absolute genesis, and is the absolute genesis of that Creator who is the Crucified God. Thus creation can only be a purely dichotomous act, and the purely dichotomous act of an absolute self-negation or self-emptying, and a self-emptying which can only be realized through an absolute dichotomy at the very center of the Godhead. That dichotomy is itself the consequence of an absolute genesis, but an absolute genesis which is actualized in that very dichotomy, a pure and total dichotomy which is the eternal willing of Yes *and* No, or an eternal willing of eternal life *and* of eternal death. This is precisely the willing and the act which is most impossible for an absolute "Being-in-itself," or for an infinite God who is and only is infinite and eternal, or who is and only is the absolutely sovereign and transcendent Creator.

Consequently, that is the Creator whose own pure reversal is fully and finally embodied in the crucifixion, but that reversal could only begin with genesis, and with absolute genesis. That is the genesis which is finally the genesis of the Crucified God, so that if the crucifixion is a repetition of the creation, it is a forward-moving repetition of the creation, and now a repetition which is a total enactment of the self-emptying or self-sacrifice of the original creation. And only now can the original act of creation be realized as the total act of self-negation, a self-negation which is an absolute sacrifice, but is totally realized as that negation only in the self-negation of the crucifixion. Thus, if an absolute genesis is the genesis of the Crucified God, it is the genesis of the Crucified God who *is* the Creator, and hence the genesis of that absolute act which is a purely and totally dichotomous act, and an act which can truly be consummated only in crucifixion. But that is the crucifixion which is resurrection, and is the resurrection of the apocalyptic Body of God, a body of God which is totality itself, and is that "body" which is the consummation of the absolute genesis of God.

6

THE GENESIS
OF FREEDOM

To be open to totality itself as the apocalyptic Body of the Godhead is
to be open to an absolutely new totality, and a totality which is itself
an embodiment of that absolute genesis which *is* absolute novum.
Only the Christian world has known genesis as the enactment of the
novitas mundi or the newness of the world, and even if that realization
does not dawn in Christianity until the closure of the ancient Christian
world, it then gradually but decisively becomes embodied with such
power as to enact the end of Christendom itself. But that enactment is the
realization of a new totality, a totality first purely known by Spinoza, and
first comprehensively known by Newton, and thereafter realizing itself
throughout both our consciousness and our society. That realization is the
dissolution of a purely transcendent Godhead, and not a simple dissolution of that Godhead, but far rather the transformation of a pure and total
transcendence into a pure and total immanence. That is the very immanence which is enacted in Nietzsche's vision of Eternal Recurrence, even as
it is abstractly embodied in the *Science of Logic,* an embodiment which is
a disembodiment of an original or a truly primordial totality.

That disembodiment is absolutely necessary to the embodiment of a
truly new and apocalyptic totality, just as the enactment of a truly new
creation can only be the disenactment of an eternal and undifferentiated
totality, or that totality which is in itself and *only* in itself all in all.
Buddhism has named that totality as Sunyata and Tathata, just as Sufism
has named it as the Barzakh or the "Nondelimited Imagination," thereby

114

knowing and realizing an original totality as being all in all. Now even if such an Imagination and such an Emptiness have never entered the Christian world, the Christian world would finally be inconceivable and unreal apart from them, for only the emptying or negation of such a totality could realize the apocalyptic totality of absolute novum.

Christianity, above all other religious traditions, is alien to both the symbol and the horizon of an original and undifferentiated totality, and at no other point has its recurrent and internal struggle with Gnosticism been so complete, a struggle which has always been a struggle to know and to affirm the fullness of the Godhead as the Creator. But that has simultaneously been a struggle to know and to affirm the crucifixion as the sole source of redemption, a crucifixion which itself is finally inseparable from an original creation, and inseparable from the creation if only because it is inseparable from the uniquely Christian God. So likewise is the crucifixion inseparable from a uniquely Christian apprehension of the fall, a fall which is not only the loss of an original paradise, but a fall which is the very arena of a uniquely Christian consciousness, a consciousness which is a consciousness embodying an eternal death or damnation. That is the very consciousness which is most deeply and most profoundly closed to an original plenitude of grace and bliss, or to an original totality which is in itself and as itself all in all, or to a primordial emptiness which is a total Emptiness. No other religious tradition has so totally "forgotten" an original plenum as has Christianity, a disrecollection or dissolution which is an inevitable consequence of a movement of total fall, and a dissolution which is finally a dissolution of every memory or image of an original or primordial totality.

Indeed, as Christianity has historically evolved, and above all so as it has evolved in the West, even a nostalgia for an original paradise or bliss has become ever more alien and empty. Nothing is more profoundly forbidden in the modern world than the backward movement of return, a movement which now and for the first time has been known and realized as the purely negative and the purely pathological movement of regression. The actuality of this Western movement is perhaps most fully manifest in the Christian epic tradition, a tradition which from Dante through Joyce has moved ever more fully and more finally into both an interior and a historical abyss, an abyss inverting and reversing a primordial totality of bliss. This is the abyss which is interiorly realized in a uniquely Christian voyage, and therein historically realized as a full and total historical necessity. Only at the closure of this voyage, a closure occurring in *Finnegans Wake*, is a primordial abyss realized as being all in all, and it is so both as an interior and as a historical abyss, but a historical and interior abyss finally realizing and fulfilling its epic predecessors. This is the very historical and interior condition which is so irrevocably our own, and if nothing could more fully distance us from a primordial totality of bliss, nothing else could make that totality so ultimately forbidden. We can see that horizon evolve in the unique historical movement of Christianity and the West, and most clearly so in our epic voyage, a voyage which dawns in the *Inferno,* and a truly new and progressive actualization of total darkness in the *Inferno* is absolutely necessary to the ever progressive evocation and actualization of total light in the *Purgatorio* and the *Paradiso.* Then that actualization passes into a new and pure dichotomy between total light and total darkness in *Paradise Lost,* an interior and cosmic dichotomy which is realized as a total dichotomy in *Milton* and *Jerusalem,* a dichotomy which finally becomes a comprehensively historical and comprehensively interior dichotomy in *Ulysses* and *Finnegans Wake.* Each of these movements of our epic voyage is not only an interior but also a historical movement, an interior movement which is simultaneously a historical movement, and nothing so distinguishes the historical movement of the West than does both its interior and its historical necessity. That is the necessity which is realized and embodied in a uniquely modern consciousness, a consciousness that finally ends and reverses the primordial movement of eternal return.

Now even if that movement is seemingly resurrected in Nietzsche's vision of Eternal Recurrence and in the eternal return of *Finnegans Wake,* neither Zarathustra's eternal recurrence nor the eternal return of the *Wake* is the return of an original totality of bliss, but far rather the return of an ultimate abyss or chaos that absolutely assaults every possible interior or historical presence. And now and only now every actual movement of consciousness is a negative actuality, and it is only in and as that purely negative actuality that it can here be celebrated or affirmed. Thereby the totality that is present and actual upon our horizon is the very reversal of that totally blissful totality that is known by Mahayana Buddhism or Sufi Islam, and is so if only because it is a truly new darkness that is a full inversion of light. Nothing more manifestly embodies this inversion than does the very language of the mature Nietzsche and the late Joyce, a language that is seemingly coincident with a purely mystical language, but a language which in that very apparent coincidence wholly inverts and reverses every image and evocation of a purely mystical realization. This inversion is most obviously clear in the continual and compulsive evocations of "God" in both Joyce and Nietzsche. Never before or since has such a total blasphemy been recorded, and that is a blasphemy absolutely essential to their epic projects. For these uniquely modern epic projects revolve about a voyage into total darkness, and they go beyond their epic predecessors by realizing a darkness that cannot be a portal into light, or not into a light that is distinguishable from darkness. Thus they demand a total assault upon the Christian God, and above all so upon God the Creator, a Creator who is here inverted and reversed as Creator so as to make possible a final and total apocalypse of finitude or the world.

God is a totally guilty God in the language of both Joyce and Nietzsche, for now God is fully and actually manifest as the ultimate ground and source of repression, a repression that is the source of history for Nietzsche and Joyce alike. That origin is now known and realized as the origin of our deepest interior, an interior that can be released from that repression not by a dissolution of God but rather by a reversal of the Creator, or by a reversal of that pure and absolutely sovereign transcendence which is the transcendence of the uniquely Christian God. At no other point were Nietzsche and Joyce such original visionaries, for even if both are Blakean in their visions of the Creator, they go beyond Blake in the comprehensive totality of their negations of God. Such negation occurs in every full expression of their language and vision, but it does so only by way of a discovery and resurrection of that original abyss or nothingness which was negated by the original act of the Creator. Now an actual nothingness is truly resurrected, a resurrection which is certainly a primal source of our nihilism, but a resurrection which is the very opposite of a spiritual resurrection, and is so in its very realization of abyss. That abyss is a pure embodiment of an absolute No-saying, an absolute No-saying which *is* absolute abyss, and therefore is the resurrection of an originally negated nothingness. So it is that an actual resurrection of nothingness could only be a reversal of the original act of the creation, and therefore a reversal of the Creator.

Only in the wake of that reversal can a genesis become manifest which is the genesis of God, and only now can genesis be fully manifest as the crucifixion of God, and a crucifixion which is finally identical with the original act of creation. That abyss of nothingness which is being enacted and embodied in our midst is surely and at the very least an echo of an originally shattered nothingness, but a nothingness which becomes an actual nothingness only in that shattering, a shattering which is the eternal *act* of creation. So that a reversal of that shattering is an embodiment of crucifixion, and an embodiment of that crucifixion which is an embodiment of death and nothingness at the very center of the Godhead. But that

117

embodiment is a self-embodiment, a self-embodiment which is a self-emptying of an original totality of bliss, a self-emptying which *is* the eternal act of creation. Consequently, the act of the Creator is the act of self-emptying, the self-emptying of an original emptiness or bliss, a self-emptying which is the ultimate act of sacrifice. That is a self-emptying realizing a dark or negative potency in the Godhead, a potency releasing an ultimate dichotomy in Godhead itself, and a dichotomy that is inseparable from the absolutely new and absolutely final act of the creation.

If it is modern Western thinking and a uniquely Christian imagination that alone has known that dichotomy, just as it is only a Christian and a Western consciousness which has known a final and an ultimate guilt, that is a consciousness, imagination, and thinking that is inseparable from an ultimately dichotomous ground, and that ground can only be what Christianity and Christianity alone has known and realized as the Creator. Although Christian theology has commonly affirmed that only Christianity can fully or truly know the Creator, that is an affirmation which has become ever more fully impossible if Christianity knows the Creator solely as the God of "light." But already Augustine could know that the act of creation and the act of predestination are identical, thereby knowing the Creator as the ultimate source of both light and darkness, or of eternal life and of eternal death. Thus, if only in the dogma of predestination, Western Christianity has known a dichotomous Creator, a realization that becomes overwhelming with the closure of the Middle Ages, and then becomes universal with the full realization of the modern world.

That dark potency of the Godhead so decisively apprehended by Boehme, and philosophically realized by Schelling and Hegel, is a potency at the very center of what Christianity alone has known as the Godhead, but a Godhead which is first fully actualized in the unique and final act of the creation. Only that actualization could make possible and real the act of creation as the act of crucifixion, so that if the act of creation is finally the act of crucifixion, then the creation is the realization of a new and actual nothingness in the actuality of Godhead itself. Now an original plenitude of bliss is realized as a pure negativity, and a pure negativity which is an actual negativity, or a negativity which is the negativity of crucifixion. Such an apprehension of creation would profoundly deepen our understanding of the act of creation as an act of absolute grace, for then the Yes-saying of the creation would be inseparable from the No-saying of God. But that No-saying is ultimately realized in and upon Godhead itself, a Godhead whose eternal act of creation is the eternal act of crucifixion, and therein and thereby is the absolute and eternal act of sacrifice. Visions of creation as the sacrifice of deity are present throughout the history of religions, but only Christianity knows an ultimate and actual sacrifice or crucifixion of God, a sacrifice which Christianity must inevitably know as the once-and-for-all and irreversible act of creation.

If Christianity is wholly alienated from a vision or recollection of an original and undifferentiated pleroma of bliss, an alienation foreclosing the possibility of a Christian repetition of that bliss, the very horizon of such a totality could open Christianity to the final ultimacy of creation and crucifixion alike, an ultimacy which is the *act* of the uniquely Christian God. While Christianity has always known that act as an eternal act, it has only all too gradually known it as a fully actual and irreversible act, and an act which is an act of absolute and total transformation. Not even Hegel could know the eternal act of creation as a once-and-for-all and irreversible act, and if Nietzsche's realization of that act marks the very point at which a deep gulf lies between Hegel and Nietzsche, that made possible a uniquely Nietzschean realization of the death of God, for now that death can be known and realized as a finally irreversible event. But that very realization is simultaneously the realization of an absolutely new "eternal now," an eternal now which once again is totality itself, but which now and only now is the purely actual now of the immediate moment. That is an immediacy which eternally recurs, but it eternally recurs only as this immediate moment, a moment which is the pure embodiment of the transcendence of "Being" or Godhead itself. That is an embodiment which Hegel could never know, for Hegel lived and thought before that night which is the consequence of an irreversible death of God, a night which Nietzsche could know as deep midnight, and a midnight releasing a joy that wants deep eternity (*Zarathustra* IV, "The Drunken Song"). That is an eternity which the "bad conscience" and the *ressentiment* of Christianity could know as Heaven, so that it is the reversal of a heavenly transcendence which releases a new and total immanence, and an immanence which is only possible as a consequence of the death of God.

Nothing is more revealing about Nietzsche than his deep centering upon the pure and alien transcendence of God, a pure transcendence that can now appear and be real as a totally alien transcendence, or that very transcendence which Hegel could know as "evil." But Nietzsche knew "evil" as Hegel did not, for Hegel could not know an evil that is truly or finally self-enclosed, or truly independent of a universal process of self-emptying. Thus Nietzsche knew a transcendence of God that Hegel could never know, but it is precisely by knowing and realizing the irreversible death of that transcendence that Nietzsche could know it as a purely and totally alien transcendence. Nietzsche's Madman, who actually smells the odor of God's decomposition, therein smells an odor that had never been smelt before, for only now is the immediacy of God's death fully incarnate, an immediacy which Zarathustra baptizes in his proclamation of Eternal Recurrence. But that baptism is the realization of a new and terrible freedom, the freedom of affirming and of totally affirming the most terrible evil, for that is precisely the affirmation that is inseparable from the affirmation of Eternal Recurrence. Yet the most terrible evil is that evil which is embodied in the purely alien God, that is the alien transcendence which is the true ground of all repression, a repression which is the interior source of every evil act. And Nietzsche understood the enactment of evil as it had never been understood before, for now it is understood as a fully willed enactment, and an enactment of that will which is the purely negative will.

But Nietzsche, even as Augustine, understood the purely negative will as a self-lacerated will, even while going beyond Augustine in understanding it as the totality of self-laceration and self-alienation. That is why a Nietzschean self-alienation is the self-alienation of God, or the self-alienation of the ultimate ground of No-saying and *ressentiment,* a ground which has truly been named only in the Christian naming of God. Accordingly, the Christian God and only the Christian God is the deification of nothingness or the will to nothingness pronounced holy (*The Antichrist* 18). That is the will which is the totally dichotomous will, and therefore a will which is self-alienated in its deepest ground, a ground releasing an actual will to nothingness. But that will to nothingness is a will to evil, and even the will *of* evil, for it is, indeed, a purely and absolutely negative will. Thus Nietzsche could know the evil will only by knowing the Christian God, or only by knowing the absolute origin of *ressentiment* and the bad conscience, an origin which is the origin of a pure negativity, a pure negativity which is evil itself. If Nietzsche was the first thinker since de Sade to understand the Christian God as pure evil itself, Nietzsche even as de Sade was able therein and thereby to affirm evil, and even to affirm pure evil, for only that affirmation makes possible and realizes a fully actual affirmation, or an affirmation that can truly and actually occur.

At no point was Nietzsche's genius more fully itself than in its apprehension of absolute will, an absolute will which is the Will to Power, and only thereby a will which is totality itself. That is the very will which Christianity has known as the will of God, but now it is apprehended as even Augustine could not apprehend it, for now and only now it is known as the will of evil itself. Nietzsche could go beyond good and evil only by knowing an evil that is totality itself, a totality that Augustine could never know as evil, because Augustine could know only the goodness of God. Augustine knew the evil will as the absence or privation of God or Being, an absence releasing that very negativity which is the evil will, for an evil choice proceeds not from nature or being, but rather from a deficiency of being deriving from our having been created from nothing (*City of God*, XII, 6). So it is that for Augustine the evil will is a will of nothingness, and a will to nothingness, a will to that very nothingness out of which the world was created. Therefore Augustine understood the death instinct as Freud could never understand it, for the death instinct is the will to eternal death, and an eternal death which is an actual embodiment of a primordial nothingness. That is the death which is the eternal death of damnation, and damnation is just as real as is an actual nothingness, and an actual nothingness which we know ourselves to will when we recognize our internal and interior chains as chains which we have fully and actually willed. If that is the very point at which Augustine discovered his own freedom, that is the very point at which Nietzsche discovered a comparable freedom, but now a freedom which is a total freedom, for it is the freedom of willing Eternal Recurrence or the Will to Power.

Just as Augustine understands the evil will as a will *of* nothingness which is simultaneously a will *to* nothingness, Nietzsche understands absolute will as a will which is beyond good and evil, but only beyond good and evil by being a will that wills everything which occurs, and therefore wills even the most terrible evil, a will which is inseparable from a will to total joy. That joy is itself the willing of evil, and therefore a will to evil, for an enactment of evil is absolutely necessary to the fullness of the will, and is so necessary precisely because of the total actuality of an absolute will. That actuality comprehends everything which occurs, so that a willing of that actuality is a willing of everything which occurs, and therefore a willing of even the most horrible evil, for only that willing makes possible that unique and absolute joy which is the *willing* of eternal return. That willing is the supreme challenge to every will, and that challenge which breaks every interior and individual will, a breakage which is the breaking of every isolated and solitary will, and therefore the dissolution of every will which is not the will of the Will to Power. At this point, too, Nietzsche is deeply Augustinian, and is so by knowing the dissolution of the individual will, a dissolution which is an inversion of that will, and an inversion of that will which is only an interior and individual will. That is the very inversion which Augustine knows as redemption, but Zarathustra, too, promises redemption, a redemption offered to all those who are bound to the past by way of a re-creation of "it was" into "thus I willed it" and "thus I shall will it" (*Zarathustra* II, "On Redemption"). Yet that is a willing which could never be a willing of an individual and interior will, but only a willing which is the willing of absolute will, or the willing of the Will to Power. The willing of our interior and individual will is totally enslaved at its very center, and is so for Nietzsche and Augustine alike, but the willing of absolute will is the willing of an absolutely free will, or that very will which Augustine knows as the will of God and Nietzsche knows as the will of the Will to Power.

Nothing more deeply unites Nietzsche and Augustine than their total affirmation of the freedom of the will, but that freedom is the very opposite of that impotence which is the actuality of the individual will, and only an inversion of that impotence can embody the freedom of the will. But that inversion occurs through a free and actual willing, and a free and actual willing of our very impotence, an impotence which is the evil of the evil will. By recognizing that impotence as an impotence which we will, even if it is the negative will of sin or *ressentiment,* we therein realize freedom as our own, and that very realization is possible only by way of a free act of the will. That act is the act of willing a total responsibility, and a total responsibility for our totally guilty or totally negative condition. This is the responsibility which Zarathustra wills in willing Eternal Recurrence, for that is a will which in willing everything which occurs wills a full and total responsibility for that occurrence, and only a willing of that responsibility could be a *willing* of eternal return. So it is that Zarathustra must will even the most terrible evil, for that is a willing which is inseparable from a total act of the will, and inseparable from a truly free act of the will. Even as Augustine identifies an evil choice as a choice of nothingness, Zarathustra identifies a free will as a willing of evil, a willing of that evil which is actual in the world, for only that willing can be an actual willing, and only an actual willing can be free.

This is a truth which Spinoza knew long before Nietzsche, and if a recognition of that truth impelled Spinoza to a denial of the freedom of the will, its recognition impelled Nietzsche to a total affirmation of freedom, and a total affirmation of absolute will, which is the only will which truly and wholly can be a free will. Even as Augustine can only know full freedom by willing the will of God, Nietzsche can only know full freedom by willing the Will to Power, a willing which is the willing of everything which occurs, just as a willing of the will of God is a willing of everything which occurs. Only in his affirmation of predestination was Augustine willing to make that affirmation, just as only in his vision of Eternal

Recurrence was Nietzsche willing to affirm all and everything, an affirmation which is the affirmation of good and evil at once. But so likewise is the affirmation of predestination the affirmation of good and evil simultaneously, which is precisely why a genuine affirmation of predestination can only be an affirmation of double predestination, a predestination comprehending redemption and damnation at once, even as a total responsibility comprehends good and evil simultaneously. Only that simultaneity can open the will to actuality itself, an actuality which is no less "evil" than it is "good," and thus an actuality that can truly be willed only by willing good and evil at once.

Only that will is the free will, for the freedom of the will is the willing of actuality itself, and therefore the willing of everything which occurs. Augustine first knew this primal truth by opening himself to the internal ground of his own bondage, only by recognizing that he himself was the source of his own bondage could Augustine know his own freedom, and that is a freedom that is truly real in its enactment of the impotence of his will. Thus we can know our own freedom only by knowing the internal ground and source of our own bondage, and the very act of accepting and willing that responsibility is the act of a free will, and a will which actually becomes free in that very acceptance. But that is a willing which freely accepts itself as the sole author of its own impotence, an impotence which is the impotence of the evil will, and thus an acceptance of a total responsibility for that impotence is an acceptance of our responsibility for the evil will. If an acceptance of that responsibility is the only freedom which we can interiorly know as the freedom of the will, we nevertheless thereby know an actual freedom of the will, and an actual freedom which occurs and is real only in an actual acceptance of our own responsibility for every negativity which is an interior negativity or every negativity which is present in and as our own interior will. Indeed, that is the very acceptance which calls forth the true interiority and individuality of the will, an individuality and interiority which have nowhere been manifest as such apart from this acceptance, for that is the acceptance which is the inauguration of the free will.

This is a primal reason why Augustine could only truly know freedom by knowing original sin, an original sin that is the consequence of freedom and of freedom alone, and an original sin that is the inauguration of the negative will, or that will which is the sole author of its own negativity. The truth is that freedom has never been deeply known apart from a realization of original sin or its counterpart, and the Nietzsche who so deeply knew the absolute freedom of the absolute will is the Nietzsche who once again

123

discovered the genealogy of the negative will, and discovered that genealogy in a sudden and inexplicable fall from an original and undifferentiated consciousness. But that is a fall which is inseparable from everything which we have actually known as freedom, and just as a true recognition of the freedom of the will has always been an interior willing of an ultimate responsibility, the willing of that responsibility is impossible apart from a full recognition of our own negative will, and a negative will which as a free *and* negative will could only be the consequence of fall. Only by knowing an original fall can we truly know our negativity as our own, a negativity that in no sense whatsoever is the product of nature or being, but is rather the consequence of our own act or enactment, and an enactment that is possible and real only because of a freedom that is so deeply our own. Augustine knew that freedom as the consequence of our having been created in the image of God, and if that is a freedom which is humanity's alone, sin is an actuality which is humanity's alone, and that sin is inseparable from our uniquely human freedom.

But Nietzsche is once again Augustinian in his vision of Eternal Recurrence, for that is an eternal recurrence which is an absolute will, an absolute will willing everything that occurs, and thereby willing a total responsibility for everything that occurs. Thus it is absolutely necessary that that will wills even the most abysmal evil, only that willing could be a true acceptance of evil, and apart from that acceptance there can be no full acceptance of actuality itself. This is just the context in which Nietzsche is so anti-Platonic, for even if his anti-Platonism is at bottom an anti-Neoplatonism, this is a profound opposition to even the most exalted attempts to dissolve the reality of evil, an attempted dissolution which for Nietzsche is simply a flight from the world. Anti-Gnosticism has never been so powerful as it is in Nietzsche, and not even in Augustine himself, and precisely because Augustine could never escape that very Neoplatonism which Nietzsche judged to be the most decadent and pathological form of philosophical thinking. This is the context in which one must understand Nietzsche's exaltation of a noble morality, a morality which is the morality of a will to power, but a morality which is only real by way of the exercise of genuine power, and genuine power is always the power of the will. So it is that Nietzsche violently assaults the weak, but the weak for Nietzsche are those who are weak in will, a weakness which is finally a refusal of actuality, a refusal arising from an internal inability to accept the earth and the world, and that internal inability is simply an absence of the will. Nietzsche's assault on the weak is an assault upon the weakness of the will, a weakness always deriving from a diminution of the will, and that diminution is here identified as an embodiment of *ressentiment.*

Accordingly, a true noble morality is a reversal of that *ressentiment,* a reversal realizing itself in the will to power, but that power is a true power only insofar as it is an act of the will. It is will itself which is all in all in Nietzsche, but that will is finally an absolute will, and an absolute will which is the Will to Power. No major philosopher has been so externally weak as was Nietzsche himself, an external and even bodily weakness which was certainly a fundamental source of his thinking, and that is a thinking which has affirmed the will as has no other thinking in history, an affirmation which is an absolute Yes-saying, but a Yes-saying which occurs and is real only by way of the realization of an absolute No-saying, and an absolute No-saying which is Nietzsche's deepest name of the uniquely Christian God.

If Nietzsche rediscovered an eternal predestination in his vision of Eternal Recurrence, that is a vision of the absolute necessity of evil, and that is the necessity of even the most horrible evil, an evil which has only truly been envisioned in our visions of Hell. Now predestination knows the necessity of Hell, even as it knows the necessity of damnation, a damnation which is a true resolution of evil, and the only resolution of evil itself which could be an eschatological or eternal resolution. Augustine could identify the act of predestination and the act of creation not just because he could know the unity of God, but rather because he could know the unity of the *will* of God, and therefore he could know the willing of creation as the willing of predestination. So likewise Nietzsche could know the willing of Yes-saying as being finally identical with the willing of No-saying, and not simply insofar as No-saying is a negation or an assault upon the impotence of the will, but rather insofar as No-saying is a violent and total assault upon every expression of the will which is not a total expression of the will. Nietzsche knew the great ascetics as the purest no-sayers, and he surely identified himself with their company, and deeply ascetic as he was in his own life, that is a life which enacted a no-saying as comprehensive as any which has ever occurred. Perhaps its only full analogy is in that apocalypticism which wills the very end of the world, and certainly Nietzsche willed the end of his world, or of his historical world, and did so as has no other thinker in our history. But that historical world comprehends everything which we can know as history, and even if Nietzsche could never bring himself to will the end of those few Greek and Renaissance figures whom he venerated so deeply, he certainly willed the end of Western history, and that is a history that begins for Nietzsche with the ancient Persian Zarathustra. As Nietzsche confesses in *Ecce Homo,* that is precisely why he chose the name of Zarathustra for his enactor of Eternal Recurrence, a new Zarathustra who reverses that very history which is most deeply our history, and most deeply our history in being the arena of *ressentiment* and the bad conscience.

In so fully knowing an ultimate No-saying as the true identity of the Christian God, Nietzsche therein finally baptized the Christian God, a baptism which is the baptism of evil itself, but only thereby is the possibility established of that absolute Yes-saying which is the total affirmation of the will. We must never lose sight of the all too significant fact that God language dominates the thinking of Spinoza, Hegel, and Nietzsche as it does no other thinkers, nor can we ignore that evolutionary movement embodied in their thinking wherein the identity of God undergoes ever more negative realizations. Only in Nietzsche among our true thinkers is God given a purely and totally negative identity, but only in Nietzsche have we been given a fully philosophical realization of evil itself, an evil that all too significantly is wholly absent from Spinoza's thinking, and an evil that is largely hidden or disguised in Hegel's thinking, only to burst forth with an irresistible power in Nietzsche's thinking. That power is inseparable from a uniquely Nietzschean understanding of absolute will, a will that must comprehend evil if it is an absolute will, and a will that must dissolve every final distinction between good and evil in its own enactment. For that is an enactment that could only be a total enactment, and thus an enactment and willing of everything which occurs, and therefore a total willing of that everything, which could only mean a willing of good and evil alike.

If nothing else, Nietzsche's revolutionary understanding of a "slave morality," a morality that is finally nothing other than our Western and Christian moral tradition, is an understanding of the morality of the "good" will, a "good" will that is wholly other than an "evil" will, and precisely thereby a will that is the diminution of the will. While Blake realized this truth before Nietzsche, it was known by no earlier modern philosopher, and unknown philosophically if only because Nietzsche is our only truly modern philosopher of the will. But Nietzsche is a philosopher of the will only by way of his understanding of the evil or purely negative will, and if thereby, too, Nietzsche is an Augustinian thinker, he is so only by way of an affirmation of evil that was all but impossible either for Augustine or for Augustinianism.

One of the more revealing dimensions of modern theology is that it has progressively lost every possibility of affirming anything that is recognizable as the providence of God. This has above all been true since the Holocaust, but this was a dissolution beginning at least as early as the Enlightenment. While it would appear that only Hegel and Schelling among our post-Leibnitzean thinkers have been able to affirm a genuine theodicy, the truth is that Nietzsche affirmed a truly negative theodicy, and did so precisely by way of his understanding of evil or the purely negative will. That pure No-saying which is a full embodiment of the purely negative will is a pure negation which is inseparable from the full activity or realization of the will itself. And absolute Yes-saying is itself a realization of No-saying, as Nietzsche confesses in his autobiographical account of how he created Zarathustra:

> The psychological problem in the type of Zarathustra is how he that says No and *does* No to an unheard-of degree, to everything to which one has so far said Yes, can nevertheless be the opposite of a No-saying spirit; how the spirit who bears the heaviest fate, a fatality of a task, can nevertheless be the lightest and most transcendent—Zarathustra is a dancer—how he that has the hardest, most terrible insight into reality, that has thought the "most abysmal idea," nevertheless does not consider it an objection to existence, not even to its eternal recurrence—but rather one reason more for being himself the eternal Yes to all things—"the tremendous, unbounded saying Yes and Amen."—"Into all abysses I still carry the blessings of my saying Yes." (*Ecce Homo*, "Thus Spoke Zarathustra," 6, Kaufmann translation)

Only an understanding and a realization of the depths of evil could make possible such an affirmation, and if that is a total affirmation, it is an absolute sanctification of evil, a sanctification apart from which no total act or affirmation of the will is possible. But such a sanctification is surely necessary for any genuine theodicy, and even if it is only after Nietzsche that we have become fully aware of this necessity, that is a necessity which is inseparable from a contemporary affirmation of the uniquely Christian God.

The truth is that Nietzsche has more deeply understood the uniquely Christian God than any other thinker since Hegel, and has done so precisely in his understanding of evil, an evil that is inseparable from reality itself, and from the depths of reality, depths which are finally the depths of Godhead itself. The Will to Power is a realization of those depths, and if the Will to Power is simultaneously the dance of Eternal Recurrence, that is a dance that could only be the dance of Godhead itself, or of that absolute will which is the Will to Power. Nietzsche could only name that will as Dionysus, and even if Dionysus is a name of a deity, and of the darkest deity, the later Nietzsche's naming of Dionysus is not a naming of the Greek, god, Dionysus, but rather the naming of a truly new deity who only dawns after the death of God. Indeed, that deity dawns in the death of God, and if Nietzsche could sign himself as Dionysus and the Crucified as he was relapsing into madness, that is surely a signature of the uniquely Christian God, or of that God who is most openly manifest in the crucifixion. If Nietzsche is the only major thinker who has truly fallen into madness, that is a madness that cannot be dissociated from the Christian God, or not dissociated from the deep depths of that God. Nietzsche, alone among our thinkers, knew those negative depths, or, if at this point, too, Nietzschean thinking parallels Kierkegaardian thinking, it is only Nietzschean thinking which knows only the negative depths of God. Yet those depths are finally positive depths, even as an absolute No-saying is finally an absolute Yes-saying, for in the deepest depths of absolute will Yes-saying and No-saying are inseparable.

Not only are they inseparable in those depths, but they are finally therein identical, an identity which Christianity has fully known only in the dogma of predestination, for that is the one point at which Christianity despite itself has been forced to affirm that God who wills light and darkness simultaneously, and eternal life and eternal death simultaneously. Both Calvinism and Augustinianism have affirmed that only predestination makes freedom possible, a freedom that would be wholly unreal apart from predestination, for a full freedom is clearly impossible in that fallen will which is our own, and yet that will is a fallen will only by virtue of its original freedom, and that is a freedom that is possible only by way of that absolute will which is the will of God.

Certainly full freedom would appear to be absent from anything which we can actually know as the interior and individual will, but if that will is a fallen will, then we have been given intimations of an original and pre-fallen freedom, but intimations which are only actually present in our acceptance of responsibility for our fallen condition. The dogma of original sin is a decisive way of realizing that responsibility, and if Augustinianism and classical Protestantism embody the fullest Christian affirmations of original sin, these are affirmations which are finally affirmations of the freedom of the will. Thus it is all too understandable that *Paradise Lost* is our fullest poetic celebration of freedom, but here freedom is inseparable from the fall, or its actualization is inseparable from the actualization of fall, and even the Son of God's free acceptance of death is a response to the inevitable destiny of that fall.

But an inevitable destiny of fall could only be a consequence of predestination, so that in Christian dogma fall and predestination are inseparably conjoined, and inseparably conjoined in the eternal will of God. And the will of God is the absolutely free will of God, so that God freely and absolutely wills predestination, and does so at the very center of His will. Augustine could know the willing of predestination as absolute grace, a grace apart from which there could be no redemption, and apart from which there could be no freedom of the will. Just as we truly realize our freedom only by realizing our damnation, or only by realizing our full and sole responsibility for our fallen condition, a realization which is the realization of the interior ground and source of our bondage, so it is that it is the very will of the negative will which most clearly bears the mark or signature of our freedom. That freedom for us can only be a terrible freedom, a freedom that we can actually know only as the source of our damnation, so that our actual freedom is a negative freedom even as our actual will is a negative will.

All too naturally, innumerable modern visionaries have known the human condition as a flight from freedom, a flight impelled by the terror of freedom, a terror inseparable from full responsibility, for that responsibility is a responsibility for our every act. That is the responsibility which Christianity has known as freedom, and if the realization of that responsibility is inseparable from grace, that grace could only be an absolute grace, for only an absolute grace makes possible the realization of freedom. Augustine could know his own acceptance of responsibility as a consequence of grace, that is the grace effecting an interior acceptance of responsibility, an acceptance which is the realization of the freedom of the will. But that very realization is the realization of the negativity of our will; only in that realization does an interior negativity become manifest and real, a negativity which is the impotence of the will, and an impotence which is most fully manifest in the very willing of the fallen will.

It is grace and grace alone which is the source of our awareness of the pure negativity of our will, that awareness is inseparable from an actualization of our freedom, so that the freedom of the will for us can only be a negative freedom, and is that negative freedom which is our freedom in the eternal will of God. Only after many years of profoundly interior struggle, an interior struggle going far beyond his exterior struggle with heresy, could Augustine realize that the actual freedom which he knew was a consequence of predestination, and a consequence of predestination precisely because it is a consequence of grace. Thus an actual freedom is inseparable from justification, a justification by grace alone, and a justification which is the realization of the eternal act of predestination.

Justification occurs only through the will of God, but that will is the one eternal act of God, and thus that will is the enactment of predestination, an enactment which is the enactment of freedom. So it is that God can will an eternal life and an eternal death only by willing that freedom which is the source of the fall. Now even if all humanity falls in that fall, and is predestined so to fall, that is the predestination which is the source of damnation and redemption alike. For redemption itself is here realized only through damnation, for those who are eternally elected to redemption pass through that same fall or damnation as do those who are eternally elected to be damned, and that grace which is realized in redemption is a grace reversing an original damnation. Therefore that is a redemption which can only be realized through damnation, so that it is absolutely necessary for God to will damnation so as to will that redemption, a redemption which is a free deliverance from the deepest depths of evil. Apart from a realization of those depths, a Christian redemption would be impossible, so that God can will an absolute redemption only by willing an absolute damnation.

This is precisely the reason why Christianity has known the fall as a fortunate fall, a fall apart from which redemption would be unreal, and a fall apart from which the Incarnation could never occur. So it is that God must will the fall, and will the fall in willing redemption, and if that is the eternal act of predestination, that is a predestination which is not only the absolutely free act of God, but is that act which is the enactment of our freedom as well. Our freedom is enacted by the will of God, and enacted in the will of God, that enactment is the act of predestination, but an enactment of that predestination in which we ourselves freely will our own damnation. Only a free act could be an eternal *act,* and that act which is our fall is that act which is uniquely our own, for even though it is eternally willed by God, it is so willed only through the actualization of our freedom. Thus our freedom is the freedom to sin, that is the only actual freedom which we have ever known, and it is the actualization of that freedom which is the actualization of fall. There has never been a human freedom which has not been actualized in sin, which is precisely why each of us is born in sin, just as each of us has fallen in the original fall. But that is the fall which *is* the fall of freedom, a fall which would be impossible apart from freedom, and a fall which is the inevitable consequence of the actualization of our freedom.

Consequently, God could not have willed our freedom apart from having willed our fall, only that fall is the actualization of our freedom, just as a subsequent realization of our freedom is necessarily a realization of our responsibility for that fall. For that is what it means to accept our bondage as our own, or to accept our will as our own, an acceptance that is only possible by way of a realization that we have freely willed our own impotence, and it is only in knowing that responsibility that we know or realize our freedom. Yet Christianity affirms that our freedom is a consequence of our having been created in the "image of God," our freedom is a reflection of the freedom of God, and it is just that freedom which makes possible our redemption. Moreover, it is just our negative freedom which makes possible that redemption, and if that is a freedom which can only be actualized in fall, that is freedom that can only be realized through damnation, a damnation that is absolutely necessary to a realization of redemption.

May we say then, that having been created in the image of God, we have been created in the image of God's negativity, a negativity which wills damnation, and therefore wills evil? None of our theologians have been able to say this, but in affirming predestination they in fact have said it, and it is all too significant that none of our truly major theologians have been unable to refrain from affirming double predestination. Double predestination may well be the deepest scandal in the Christian tradition, but it is embedded at the very center of the Western Christian tradition, and this is a center which no true theologian has been able to unthink or dissolve.

Nietzsche, in understanding the Christian God as the pure embodiment of evil, is therein and thereby the thinker who has most deeply understood the uniquely Christian dogma of predestination. For Nietzsche and Joyce alike, God wills eternal judgment simply and only because God is God, the act of God can only be a purely and totally negative act precisely because God *is* God. Thus both could know God's willing of redemption as the willing of damnation or eternal judgment, just as each could know in their all too distinctive ways that what Christianity has celebrated as redemption is, at bottom, damnation, or an absolutely impotent state or condition of the will. A constantly repeated prayer in *Finnegans Wake* is a prayer for sleep—"Grant sleep in hour's time, O Loud!" (259.4)—a sleep which is the deepest sleep in the "Ainsoph" or En Sof, the mystical center of this Christian Kabbalah. Yet arising from the center of this sleeping Godhead is original sin or "original sun," a "felicitous culpability" or *felix culpa,* and a *felix culpa* which our final epic poet has derived from "*Hearsay in paradox lust*" (263). Thus if the dominant movement in *Finnegans Wake* is the movement of fall, that is finally a fall of Godhead itself, a fall which is the crucifixion of God, and a fall which is finally reversed in the Easter celebration of book four of the *Wake*. That celebration is embodied in the apocalyptic resurrection of Anna Livia Plurabelle, which can issue in her cry: "Rise up now and aruse! Norvena's over" (619.28). "Norvena" or Nirvana is over when "Far calls" but "End here" (628.13), an end which is the end of "my cold mad feary father" (628.2), and an end which can only be pronounced by "Yes" or "Lff!"

A cosmic and apocalyptic Eucharist is reborn and renewed again and again in *Finnegans Wake,* and above all so in that tavern orgy occurring in the axial chapter of the *Wake,* an orgy immediately following the execution or crucifixion of "Haar Faugher," and an orgy which is a cosmic repetition of an Easter which is Good Friday, an Easter or resurrection which is an ecstatic consumption of the crucified body of God. But this cosmic Easter is possible only as a consequence of the breaking of the Host:

> How Buccleuch shocked the rosing girnirilles. A ballet of Gasty Power. A hov and an az and off like a gow! And don't live out the sad of tearfs, piddyawhick! Not offgot affsang is you, buthbach? Ath yetheredayeth noth endeth, hay? Vaersegood! Buckle to! (346.20)

The Dublin "ostman" or Norseman, H. C. Earwicker, is both "Haar Faugher," and the ancient Celtic hero, Finn MacCool, but he is also Yggdrasil or the cosmic Tree, which in the Eddas symbolizes the universe, a universe which goes on trial as the "Festy King," in this chapter. The fall, condemnation, and crucifixion of H.C.E. is the dominant epic action in the *Wake,* it is repeated again and again, even as the Host is ever broken in the Mass. And just as the liturgical acts and action of the Mass culminate in communion, so fall and death culminate in a festival of orgiastic communion in this apocalyptic epic, a communion whose very blasphemy, and scatological blasphemy, undergoes a constant ritual repetition in the text. But lying at the center of this epic, even as the breaking of the Host lies at the center of the Mass, is the execution or crucifixion of "Haar Faugher," an execution which becomes most dramatic and most scatological in the television skit by the comics Buff and Tuff of "How Buckly Shot the Russian General."

After the announcement of this primal event, H.C.E. is himself accused of the crime; he pleads guilty (363.20), and goes on to identify himself with his own executioner:

> I am, I like to think, by their sacrereligion of daimond cap diamond, confessedly in my baron gentilhomme to the manhor bourne till ladiest day as pantoposopher, to have splet for groont a peer of bellows like Bacculus shakes a rousing guttural at any old cerpaintime by peaching (allso we are not amusical) the warry warst against myself in the defile as a liebarretter sebaiscopal of these mispeschyites of the first virginial water who, without an auction of biasement from my part, with gladyst tone ahquickessed in it, overbhowe and underwhere, the totty lolly poppy flossy conny dollymaukins! (365.3–12)

Here, the death of God is the self-sacrifice of God, and not only is the executed the executioner but the condemned one is the Eternal Judge, and nothing whatsoever distinguishes guilt and condemnation or crime and execution, because Victim and Judge and Host and Creator are one. If *Finnegans Wake* is our only imaginative text which is simultaneously a liturgical text, only here does our uniquely Western liturgy undergo a full imaginative metamorphosis, and even if the awe and sublimity of the Mass now passes into a cosmic ribaldry, there an ultimate transgression occurs, and one inverting and reversing the Eucharist, as the language of the Roman rite becomes the very opposite of itself in *Finnegans Wake*. Yet thereby there occurs an awakening of the Christian God, an awakening in a world or cosmos in which God is dead, only now is a Christian reversal of God liturgically enacted, and enacted in a purely transgressive language which is simultaneously the ecstatic and universal language of Here Comes Everybody.

The Yes-saying of Nietzsche and Joyce alike is a Yes-saying inseparable from an absolute No-saying, and that is a No-saying which Christianity has known as God's eternal act of predestination, an act which is the innermost act of God Himself, or which is manifest in a uniquely Christian faith as God's innermost act and actuality. That is an actuality which can only be known in Christianity, for only Christianity knows the absolute No-saying of God, and a No-saying which is the genesis of what the Christian knows as freedom. So it is that the Christian can only know that freedom which is grounded in an absolute bondage or impotence of the will, and if the very identity of the will itself has only been called forth by an interior recognition of that bondage, that is a recognition of the only freedom that can be actual for us. But that freedom does make possible an eternal act, an eternal act which is the actualization of freedom, and an actualization of that freedom which can only culminate in fall. Yet by recognizing that we ourselves are the authors of our fall, we thereby realize an autonomous freedom, for even if that freedom is a purely negative freedom, it is a freedom which is our own. And it is our own because we were created in the image of God, and that is an image which we actualize when we actualize our freedom, and actualize it eternally in our own free act. That act is our eternal act, and our only eternal act, the only eternal act which is fully our own, and is our own by virtue of the eternal act of predestination.

So it is that the absolute act of predestination is that act which actualizes our freedom, a freedom which is a total responsibility, and a total responsibility which is our freedom. That freedom is our only glory, and even if it is the glory of damnation, that is the glory making possible our redemption. For even if our redemption is solely the consequence of the eternal act of God, so likewise is our freedom the consequence of that act, but our freedom, unlike our redemption, is fully our own. And it is fully our own in our having been predestined to damnation, a damnation which is the inevitable destiny of our freedom, but a damnation actualizing our freedom as a freedom which is uniquely our own. Only in that damnation can we know our freedom as uniquely our own, and if to know the absolute No-saying of God is to know that damnation, that is a damnation in which we can recognize our freedom. And we can recognize it here as we recognize it nowhere else, and recognize ourselves in that damnation as we can recognize ourselves nowhere else, for only here can we truly know the freedom of our will.

Yes, our freedom is a terrible freedom, but it is also a glorious freedom, for it is a freedom embodying a total responsibility, and that is precisely the responsibility which fully embodies the will. Not until Paul is there a recognition of that responsibility, and if that is a recognition of original sin, that is a recognition of our freedom, a freedom apart from which there could be no sin.

Thus a recognition of freedom is the recognition of an internal and interior negativity, an interior negativity which is the negativity of the free will, for it is precisely the free will which is the purely negative will. If that negativity is the negativity of evil, that is a negativity which is inseparable from freedom, and inseparable from that freedom which is the purely interior source of our negative acts. When we know our acts to be our own, we know our freedom to be our own, and that is a freedom which is the freedom of the will, and a freedom which is actualized when we accept

134

responsibility for our acts. That is the will and that is the only will which is the free will, and if that is the will which most fully activates or actualizes the will, that is a will which is only truly manifest in our acceptance of our negativity as a negativity which is uniquely our own.

Augustine could understand his conversion as a conversion revealing his own will as a will which had willed every possible evil, and if that revelation is truly a revelation of the will, it is a revelation revealing that will which embodies the deepest depths of evil, and embodies those depths in its deepest center. An act of freedom is an act accepting those depths as our own, thereby accepting our full responsibility for those depths, a responsibility which is quite simply the responsibility of freedom. That is the freedom which is the power of the will, a power that is only truly actual in that acceptance, and a power that is only possible as a consequence of the eternal act of predestination.

Accordingly, if the act of predestination is an act which eternally wills evil, that is an act which is inseparable from freedom, or inseparable from the actualization of freedom. For that actualization can occur only through the actualization of the purely negative will, an actualization which is the realization of freedom, and therefore the genesis of the freedom of the will. Freedom is simply impossible if it is not simultaneously the freedom of either life or death, but a freedom which is realized only in eternal life could never be an actual freedom, and could never be an actual freedom because it could never be actualized as a freedom which is truly our own. That would be a freedom which is only the freedom of grace, and never a freedom which is uniquely our own, and thus never a freedom which is the consequence of our will.

It is damnation and damnation alone which is fully the consequence of our will, that is the damnation which is the actualization of our unique freedom, which is a freedom to be the full author of our own acts. That freedom could never be realized in redemption, or not in a redemption which is not a reversal of damnation, or a redemption in which grace and grace alone is present. Nietzsche could justly recognize *that* redemption as an absolute impotence of the will, whereas an actual recognition of the impotence of the will is a realization of our responsibility for that will, and hence an awakening of the power of the will. Now that is just the awakening which occurs in the realization of freedom, and if the actualization of freedom is the actualization of fall, that is a fall apart from which there could be no true actualization of freedom.

Consequently, our predestination to damnation is a predestination to freedom, and even as all humanity is predestined to damnation—for even the redeemed are redeemed from the actuality of that damnation—so are we thereby and only thereby predestined to freedom. The absolute No-saying of God is a No-saying actualizing freedom itself, a freedom which would be impossible apart from that No-saying, and would be so impossible because apart from that eternal judgment there could be no actual acceptance of responsibility, and thus no full responsibility, and therefore no actual freedom. Even Augustine could not conceive that real freedom which he believed to be present in the saints in Heaven, just as the Dante who could so gloriously envision those free acts which culminate in damnation could not envision the freedom of beatitude, just as he could not envision those acts which culminate in beatitude as being free acts of the will. The only acts which we can know to be truly and uniquely our own are purely negative acts, negative acts realizing an interiority which is fully our own, and that is the interiority which is the sole arena of an actual freedom. But that is an interiority which could be born only through fall, a fall which is a fall from all possible positive identity, and therefore a fall reversing an original identity so as to realize its opposite. That is the opposite which is the negativity of sin, and the negativity of an original sin, but an original sin which is possible only by way of the actualization of freedom. So it is that a predestination to freedom is inevitably a predestination to sin, and to original sin, and that is the sin which is the actualization of an eternal death.

Certainly God wills that death, and wills it in the eternal act of predestination, for that is a predestination to sin, a predestination apart from which there could be no actualization of freedom. Our freedom to sin is freedom itself, a freedom which is only actualized in sin, and even if that sin is solely a self-laceration, that is a laceration that is inseparable from the activity of the will, and from the activity of the free will. Every negative embodiment of the will is an embodiment of evil, an evil which is a pure negativity, but a pure negativity which can only be actualized in freedom. Evil cannot have its source in nature or being, but only in the negative will, and just as the refusal of that will is the refusal of the possibility of an intrinsic evil, a refusal of that will is also the refusal of the possibility of an actual freedom. If there has been no understanding of freedom in the West apart from an Augustinian ground, there has been no understanding of evil in the West apart from that ground, and not even by Augustine himself in his Neoplatonic mood. For we have been given a tradition in which evil and freedom are dialectical twins, neither has ever actually been known apart from the other, and just as an identification of evil with matter or natural instinct is an identification which dissolves its human or interior

136

ground, an identification of freedom with external power is an identification which is a dissolution of freedom. All too significantly, the freedom of the will has never been known apart from the Biblical tradition, and that is a tradition embodying a total and an eternal judgment.

Freedom as freedom is inevitably an internal and interior power, and it can be realized only in the activity of the will, a will which is a free will only insofar as it is a negative will, or only insofar as it embodies a movement of negativity. That deeply divided and doubled consciousness which is a self-consciousness, is a consciousness which is conscious of its freedom, but it is so only insofar as it effects a negation of itself. That negation is the realization of freedom, but it can only be a negative realization, for it can realize its own freedom only in realizing its own bondage, and when that bondage is known as its own, then freedom is known as its own. So it is only in realizing the pure negativity of the will that we realize the freedom of the will, and if that realization is the realization of judgment, then that is the judgment which is the birth of the freedom of the will. Hence that freedom is born only through fall, and through a conscious realization that we are the authors of our fall, a realization that is truly possible only by an acceptance of our own responsibility for the depths of our fall. That is a responsibility which is impossible apart from judgment, and finally impossible apart from an eternal judgment, which is the eternal judgment of predestination. And if the act of predestination is identical with the act of creation, then the creation itself is destined to fall, for it is eternal death which is the center of predestination, and is inevitably that center if only because redemption itself can only be realized through fall.

Thus if God wills predestination, God wills the fall, and wills the fall in an eternal act of grace, a grace which is the sole source of redemption. That is the grace which is embodied in the absolute No-saying of God, a No-saying which wills the damnation of all, and wills that damnation as the only way to the freedom of all. Predestination is the genesis of freedom, and the sole genesis of freedom, and if that is the genesis of the absolutely negative will of God, that is a genesis apart from which there could be no actual freedom, and apart from which there could be no actual activity of the will. It is precisely when predestination is hidden or silent that there is no awareness of the will, a will whose awakening is inevitably an awakening to the act of predestination, an act apart from which there could be no freedom of the will. Every thinker who has understood the will as a self-embodied will has thereby understood predestination, and if Nietzsche is the most atheistic of our thinkers, it is Nietzsche who most passionately affirms predestination, and does so in his affirmation of

Eternal Recurrence or the Will to Power. So likewise that imaginative tradition which most deeply or most manifestly embodies the will, our epic tradition from Dante through Joyce, has continually been an enactment of predestination, and has perhaps been most deeply so in its very reversals of predestination. Just as there can be no awareness of the freedom of the will apart from an awareness of a profoundly interior evil, there can be no actualization of that freedom apart from a purely negative actualization, and that is an actualization which is an actualization of judgment, and an actualization of the eternal and total judgment of God.

7
THE GENESIS
OF NOTHINGNESS

Now just as a realization of interior freedom has been so intimately and so fully conjoined with a realization of interior negativity or evil in our history and consciousness, so it is that our deep understanding of evil has always been an understanding of nothingness, and of that nothingness which can be known as a primal ground of our will. Only a Western and Christian tradition has known an actual nothingness, or a nothingness which can be an embodied nothingness, or a nothingness which can be embodied in the actuality of the will. If Nietzsche was inspired by Schopenhauer to realize an ultimate negativity as the negativity of the will, that negativity for Nietzsche is an actual nothingness, and an actual nothingness that Augustine could know as the fallen or evil will. Just as that fall is a fall into nothingness, the nothingness out of which the world was created, that fall is an actual fall, and an actual fall which is original sin. Augustine knows that fall as the genesis of sin, even as Nietzsche knows it as the genesis of the bad conscience or *ressentiment,* and for both Nietzsche and Augustine our interior consciousness is a negative consciousness, and a negative consciousness assaulting itself in its deepest act, an act that is an absolute self-negation. That is a self-negation calling forth the depths of our interiority, and just as those depths can only be negative depths for us, they are depths embodying an actual nothingness, an actual nothingness which is a pure negativity. Thus if our consciousness is a self-lacerated and self-lacerating consciousness, it is a consciousness embodying an alien nothingness, or an

139

emptiness which is a negative emptiness, and an actually negative emptiness which is fully actual in its very assault upon itself.

No other historical tradition has known such an actually negative emptiness, just as no other tradition has known a self-consciousness which is a consciousness of freedom, but is a consciousness of freedom only insofar as it is alienated from itself. That self-alienation which we have known as self-consciousness, is a self-alienation which is an embodiment of an interior emptiness, and an interior emptiness disrupting the very center of our consciousness. Therefore such an emptiness could only be an actual emptiness, an actual emptiness which is finally an actual nothingness, and is nowhere so manifestly an actual nothingness as it is in an interior realization of freedom. It was precisely by undergoing that interior realization that Augustine could know the actual nothingness of the negative will, a will that is an impotent will just because of its embodiment of that nothingness, but only a realization of our interior negativity as a negativity that is fully our own makes possible the realization of a freedom which is our own. Thus our freedom is a freedom inseparable from an actual nothingness, just as our self-consciousness is inseparable from a realization of an interior negativity, an interior negativity alienating consciousness from itself, so that the self-consciousness which we have known is a fully dichotomous consciousness.

Now just as a dichotomous consciousness has ever more fully and more finally realized itself in the course of the evolution of our consciousness, then so, too, has an actual nothingness become ever more fully embodied in that evolution or that history. Nietzsche was the first thinker to know that actual nothingness as a total nothingness, or as a nothingness which is inseparable from every act of the will, for even if this is an Augustinian apprehension, it goes far beyond Augustine in apprehending the totality of that nothingness. This is a totality which is fully incarnate in a uniquely modern imagination, and a totality which has wholly triumphed in a fully modern poetry and painting, a painting and poetry which has dissolved or reversed every interior presence or voice, but has done so only by realizing the actual nothingness of every interior voice and presence, a realization which is the realization of a truly new and apocalyptic nothingness. That is the nothingness which Nietzsche celebrates in his vision of Eternal Recurrence, just as that is the nothingness which is willed in the Will to Power. But therein and thereby that is an actual and not an empty nothingness, or a nothingness which is willed in *a total act of the will,* and it is only the totality of that willing which realizes the totality of an actual nothingness, a totality dissolving every echo or trace of "God" or "Being."

The Genesis of Nothingness

If Nietzsche could know the uniquely Christian God as the will to nothingness pronounced holy, the Will to Power is a reversal of that will, a will reversing an empty nothingness into an actual nothingness, and an actual nothingness which is finally and wholly empty of God. Only the full realization of an actual emptying of God makes possible the realization of the totality of an actual nothingness, and just as the dawning of that totality is the dawning of our nihilism, that is a nihilism which is an actually embodied nihilism, and a nihilism which is the nihilism of an actual and not an empty nothingness.

Certainly we can know our nihilism to be a truly new nihilism, for just as the horrors of the twentieth century are historically unique, so likewise have been our imaginative embodiments and celebrations. If those celebrations and embodiments culminate in *Finnegans Wake,* that culmination is an epic culmination, and an epic culmination of our consciousness and history. It was the mature Nietzsche who realized that thinking and that consciousness which is a primal center of *Finnegans Wake,* and that realization is the calling forth of a total nothingness, and an actual nothingness which undergoes a resurrection at the conclusion of *Finnegans Wake.* But that conclusion is also the beginning of our final epic, and if that "the" which concludes this epic makes possible its very beginning, that is a beginning which is an apocalyptic beginning, and an apocalyptic beginning of a final nothingness. Only in full modernity is there an enactment of an apocalyptic nothingness, a nothingness which is a total nothingness only by being an apocalyptic nothingness, and therefore a nothingness which is a full reversal or inversion of an original or primordial nothingness. So it is that the nihilism which we know is alien to every archaic consciousness, just as it is alien to every ancient form of consciousness, for ours is a nihilism that is both interiorly and historically manifest and real, and historically real precisely by way of a voiding or dissolution of an interior consciousness.

That voiding historically dawns in the very advent of self-consciousness, an advent which is the advent of Christianity, and the advent of an apocalyptic Christianity revolving about a total ending or apocalypse. Hegel and Nietzsche know that apocalypse as do no other thinkers, and they know it as the total embodiment of an absolute negation, and an absolute negation which is an absolute self-negation or self-emptying. While Nietzsche and Hegel profoundly differ in their understanding and realization of that self-negation, each understands it as an absolute negation, and an absolute negation which is internal and historical at once. At no point are Hegel and Nietzsche so deeply united as

THE GENESIS OF GOD

they are at this point, but Nietzsche was able to realize it interiorly as Hegel was never able to do, an interior realization which is the realization of absolute negation as the absolute will. If absolute will is absolute No-saying and absolute Yes-saying at once, that is an enactment which is a totally *willed* enactment, but a willing which is absolute affirmation and absolute negation simultaneously. This is the willing which Augustinianism can know as the will of God, and the will of God in the willing of a double and eternal predestination, and an eternal predestination in which redemption and damnation are inseparable. So it is that here God wills the nothingness of eternal death in willing the glorification of redemption, a willing which is the willing of eternal death and of eternal life at once, and only the simultaneity of that willing is or could be an eternal *willing,* an eternal willing which is the willing of actuality itself.

That is an actuality which is positive and negative at once, or "good" and "evil" at once, or "life" and "death" at once. Such an actuality could only be the embodiment of an actual as opposed to an empty nothingness, and an actual nothingness in its very realization of death and evil, and a realization of evil and death as an ultimate negativity. That is the negativity of an actual but total nothingness, and even if the totality of that nothingness only all too gradually becomes actualized in that consciousness which embodies it, that very actualization is an irreversible actualization, and is so if only because of the irreversibility of that history in which it is realized. Already Meister Eckhart could know the nothingness of the creature, a nothingness which is pure of all being (*puritas essendi*), but precisely thereby a nothingness which is not less than being, but rather beyond being. That is a beyondness of being that Augustine could not know, for Augustine could not know a positive as opposed to a negative nothingness, just as Augustine could not know an "I" that is an interior "I" as an "I" that is the "I" of God. Or, rather, that interior "I" that Augustine can know as the "I" of God is an "I" that is wholly other than our own. Yet Eckhart realizes an actual interior self-annihilation that is a genesis of God in our interior: "He gives birth not only to me, His Son, but he gives birth to me as Himself and Himself as me as His being and nature" (sermon 6, Colledge translation). That is a birth occurring in that nothingness which is pure of all being, but a nothingness which a uniquely modern mysticism can know as the womb of God, and the womb of that Godhead which is beyond God.

Indeed, a uniquely modern mysticism can know a dark night of the soul which is a purgation of every interior image and identity of God. But that is a purgatory which is a truly modern purgatory, and just as a real purgatory is only interiorly and historically born in the Middle Ages, a birth which is consummated in Dante's *Purgatorio,* it is only a deeply modern Catholic mysticism which knows a total purgatorial negation, a negation which is the negation of that God which is known by Catholic scholasticism, and thus a negation of that God which simply is "Being." Or, rather, that God whom Aquinas and Dante could know as the "act of being" or *ipsum esse* disappears or dissolves in a post-Gothic consciousness, a dissolution which is the dissolution of the actuality of being as being, even while being the advent of a nothingness which is "beyond" being. That nothingness is present in that Godhead which is beyond God, even as it is present in the "dark night of the soul," a dark night which Hegel could know as the death of God and Nietzsche could know as the advent of Zarathustra. For that dark night is an interior nothingness, and an interior nothingness which is an actual nothingness, and an actual nothingness ever more fully realizing itself as a total nothingness. While Hegel could know that nothingness as a dialectical emptiness eternally realizing that crucifixion which *is* resurrection, Nietzsche could know it as an irreversible nothingness, and an irreversible nothingness which *is* absolute will, and is absolute will precisely because it is nothing but will.

Not even Augustine could so purely know the will of will, for Augustine could not dissociate will and Being, so that he knew the fallen will as the absence or privation of Being, just as he ever strove to know the will of God as Being itself. That is a striving that is inevitably an impossible or self-lacerating striving, for the God whom Augustine knew as the God who *is* love could not and cannot be the God who *is* Being. Just as will must finally be absent from every pure apprehension of Being, as it is finally absent in Aquinas, love must likewise be absent from that Being which is finally conceptually and interiorly unknowable, or absent as a love which can be interiorly celebrated or affirmed. The history of the understanding of the will is a history of the progressive diminution of the very idea or apprehension of "Being," a history that begins with Augustine and is consummated in Nietzsche, and a history which is not simply a "forgetting of Being," but rather a real and actual negation of Being, or a negation of that Being which is simply and only Being. In a fundamental sense, the end of metaphysics occurs in the deepest metaphysical thinker of early modernity, Spinoza, if it did not already occur in a pure nominalism. For even if nominalism realized an infinite chasm between God and the world, that is a chasm dissolving a purely metaphysical God, even as Spinoza's infinite Substance dissolves that Being which is Being and only "Being," and does so by virtue of the real identity which it establishes between infinity and finitude. That is an identity that was mystically known by Meister Eckhart, even if Eckhart knew a real finitude as nothingness, for that is the nothingness which is finally the nothingness of Godhead, and the nothingness of that Godhead who *is* love.

So it is that the uniquely Christian God embodies nothingness, and not a nothingness which is an empty nothingness but rather a nothingness which is an actual nothingness. That is a nothingness which is enacted in the eternal act of creation, and enacted in that world which is the creation of the uniquely Christian God, a world which is a fallen world, yes, and already fallen in the eternal act of creation. Just as fall is willed in the eternal act of predestination, fall is willed in that act of creation which is identical with the act of predestination, and is so willed precisely because that is a will which wills actuality itself. While that is an actuality that Aquinas could not know, this is an actuality that is inevitably absent in a purely metaphysical thinking, and absent in that thinking because that thinking cannot know the being of nothingness itself. Such a being is wholly absent from the ancient world, even as is an actual nothingness itself, but that is an absence which is simultaneously the absence of self-consciousness, even as it is the absence of a consciousness of freedom.

Perhaps the deepest realization of freedom which occurs in the Classical world occurs in the deepest moments of Greek tragedy, and there most clearly in the Oedipus of *Oedipus Tyrannus,* for if that Oedipus is the most fully individual figure in Greek tragedy, this is an Oedipus who enacts a preordained fate which is here an individual act and decision. Destiny is an overwhelming presence in Greek tragedy, if not in the Classical world as a whole, but in this tragedy destiny is individually enacted, an enactment wherein a primordial fate becomes an individual destiny, and a destiny which is necessarily and perhaps even freely chosen by Oedipus. If the plot of *Oedipus Tyrannus* is the purest plot in all tragedy, for every step in its development is a necessary realization of all that has happened before, this realization most fully occurs in the words and the acts of Oedipus himself. Plot and character are one in this tragedy, a full union between individual consciousness and tragic action which is achieved nowhere else in tragedy, and a union which perhaps is consummated in the apotheosis of Oedipus in *Oedipus at Colonus.* That apotheosis is the most exalted moment of Greek tragedy, but it is an apotheosis in which Oedipus disappears, a disappearance which is the purest moment of grace in Classical literature. That disappearance is the disappearance of evil and destiny at once, and if this occurs nowhere else in Greek tragedy, that is an absence which is the absence of a fully embodied nothingness.

A fully embodied or actual nothingness has only been known in the Christian and Western world, and the vast and uncrossable distance between our nothingness and a Buddhist nothingness is a decisive sign of a uniquely Western and Christian mode of consciousness, a consciousness which is a truly interior consciousness, yes, but precisely thereby and therein a realization of an actual nothingness. Just as our interior consciousness is a dichotomous consciousness, and a consciousness which can never fully realize its own intention or will, that will which is a free will is a deeply divided will, and so divided or doubled in its very center. Once our deeper interior is manifest and real as will itself, that will is real as a self-alienated will, a self-alienation and self-estrangement which is inseparable from the true center or subject of our consciousness. Even as an individual and interior will is finally an impotent will, that impotence is most deeply an interior impotence, and an interior impotence which is actually willed by the interior and individual will. So that willing is not only a dichotomous willing, but a dichotomous willing arising from the very center of the will, a center apart from which the will could not be an individual and interior will. Consequently, the willing of that center is an inverted willing, a willing finally willing against itself, and that is the very negativity of willing which calls forth the center or the subject of consciousness itself. No such center or subject is manifest in the ancient world, an absence which is the absence of self-consciousness, and that absence is the absence of a purely negative center of consciousness.

Now if a negative center of consciousness is a self-lacerating center, a center of consciousness which continually and compulsively assaults itself, that internal and interior assault is a necessary and inevitable response to a pure negativity which is fully present at that center. And that negativity could only be an actual negativity, and an interiorly actual negativity, a negativity which is the negativity of the internal will, and a negativity which is the inescapable actuality of that will. So deep is that negativity that that very willing which is so uniquely and actually our own is inevitably a negative willing, and a negative willing which is necessarily directed against itself, and directed against itself in its own deepest center. We can clearly see this negativity in the tragic heroes and heroines of Shakespearean tragedy, for unlike their ancient Greek counterparts, these primal figures of the modern imagination can act only by acting against themselves, a self-laceration which is the very arena of all fully modern tragedy, and a self-laceration releasing a uniquely modern soliloquy, a soliloquy in which the very presence of an individual and interior voice is the presence of a self-negating or self-lacerating voice. Nothing like this is present in Greek tragedy, and just as that tragedy veils the human face with a tragic mask, its individual actors are inseparable from a cosmic destiny, a cosmic destiny which is a total destiny, thereby foreclosing the very possibility of an interior conflict or *agon*.

But it is precisely interior conflict which is the true arena of the individual and internal will, an arena which is not only the arena of modern tragedy, but is the very domain of everything which we have known as self-consciousness. Just as that will is absent from Greek tragedy, and from the Homeric epics as well, an *ananke* or necessity is present which is its counterpart, for that necessity or destiny is the human arena of the Classical world. No such necessity reigned in what a Classical consciousness could know as the natural world, or did not do so until the advent of the Roman Empire, and no such interior conflict is manifest in anything that we can know as nature. Perhaps that is yet another reason why we have been so overwhelmed by an internal and interior conflict, just as the Classical world was overwhelmed by destiny or fortune, each such presence has been the horizon of a whole historical world, a presence apart from which that world would lose its own historical or individual ground. Yet the necessity of destiny does appear to be absent from Greek philosophical thinking, an absence making possible the abstract moralizing of Aristotle's *Poetics,* just as it made possible a Platonic idealism. Yet that idealism is transcended if not reversed in the late Plato, even as all real traces of a Platonic idealism are absent from the mature Aristotle, for ancient philosophy never knew idealism in the modern sense, and could not do so if only because it could not know a true subject of consciousness. That subject is only philosophically born in Augustine, and if it does not realize a pure philosophical expression until Descartes, that expression is the expression of a profoundly divided consciousness. A Cartesian doubt cannot be found in the ancient world, for there there is no internal subject which is capable of such a doubt, no possible doubling of the subject of consciousness, for there there is no subject of consciousness which is an internal subject. An ancient *ananke* or destiny foreclosed the very possibility of such an internalization of consciousness, even as a philosophical thinking in which there is a full coincidence of the object and the subject of thinking foreclosed that possibility, and only the true ending of that ancient world made possible the birth of the internal and interior subject of consciousness.

That interior subject which first speaks in Paul, or is first recorded in writing in Paul, is an interior subject only by way of that assault which it conducts upon itself. That assault is the initial voice of a truly interior guilt, an interior guilt wholly transcending that evil which could be known by the ancient world apart from Israel, and transcending it by realizing it as an evil that is a fully internal evil, and thereby and only thereby a truly interior guilt. If that guilt is the initial realization of an interior consciousness, that consciousness is a truly divided consciousness, a divided and doubled consciousness which can know itself only by knowing its own intrinsic "other." Such an intrinsic and interior "other" was never manifest in the ancient world, just as an interior subject was never manifest in that world, for only an interior subject can know and realize otherness as its own, a realization which is the realization of the dichotomous center or subject of consciousness. Now, an absolutely alien subject is inseparable from the center of consciousness, an alien subject which is the intrinsic "other" of consciousness itself, and therefore a subject effecting a division or a doubling of consciousness, and a doubling wherein consciousness itself *is* its own intrinsic "other." That doubling is not a simple fantasy or illusion, as witness its overwhelming impact upon our history, an impact wherein an ancient cosmic necessity becomes an interior necessity, and an interior necessity which is just as destructive and catastrophic as is the *ananke* of Greek tragedy.

Indeed, that interior necessity which we so deeply know, and which is overwhelmingly manifest in our history and world, is a necessity which is not only intrinsically other than ourselves, but intrinsically other than everything which is simply given us as world. So it is that nature or world can be for us only a wholly alienated world, an alienation never so present in the ancient world, and even if such an alienation made possible the triumphs of modern science and technology, those triumphs are inseparable from the pure alienation of the subject of consciousness, a self-alienation which itself is inseparable from our historical catastrophes. And those catastrophes are perhaps most purely present in the deepest expressions of our imagination, so that even as the horrors of political totalitarianism are prophetically foreknown by Dostoyevsky and Kafka, the abyss of cosmological and historical disintegration is prophetically foreknown by Mallarmé and Beckett, and even the ecstatic celebrations of Rilke and Stevens are inseparable from an interior realization of total abyss. Neither such an abyss nor such celebration was possible in the ancient world, or known only by the prophets of Israel, prophets who seemingly have been reborn in our world, and reborn in our own prophetic visionaries. Certainly Blake and Nietzsche are such visionaries, but it is Nietzsche above all who is the prophet of our destiny, and one whom like the prophets of Israel could realize an ecstatic celebration only by

147

knowing, and by deeply and purely knowing, an ultimate eschatological or apocalyptic ending and disaster.

The early Nietzsche could understand Greek tragedy as an ecstatic return to the night of unconsciousness, an unconsciousness which is an undifferentiated consciousness, and an undifferentiated consciousness reversing that *principium individuationis* which was the unique creation of ancient Greece. While Nietzsche's early understanding of a Dionysian ecstasy is very different from his late understanding of Dionysian joy, both are united in seeking a radical overcoming or transcendence not of an ancient individuality but rather of a uniquely Christian interiority, an interiority which is the interiority of the bad conscience and *ressentiment,* and an interiority which is the embodiment of a uniquely Christian nothingness. Indeed, Nietzsche ever more decisively came to know a true interiority not only as a purely alien interiority, but as an annihilating interiority, an interiority which is the *will* to nothingness pronounced holy. Only a Christian interiority knows a deification of nothingness, a deification embodied in the uniquely Christian naming of God, and only that naming calls forth or evokes the absolute No-saying of God. Eckhart and his disciples could know a mystical divination as the consequence of a profound self-abandonment, so that Eckhart could declare that the man who has truly abandoned or annihilated himself, and therein abandoned both God and the world, will thereby take possession of the lowest point, and then God "must" pour the whole of Himself into this man or God is not God (sermon 48). Nietzsche understood that lowest point as an actual nothingness, and an actual nothingness which is inseparable from the Christian God, for only a realization of that God embodies such a nothingness, a nothingness which is an absolutely alien center.

Even as Buddhism can know and embody an absolute nothingness as an absolute totality, Eckhart could know the "lowest point" as that point which impels the Godhead to release the totality of itself, and Nietzsche could know an absolute nihilism as the very arena of the totality of Eternal Recurrence or the Will to Power. At no other points has our history evoked a more total nothingness, and if a total nothingness is therein and thereby a total grace, that grace is inseparable from nothingness itself. The apotheosis of Oedipus in *Oedipus at Colonus* may well be such a point, and if that is the purest grace which is realized in a uniquely Greek imagination, that is a grace which is a portal to a uniquely Christian resurrection, a resurrection which is the resurrection of eternal death. That is the resurrection which is realized in the genesis of the uniquely interior "I," an "I" that is eternal life and eternal death at once, but is so only by way

148

of its embodiment of an apocalyptic nothingness. While an apocalyptic nothingness may well be the opposite of a Buddhist nothingness, and is so if only because of the actuality of its occurrence, that occurrence does release a pure and total nothingness, and a nothingness which apocalypticism knows as the end of the world. For the apocalyptic symbol of ending is unquestionably a nihilistic symbol, which is just why it has been so deeply resurrected in an all too modern nihilism, and that nihilism is a voyage into nothingness, and a voyage into that nothingness which is the consummation of our history.

But if an apocalyptic nothingness is a real and actual nothingness, and an actual nothingness which is a total nothingness, not only is it the arena of an interior pathology and guilt, but also the arena of a disenactment of consciousness itself, and a disenactment which is not a dissolution. For it cannot be the dissolution of consciousness if it is the embodiment of an actual nothingness, and precisely because an actual nothingness is not an empty nothingness, not a nothingness which is simply and only nothing. That is all too clear in Eckhart's enactment of the lowest point, just as it is overwhelmingly clear in Nietzsche's calling forth of the Will to Power, for that nothingness which is the Will to Power is a nothingness that is free of everything whatsoever that has ever been known or manifest as "God" or "Being." Only that disenactment releases what Nietzsche knows as absolute will, and that will is the will *of* nothingness only by being the absolute reversal of every possible will *to* nothingness. So it is that absolute will is here the absolute reversal of the will of the Christian God, and in being the full inversion of that God it is the full inversion of an absolutely sovereign transcendence, and therefore is that pure immanence which is free of every possible teleological end or goal. Its total voiding of that end is a realization of nothingness, but is a realization of that nothingness which *is* absolute actuality, and therefore is the total reversal of the uniquely Christian God. Just as that nothingness is a new nothingness, and a totally new nothingness, it is thereby an actual nothingness, and an actual nothingness which is actuality itself.

No one has understood cruelty so deeply as did Nietzsche, and above all so in his continual evocation of the great ladder of religious cruelty, a ladder which will culminate in an ultimate sacrifice:

> Finally—what remained to be sacrificed? At long last, did one not have to sacrifice for once whatever is comforting, holy, healing; all hope, all faith in hidden harmony, in future blisses and justices? Didn't one have to sacrifice God himself and, from

cruelty against oneself, worship the stone, stupidity, gravity, fate, the nothing? To sacrifice God for the nothing—this paradoxical mystery of the final cruelty was reserved for the generation now coming up: all of us already know something of this. (*Beyond Good and Evil*, 55, Kaufmann translation)

This is that apocalyptic sacrifice which is the embodiment of an ultimate nihilism, an ultimate nihilism which is a sacrifice of God for "the nothing," and a nothing which only truly becomes manifest and real in that very sacrifice. If that nothing is deeper and thereby more vacuous and abysmal than every previous epiphany of the nothing, it is also thereby more actually real, and more actually real as that nothing which is our deepest origin and ground.

Only in this perspective can one realize how innocent are all Freudian images of the womb, images disguising an eternal death that is an eternal nothingness, and disguising them so as to make possible a uniquely modern therapy. If that therapy has now broken down, and broken down by returning to its original source, that source is a nothingness which is our own, but only now is actually and finally our own. Yet precisely thereby we can know our nothingness not simply as a contemporary nothingness, nor even only a truly new nothingness, but a nothingness which is the embodiment of an original nothingness. And it is just in knowing the actuality of nothingness that we can know a genesis of nothingness, a genesis or actual beginning that is wholly alien to a Buddhist nothingness, and so alien to every nothingness which is and only is a pure emptiness. For it is exactly that emptiness that our nothingness is not, and that pure otherness from a purely empty nothingness is a decisive sign and seal of a nothingness that is the consequence of the genesis of nothingness, and of an actual genesis which is an actual beginning. Just as it is only the Biblical tradition which has known a once-and-for-all and irreversible beginning, it is only that history and that consciousness which is a consequence of that tradition which has known an actual nothingness, and an actual nothingness that could only be the consequence of a genesis of nothingness.

Nothing more clearly calls forth the necessity of genesis than the realization of a real and actual evolutionary movement, that is a movement which has historically evolved in the evolution of our consciousness, and if that purely negative consciousness which is so fully and so finally our own is the consequence of an evolutionary expansion and deepening of negativity itself, that negativity must have a real and actual origin. The

150

dissolution of an image or echo of absolute or ultimate origin has been a way for us of loosening or disguising our deep interior negativity, and if a fully modern consciousness is inseparable from "bad faith," such an illusory and deceptive faith is at no point more pervasive than it is in our continual and compulsive efforts to transform our birth into unbirth or our actual origin into a disappearance or dissolution of origin. The dissolution of that origin would be the dissolution of guilt, or the dissolution of an interior guilt, thereby evil or negativity could be known as a wholly exterior or external negativity, and therefore as a negativity which is precisely not our own. An ancient consciousness could know such a negativity as *ananke,* a cosmic necessity or destiny transcending the power of the divine realm itself, and a necessity which is directed against all human individuality as an individuality that is wholly other than itself. But that is a necessity which has never been renewed or resurrected in the modern world, and the impossibility for us of such an *anamnesis* or renewal is a decisive sign of the transformation of consciousness itself, a transformation foreclosing the possibility of a return to an earlier form or mode of consciousness. While an ancient consciousness could know beginning itself as the beginning of a cosmic chaos, we can know it only as the beginning of a chaos which is our own, and is our own precisely at the center of our consciousness.

Now even if center as center has disappeared from our consciousness, that is not a disappearance which is the disappearance of an interior negativity, but rather a disappearance which profoundly deepens that interiority, and deepens it by knowing a chaos that is interior and exterior simultaneously. Nothing more fully evades or flees that chaos than does an intention or will to annul origin itself, a will which would, indeed, be a will to nothingness, or a will to a primordial origin which is all and all. That is the very origin in which an actual origin is impossible, an impossibility which is most profoundly understood by a Buddhist realization of dependent origination, and which has been inversely or negatively understood by the Freudian understanding of the Oedipus complex. For if the Oedipus complex is the origin of our interior, that is an origin which is a pathological origin just because it compulsively wills that ultimate womb which is the womb of all and everything. Only such a willing could be an exit from our interior, and if our actual interior is a consequence of such willing, that is the consequence of a profoundly negative will, but a will which is possible only because of a deeply interior alienation from womb or plenitude itself. It is our compulsive will to reverse that alienation which is the genesis of the Oedipus complex, and if that is the will which is the

151

individual will, that is a will which originates in that alienation. Only when Freud came to understand the death instinct did he become open to the deeper consequences of the Oedipus complex, and it was exactly in understanding that instinct that he understood the impossibility of resolving the Oedipus complex, an impossibility which is the impossibility of an exit from our origin.

But a realization of the impossibility of that exit is a realization of the impossibility of a real or actual return, only now does the backward movement of involution become fully manifest as a pure and actual impossibility, an impossibility calling forth the purely negative and pathological identity of regression. If that regression is our deepest interior pathology, it is a pathology with an interior and exterior ground, and its exterior ground is the impossibility of historical return, an impossibility which is inseparable from the pure irreversibility of a fully actual moment of time. Buddhism, in knowing and realizing an original pleroma of emptiness, can know a time which is present, past, and future simultaneously, a pure simultaneity of time which is an absolute disenactment or voiding of the actuality of time. Thereby Buddhism can only know a primordial origin, an origin which is the very opposite of an actual origin, and thus an origin which voids the very possibility of an actual origin. That is a voiding which is the voiding of the very possibility of an actual nothingness, a voiding which is also the voiding of the very possibility of the will, and hence the dissolution of the possibility of a center of consciousness. That is a dissolution which is only pathologically present in that death instinct which we can know, for that death instinct is an *instinct* or will, and precisely as such it cannot realize its own intention, which is the instinct or will of returning to an original moment of time. For that moment for us can only be an actual birth or origin, and therefore a moment which is alienated from an original totality or plenitude, and self-alienated from that pure emptiness by virtue of the actuality of its origin. Augustine knew that origin as original sin, just as Nietzsche knew it as a fall from an original and undifferentiated consciousness, and *Finnegans Wake* enacts it as the fall of all and everything. Thus if origin is fall, origin is an actual origin, and an actually evolving origin, an evolution which is the progressive totalization of an original and actual fall.

Such an evolving actualization could only be a truly evolutionary movement by way of a full and actual origin, and if the will to reverse or dissolve that origin is a will to an original pleroma which is wholly beyond every actual origin, that is a will to that nothingness which is beyond the actuality of genesis or beginning. So it is that this is that instinct or *Trieb* which is the death instinct and the Oedipus complex at once, an ultimate pathology which Nietzsche knew as the will to nothingness, and a will to an empty nothingness which is finally a flight from the actual nothingness of our will. Yet it is will itself which forecloses the actual possibility of that flight, and if a refusal of actuality is for us a refusal of the will, that is a refusal which is not only an annulment of the very possibility of freedom but simultaneously an annulment of the very actuality of consciousness.

Accordingly, that is an annulment which is the embodiment of a pure *ressentiment,* a bad conscience demanding a dissolution of consciousness itself, and a dissolution of that consciousness which is a negative consciousness. But that is the only consciousness which we can actually know, so that for us the dissolution of origin could only be the dissolution of consciousness, and not a dissolution realizing an absolute emptiness, but only a dissolution realizing death itself. While Freud could call the death instinct the Nirvana principle, it is such only in a modern secular perspective, a perspective knowing life and death as inseparable, true, but therein knowing both life and death as cosmic or universal, a universality which is the universality of cosmos or nature itself.

If an ancient Stoicism was reborn in Freud, that is not a rebirth which is a historical return, for Stoicism knew nothing of that negativity of consciousness which Freud so deeply unveiled, just as Stoicism could only know freedom as an *apatheia* or detachment from the actuality of consciousness. Such an *apatheia* is fully alien to our consciousness, and is so because our consciousness is an interior consciousness, and even if that consciousness is being voided in our midst, it is being so voided by both an interior and an exterior movement. So it is that we can only detach or dissociate ourselves from consciousness by an actual willing of death, and if that willing is a death instinct or drive, it is not a willing of a cosmic *ananke* which is actuality itself, but rather the willing of a real and actual inactuality, or an inactuality which is the emptiness of an actual nothingness. Thus that is a willing which can never realize itself, and can never realize itself because of the very actuality of its own nothingness, hence that nothingness can never become a pure emptiness, but far rather an emptiness which is a purely alien emptiness. The Platonic Socrates could accept his own death as a wholly innocent and even sacred death, but no such death has either been portrayed or embodied in either our imaginative or our conceptual enactments, and could not be so if only because of the pure actuality of death for us, an actuality foreclosing the possibility of either an innocent or a natural enactment.

The Spinoza who could foreswear all meditation upon death is the

Spinoza who could then immediately affirm that if the human mind had only adequate ideas it would form no conception of evil (*Ethics* IV, Proposition LXIV). That is surely a pure innocence which is impossible in our world, even as it is a pure thinking that is likewise impossible in our world, and impossible if only because we are inevitably grounded in a pure rupture or chasm that is wholly alien to Spinoza. But if alien to Spinoza, it is not alien to the evolutionary movement of a Christian and Western consciousness, and if that is the only movement of consciousness in history that can, indeed, be apprehended as an evolutionary movement, that is a forward movement revolving about fall, and revolving about an ultimate fall into an actual nothingness. Fall itself, by an inescapable and irresistible necessity, must have an actual beginning or origin, otherwise it would not be fall, or could not be an actual fall. Accordingly, attempts to annul our origin are also attempts to annul our fall, but if that fall is an illusion, then so likewise is the whole movement of a Christian and Western history, to say nothing of a uniquely Christian scripture or writing.

Yet, if fall as an actual fall, could only be a fall with an actual beginning, then so, too, nothingness as an actual nothingness could only be a nothingness with an actual beginning or genesis. An actual nothingness could only be an actually embodied nothingness, and therefore it has a genealogy, a genealogy which is also the genealogy of guilt, yes, but precisely thereby a genealogy of nothingness. Even if guilt is finally an Augustinian "deficiency of being" deriving from our having been created from nothing, that deficiency is a real deficiency, and it is embodied in what Augustine knows as the fallen will. That will has an actual origin, and even if that origin is ultimately the eternal act of predestination, or the eternal and simultaneous act of predestination and creation, that eternal act is an act enacting an actual origin, even as the act of creation is the actual origin of the world. So it is that an actual nothingness is inseparable from an actual beginning, and if that beginning is a forward-moving beginning, or a beginning realizing itself in ever more comprehensive enactments of nothingness, then those enactments are a necessary and inevitable consequence of a real and actual genesis. Thus, if the Classical world could know a cosmic and even metaphysical *ananke* or necessity which is an absolutely unmoving necessity, the post-Classical Western world has ever more comprehensively and ever more overwhelmingly known an absolute necessity which is an evolving necessity, and most clearly and most manifestly an evolving necessity in the realization of that actual nothingness which we have finally come to know and realize as a total nothingness.

The ancient world knew an *ananke* that is deeper than deity, and not only deeper than deity but more comprehensive than deity itself, this is that *ananke* which is the ultimate power in Greek tragedy, and an *ananke* which could have no possible origin. Indeed, nothing is a deeper mystery in *ananke* than its independence of origin, that is precisely what makes it anonymous or nameless, an anonymity which is the absence of beginning. Only that which begins can actually be named, so that all of the ancient deities are deities who have begun, and only an awareness of their beginning makes possible a naming of the Greek gods. And that beginning is not only named, it can actually be envisioned, as witness Athena's miraculous birth which is enacted among the mutilated sculptures which remain to us from the east pediment of the Parthenon. Aphrodite is a primal witness to this birth, and here she is reclining next to and upon her mother Dione, as the goddesses themselves embody the ecstasy of the birth of deity. It is *ananke* alone among the primal powers that can neither be named nor envisioned, but that is a decisive sign of its ultimate power, and of its ultimately destructive power, a power which is the source of that one true negativity which was known to ancient Greece. While Dionysus does exercise such a power in *The Bacchae,* that is nevertheless a power which here transcends Dionysus, just as it transcends every divine or human presence in the Greek sensibility, a transcendence which is the transcendence of purely negative power.

Perhaps only Goethe has attempted an *anamnesis* or renewal of that power, and if this occurs most fully in *Faust,* there it occurs in the second part of Goethe's ultimate drama, as the passionately subjective Faust of the first part has now realized a trans-individual status and power, a power that Goethe envisioned as being directed to a reversal of the damnation of Faust. Already in the first act of the tragedy's second part, a descent to the realm of the Mothers occurs in "Dark Gallery," a descent which is Faust's way to an ultimate creativity. Mephistopheles informs Faust that these goddesses are enthroned in sublime solitude, a solitude where there is neither space nor time, just as there is no way to this solitude, where Faust will see "Nothing." Faust accepts this summons to the void, and can even say: "In deinem Nichts hoff' ich das All zu finden," I hope to find the All in your Nothing (6256). For if that All is the Nothing of Mephistopheles, that All will be a triumphant fulfillment of the wager in the first part (1692–1706), and a fulfillment reversing the initial damnation of Faust.

Now a descent occurs into the unbound realms of forms, realms which have long since been dissipated, and a descent which Mephistopheles can identify with ascent. Only when Faust has arrived in the deepest abyss, will he behold the radiant glow of the Mothers, and then encounter that formation and transformation which is eternal re-creation. As Faust majestically declares, the Mothers have their throne in boundlessness, a boundlessness which is the womb of all and everything, and a boundlessness which is the final destiny of Faust.

That destiny is enacted at the conclusion of the drama, as now Oedipus at Colonus is reborn, and reborn in the triumphant death of Faust, a death which once again is invisible, and a consummation of the tragic hero which once again is an ultimate disappearance. Now that disappearance occurs by way of a union with the Eternal Feminine, an Eternal Feminine which is a resolution of those deep feminine powers which occur throughout the drama, but which are only unveiled in Faust's descent to the realm of the Mothers. Those powers are embodied in the Catholic Mother of God, who is here the one source of salvation in the Christian world, and even as the conclusion of *Faust* is a reenactment of the conclusion of the *Paradiso,* the Mothers are here the primal source of the Virgin and Beatrice alike, a source which is ecstatically celebrated in the lines which conclude the drama. This is an ultimate hymn of celebration, intoned by the chorus mysticus, celebrating that "Ewig-Weibliche" or Eternal Feminine which draws us on high: "Das Unzulängliche, hier wird's Ereignis." Now what is empty or deficient or nothing finally becomes *Ereignis,* a holy and disembodied action which is the action of the redeemed Faust, for that redemption is the eternal transfiguration of an original or primordial nothingness. Apparently no other epiphany has had such a deep effect upon the modern German mind, and if that is the mind which has given us our deepest understanding of nihilism, an understanding which is present in Heidegger and Wittgenstein as well as in Nietzsche, and is nowhere so purely embodied as it is in the purest poetry of Rilke and the purest prose of Kafka, that is an understanding which has lost all actual point of contact with the Classical world.

No one has ever sought the profoundest depths of the Greek world more deeply than did Goethe, Hölderlin, Hegel, Nietzsche, and Heidegger, yet no one has ever so reversed those depths as have these poets and thinkers, a reversal which is most clearly manifest in Nietzsche's vision of Eternal Recurrence. Nietzsche's professed *amor fati* is clearly a reversal of any possible Classical *amor,* and is so precisely because it dares to be a love of *ananke.* Thus, in June of 1882, while anticipating the opening of a new phase of his life, Nietzsche could write to Overbeck that he is in a mood of fatalistic "surrender to God," which he calls *amor fati*. Only in his notebook does Nietzsche fully draw forth the meaning of this all too modern *amor fati*, and then it does not occur until one of his last entries:

> *My new path to a "Yes."*—Philosophy, as I have hitherto understood and lived it, is a voluntary quest for even the most detested and notorious sides of existence. From the long experience I gained from such a wandering through ice and wilderness, I learned to view differently all that had hitherto philosophized: the *hidden* history of philosophy, the psychology of its great names, came to light for me. "How much truth can a spirit *endure*, how much truth does a spirit *dare?*"—this became for me the real standard of value. Error is *cowardice*—every achievement of knowledge is a consequence of courage, of severity towards oneself, of cleanliness towards oneself—Such an experimental philosophy as I have lived anticipates experimentally even the possibilities of the most fundamental nihilism; but this does not mean that it must halt at a negation, a No, a will to negation. It wants rather to cross over to the opposite of this—to a Dionysian affirmation of the world as it is, without subtraction, exception, or selection—it wants the eternal circulation: the same things, the same logic and illogic of entanglements. The highest state a philosopher can attain: to stand in a Dionysian relationship to existence—my formula for this is *amor fati*. (*The Will to Power*, 1041, Kaufmann translation)

Certainly nothing could be more alien to an ancient consciousness and sensibility than this affirmation, and if this is a total affirmation of *fati* or *ananke*, it thereby is a total transformation of everything which the ancient world could know as destiny or necessity. If only at this point, Nietzsche's profound Christian roots are all too manifest, for it was Christianity that shattered an ancient destiny, and even if Nietzsche could understand the Christian God as the origin of our nihilism, that is an origin which voids *ananke*, a voiding which is fully embodied in a uniquely modern consciousness and world.

But that voiding is not a simple negation of *ananke*, but rather a dialectical negation, and a dialectical negation in the Hegelian sense, for it negates *ananke* only to preserve it. If that is a transcendence of *ananke*, it is a transcendence embodying a totality of *ananke* that was never manifest in the ancient world, as witness the vast and uncrossable distance between *Oedipus at Colonus* and *Faust*. This is the totality which Nietzsche knows as the Will to Power, and if that power is free of any possible conscious intention or will, that is a power which is a totally negative power, and it is pure power itself precisely because of that. But just as the *Science of Logic* can know pure Being as pure nothingness, Zarathustra can know pure power as pure nothingness, and it is precisely thereby that he can celebrate and enact it. Only such a nothingness makes possible a celebration of pure power or pure will, for only that nothingness inactivates an absolute assault that otherwise would occur, a disenactment or disembodiment which is the willing of eternal recurrence. But the willing of eternal recurrence is the willing of responsibility for eternal recurrence, a total willing *willing* a total responsibility, and that is a responsibility wherein the will is the origin of eternal recurrence. Only an absolute will can embody that willing, and the absolute will is the origin of that willing, an origin apart from which such a willing could never occur. Even as Nietzsche is that modern thinker who most compulsively speaks the name of God, Nietzsche is that one modern thinker who understood an absolute will, and understood absolute will as absolute origin itself. That is the origin which Nietzsche willed as the origin of our nothingness, and even as a total nothingness has been enacted again and again in the deepest and purest expressions of a uniquely modern imagination, that very enactment is an enactment of origin, for each of the primal works of that imagination have been genealogies of nothingness, and genealogies of nothingness which ecstatically celebrate that nothingness precisely in calling forth its origin.

Even the darkest prose of Kafka is finally a celebration, and a celebration even if only because it is embodied in writing, and if that writing induced in Kafka an ultimate guilt, that is a guilt inseparable from what he realized as pure writing, for that writing is inevitably a celebration of darkness. Kafka knew a solitude that has been realized by no other writer, a total solitude which he knew as writing itself, and if that writing is the clearest prose which has ever been written, its very clarity is an embodiment of darkness, and a darkness far darker than any that has entered either a poetic or a mythical language.

Yet that darkness here realizes an origin, an origin which is now spoken by pure writing itself, and an origin that now and for the first time is inseparable from all writing. Even Nietzsche's prose threatens to fall back into a mythical ground in the perspective of Kafka's writing, and if Kafka's writing is an ultimate challenge to all subsequent writing, that is a challenge that is only fully met by the language of *Finnegans Wake*. For it is fantasy of every kind which has now ended, and just as the most grotesque fantasies of *Finnegans Wake* are fully and actually spoken, that is a speaking which is the end of fantasy, and the end of fantasy because here there is nothing whatsoever that is not actually embodied. While that embodiment is more fantastic than any fantasy which has been recorded, here fantasy becomes actuality itself, and even a factual and historical actuality, for no other major work has been written which such a total attention to exact detail. That is an exactitude which reverses fantasy, a reversal that begins with Dante in our modern epic voyage, and even as Dante's is the major presence in the *Wake,* that is a presence which is the presence of origin, and the presence of that origin which is here embodied in a total nothingness.

So it is that the reversal of fantasy is the epiphany of origin, and of an actual origin, but an actual origin that is an embodiment of nothingness. That is a nothingness that is inseparable from actuality, and from a pure actuality, and a pure actuality that is a pure and total will. Only pure will *is* pure nothingness, a nothingness that is an actual nothingness, and therein is inseparable from actuality itself. That is the nothingness which is a willed nothingness, for will itself is inseparable from a willing of nothingness, inasmuch as the will is possible and real only by way of a profound internal division, a division apart from which there could be no actual act of the will. Just as the act of the will and willing itself is a willing of otherness, that otherness is necessary and essential to willing itself, for apart from its realization, there could be no act of the will which is an actual enactment or an actual realization. Such a realization or such an enactment must be an embodiment of that which is "other" than the will, and hence it could be willed only when the will is other than itself, an "othering" of the will that is the pure act of the will itself. Christianity could know that "othering" as an eternal predestination to eternal death, a predestination which is eternally willed by God, and eternally willed by that act of the will which *is* the will of God. Nietzsche could know that willing as the willing of Eternal Recurrence, an Eternal Recurrence which *is* the Will to Power, but is the Will to Power only because it is an absolute act of the will. Yet that is the act of the will which is an embodied nothingness, and is an embodied nothingness precisely because it is a total act of the will, and therefore is a total reversal or inversion of a pure passivity or emptiness of the will. Buddhism can know that emptiness as a total emptiness, but Christianity in knowing God the Creator knows a total inversion and reversal of the emptiness of emptiness, a reversal which is the genesis of the will, and therefore is the genesis of an actual nothingness.

8

THE GENESIS
OF GOD

I f Christianity knows the will of God as absolute will, an absolute will
which is absolute actuality, that actuality is ultimately an absolutely
dichotomous actuality, and a dichotomous actuality in its ownmost
center or ground. Only a dichotomous actuality could make possible or
could embody an act which is pure and total *act,* an act which is absolute
enactment, and an enactment which is the real and actual realization of
itself. Such realization is impossible in a pure and total emptiness, an
emptiness which is all in all, and only a self-negation or a self-emptying of
that emptiness could realize a pure and total *act,* an act which is the
embodiment of a pure and total dichotomy. That is the dichotomy which
is the embodiment of absolute will, a dichotomy apart from which
absolute will could not be will itself, and impossible because will could not
be will apart from otherness, an otherness which is that center apart from
which there could be no act of the will.

Nothing was more revolutionary in primitive Christianity than the very
discovery of the will, and if this occurred in Paul, and was renewed in
Augustine, that is a discovery and renewal which embodies the end of the
ancient world, an ending which is, indeed, the very realization of the will
of will, a will which is an absolute energy or act. Aristotle's pure actuality
or *energia* is the divine or metaphysical activity of pure thought (*nous*)
eternally contemplating itself, but that contemplation is the contemplation
of the unmoved Mover, an unmoved Mover who is the very opposite of
absolute act. Even the Demiurge of Plato's *Timaeus* is a mythical embodi-

ment of a chasm between the unchanging realm of true being and the lower and contingent realm of becoming. While that chasm is truly challenged in the late dialogues of Plato, and is transcended in Aristotle's metaphysics, that is a transcendence which forecloses the possibility of a pure actuality which is not simultaneously a pure inactuality or quiescence, a quiescence which is the absolute passivity of ultimate ground.

That is a quiescence which was shattered by the birth of Christianity, and even if that quiescence was reborn as the absolute passivity of God in Christian and medieval scholasticism, that very rebirth is inseparable from its own ending, an ending which most purely occurs in Spinoza. That ending is the ending of an actual possibility of thinking an actuality that is a pure quiescence, an ending which is the conceptual ending of a disembodied *nous,* and that ending is inseparable from the final disenactment of an original and a total calm. That is a disenactment which Christianity has known as creation *ex nihilo,* a creation out of nothing, and out of "nothing" if only because the act of creation is absolute act. But that absolute act is absolute disenactment, the disenactment of an original "nothing," a disenactment which is the embodiment of dichotomy, and an embodiment of that dichotomy which is the realization of a pure and total act. Just as a thinking of that dichotomy is wholly alien to the thinking of the ancient world, that ancient thinking is closed to the very possibility of a once-and-for-all and irreversible creation, a creation which is a creation *ex nihilo,* and therefore is the embodiment of an actuality which is actuality and inactuality at once. Yet that actuality is wholly other than an Aristotelian or Classical actuality, and is so if only because it embodies a "deficiency of Being," a deficiency which is an actual nothingness, and an actual nothingness which is the very center of the fallen will. That is the will which Paul discovered as our ownmost will, a will which is the will to eternal death, and a will which is a reverse and inverted image of the will of God. Even as that will is wholly absent from the ancient world, it is totally present in an original and apocalyptic Christianity, a Christianity that can celebrate God only by celebrating the end of the world, for that apocalyptic ending is the necessary and inevitable consequence of the original act of creation.

It is precisely because original Christianity is an apocalyptic Christianity that it can celebrate and know an absolute dichotomy, an absolute dichotomy between "flesh" and Spirit or between sin and grace or between darkness and light, and that is a dichotomy calling forth the very will of will, a will that would be impossible apart from the embodiment of dichotomy. An apocalyptic embodiment of dichotomy not only made possible a discovery of the will, but did so just because that apocalyptic embodiment is a celebration of the will of God, an absolute will that even now is realizing its own consummation, and realizing that consummation in a total and apocalyptic ending. That is the very ending which interiorly occurs in the death of the old Adam, a death which is an apocalyptic death, and therefore a death which is only possible by way of the final triumph of the new aeon or the Kingdom of God. While the Fourth Gospel could know the Kingdom of God as "life" or "light," that light is ultimately an apocalyptic light, and is so if only because it brings a final end to darkness. That is the realization which is the apocalyptic realization of the will of God, and if the will of God is absolute will itself, that is a will which wills an absolute ending even as it wills an absolute beginning. Apocalyptically, absolute ending is inseparable from absolute beginning, so that the willing of absolute beginning *is* the willing of absolute ending. Here, beginning can be beginning only insofar as it is ending, or is finally ending, and if this conjunction of beginning and ending could only be a dichotomous conjunction, that is the conjunction which is the embodiment of absolute will.

We find no ancient witness to the embodiment of dichotomy until the advent of apocalypticism, and if apocalypticism is a consequence of prophetic Israel, it is so most clearly in its very apprehension of the final and eschatological act of God, an act of God which is an absolute disenactment of darkness or sin, and therefore a disenactment or reversal of fall. Not until the advent of apocalypticism may we discover the advent of the symbol of an actual and total fall, a fall which is the fall of the creation itself, and therefore a fall which is a realization of an original nothingness. That is the fall which is reversed in an apocalyptic ending, but only the advent of that ending makes possible an epiphany of that fall, so that fall as a total and actual fall is an apocalyptic fall, and an apocalyptic fall inseparable from the apocalyptic God. The apocalyptic God is the God who wills an apocalyptic ending, and to know that God is to know an apocalyptic ending, an ending which is itself the historical beginning of an original Christianity. Just as that beginning is the beginning of an apprehension of the will, it thereby is an apprehension of the will of God as an apocalyptic will, and an apocalyptic will which is interiorly manifest and real in the birth of that "I" which is a purely negative "I," and a purely negative "I" in that absolute assault which it conducts upon itself. That assault is an apocalyptic assault, an assault not only unveiling that dichotomy which is the center of consciousness, but embodying that dichotomy which is the dichotomy of the apocalyptic God. Only the advent of that dichotomy makes possible an apprehension of the will of will, and if that apprehension is a purely negative apprehension, it is negative above all in knowing the will of God as an apocalyptic will, and therefore as that will which wills a final and absolute ending.

Now if that will is a will which simultaneously wills an absolute beginning, it is absolute will in the simultaneity of that willing, and if Christianity has known the act of creation as an eternal act, and an eternal act which is genesis and apocalypse at once, it is and can be so only as eternal act of absolute will itself. Here, absolute will can only be an apocalyptic will, and an apocalyptic will in willing beginning and ending at once. Yet just as that beginning is a real and actual beginning, that ending is a real and actual ending, and the actuality of each is inseparable from the apocalyptic actuality of absolute will. Absolute will *wills* absolute beginning even as it wills absolute ending, and it is just because that willing is an absolute willing that it is an actual willing, and yet an actual willing that *is* actual only insofar as it wills beginning and ending at once. That is the actuality which is unknown in the ancient world, or unknown apart from Israel, and even as that world is innocent of an absolute beginning, so likewise is it innocent of an absolute ending. But the conjunction of that beginning and ending could only be a dichotomous conjunction, and a dichotomous conjunction precisely because here beginning *is* beginning, even as ending *is* ending. All too significantly, it is only with the closure of ancient Israel that Israel could know a truly absolute beginning, just as it was only an apocalyptic Israel that could know a pure and total ending. That is the Israel which is the historical womb of Christianity, and the womb of that Christianity which knows and only knows the apocalyptic God, for even if that God was negated and reversed in the historical evolution of Christianity, the negation of that negation is a resurrection of the purely apocalyptic God.

So it is that that resurrection is an apocalyptic resurrection, and therein and thereby an ultimate and final renewal of an apocalyptic ending, an ending of that God which is wholly other than the apocalyptic God, and an ending of that world which is wholly other than an apocalyptic darkness. But just as that renewal is the renewal of apocalyptic ending, then so likewise is it the renewal of absolute beginning, but now an absolute beginning which is not only inseparable from absolute ending, but is itself a beginning which *is* that ending. Therein and thereby it cannot stand forth as beginning alone, as that beginning itself is now ended, and ended in an ending that is wholly and only ending. But that ending does call forth the necessity of an ultimate and absolute beginning, an actual beginning apart from which there could be no actual ending, and apart from which there could be no realization of the apocalyptic God.

Even as that realization is an actual realization, the very actuality of that realization is inseparable from an actual beginning, and an actual beginning of the realization of Godhead itself. No imagery more clearly makes manifest that necessity than does the dogma of predestination, a predestination which *is* creation, and is creation in its very willing of eternal life and eternal death at once. That is certainly a willing which must begin, and must begin if only because it is an actual act of the will, and is, indeed, that willing which is the will of absolute will. That will must begin, and must actually begin, otherwise it could not be an act of the will, or an act of the will which is actually enacted. For the actuality of that enactment could only be a dichotomous enactment, and not only dichotomous in the willing of eternal life and eternal death at once, but dichotomous in the very actuality of its act, an act which could only be an actual act by way of its embodiment of a real and intrinsic otherness.

The symbol of an ultimate and intrinsic otherness has only been fully realized in apocalypticism, and just as it is only apocalypticism which has known both an actual and a total fall, it is only apocalypticism which has celebrated and proclaimed a total transfiguration of all and everything. That transfiguration is the total triumph of the Kingdom of God, a Kingdom of God which even now is becoming all in all, but is becoming all in all only by way of an ultimate and final triumph over a totality of sin and darkness. That totality is the kingdom of Satan, a kingdom which is not even named until the advent of apocalypticism, for even if such a kingdom was named as early as Zarathustra's naming of Angra Mainu, that naming, if it occurred, could only have been an apocalyptic naming. For an apocalyptic naming is a simultaneous naming of total light and total darkness, therefore it is a dichotomous naming, and an ultimately dichotomous naming, inasmuch as the ultimate triumph of light is inseparable from the final ending of darkness. Nowhere in the realm of mythical naming may we discover such a pure and total dichotomous naming, for here "light" itself is unreal or unmanifest apart from the epiphany or realization of a pure and total "darkness," a darkness which itself becomes visible only with the advent of total light. So it is that a real Satan is only manifest in Israel or Judaism with the beginning of a Jewish apocalypticism, that is a beginning which is consummated in the birth of Christianity, and nowhere more clearly so than in Jesus' continual naming of Satan.

That naming manifestly distinguishes Jesus from every earlier prophet of Israel, and even as Jesus was the first prophet to proclaim the actual dawning of the Kingdom of God, that dawning itself occurs by way of an apocalyptic war with Satan and the kingdom of darkness. No scripture in the world more fully embodies demonic powers than does the New Testament, and just as the New Testament is the only scripture which fully names Satan, the New Testament is our only full scripture which is an apocalyptic scripture, or is an apocalyptic scripture in its original ground. While that is a ground that is already being eroded in the New Testament itself, for there is no greater internal conflict and opposition in the New Testament than that between its apocalyptic and its non-apocalyptic poles, no corpus of writing has engendered such profound conflict as has the New Testament, just as no other religious tradition has undergone such a profound transformation as has Christianity. Already such a comprehensive transformation occurs within the first three generations of Christian history, a transformation embodied in a dissolution of apocalypticism, and a dissolution which is complete with the triumph of the Great Church or the Catholic Church in the second century. Now even if apocalypticism has arisen again and again in Christianity, and all too significantly has done so at the great turning points or crises of Christian history, Christianity has never evolved an apocalyptic theology, and it is only in the realm of the imagination that Christianity has fully realized an apocalyptic vision.

This has most fully occurred in the Christian epic tradition, and that tradition has become ever more fully apocalyptic as it has evolved, as can be seen in the transformation of our epic voyage as it is enacted by Dante, Milton, and Blake. Not only does that voyage therein become ever more fully apocalyptic, but its enactment becomes ever more purely and more totally a dichotomous enactment, and even if dichotomy as such is seemingly absent in the *Commedia,* the integral and comprehensive unity of the *Commedia* is the unity of the *Inferno,* the *Purgatorio,* and the *Paradiso,* and that unity between Heaven and Hell is inevitably destined for a dichotomous resolution, and a resolution which does historically occur in the ending of Christendom. Each of our great epic poets have been apocalyptic prophets, and apocalyptic prophets in their very enactment of an epic voyage, a voyage which is a cosmic voyage and an interior voyage simultaneously, and a voyage which embodies a truly new historical world. That historical world is ever more fully an apocalyptic world, for the full realization of Christian epic poetry in Dante was made possible by that full apocalyptic faith which is first recorded in *De Monarchia,* just as *Paradise Lost* is deeply grounded in that new apocalypticism embodied in the English Revolution. With Blake, Christian epic poetry is a totally apocalyptic poetry, a poetry which is not only a rebirth of an original Christian apocalypticism, but is also and even thereby the inaugural realization of a uniquely modern apocalypticism.

A seldom noticed identity of true epic poetry is its subversive religious identity, just as the *Iliad* and the *Odyssey* effect or record the first comprehensive negation of a primordial religious world, so, too, *The Aeneid* is a negation of a Classical and pre-Hellenistic religious world. And Dante is surely the greatest "heretic" of the Middle Ages, and not simply because of his primal conflict with the Papacy, but above all by way of his very creation of the *Commedia,* a work which not only subverted the authority of the Church, but did so in realizing a total vision in which there is a full and integral unity and harmony between the human, the cosmic, and the divine realms. That harmony and unity break asunder in *Paradise Lost,* and does so in its very vision of God, a God who must "retire" to effect the creation, and a wholly solitary God who by His very solitude is wholly removed from the redemptive action of the Son. That is the very God who is named as Satan in Blake's prophetic and epic poetry, and if a fully apocalyptic poetry is an ultimately heretical and subversive poetry, that poetry itself is a rebirth of an original Christian apocalypticism, an apocalypticism which is itself heretical by the second century. At no point is Joyce more fully in continuity with his epic predecessors, and if Joyce is the most heretical or most subversive visionary in the twentieth century, that would be yet another sign of the fully epic identity of his work. But Joyce's vision is also our most dichotomous vision, and even as Joyce himself chose Dante and Blake as his fullest predecessors, *Ulysses* and *Finnegans Wake* are our *Commedia,* and our *Milton* and *Jerusalem* as well.

No embodiment of the imagination is in more integral continuity with the Bible than is the Christian epic tradition, and even as that tradition becomes ever more "heretical" as it evolves, that subversive evolution is simultaneously an apocalyptic evolution, and one which echoes if it does not embody the subversive movement of ancient apocalypticism. At no point is that ancient subversion so clear as it is in its progressive enactment of the apocalyptic God, an epiphany of God in ancient apocalypticism ever distancing itself from the God of Torah and of Torah alone, and an epiphany of God in modern apocalypticism ever distancing itself from the God of Christian orthodoxy. Even Dante's vision of the "Infinite Goodness" and the "Eternal Light" of the Godhead in the final canto of the *Paradiso* is an assault upon the Christian dogma of the absolute transcendence of God, and is so if only because it can envision the love of that Godhead as dispersed in "leaves" throughout the universe, so that the book of the universe itself is contained and bound in God. No vision could be further from a scholastic understanding of God, and just as Dante scholarship has long since demonstrated that Dante was not theologically a Thomist, the long delayed publication of Milton's one full dogmatic treatise, *De Doctrina Christiana,* has fully unveiled the immense theological distance between Milton and orthodox Protestantism, and above all so in Milton's understanding of both God and Christ. The very enactment of the Christian imagination is an assault upon Christian orthodoxy, but an assault which is itself a renewal of the Bible, and a renewal of that Biblical ground which itself had been subverted by Christian orthodoxy, and nothing was more profoundly subverted by that orthodoxy than the original apocalyptic ground of Christianity.

The scholastic idea and image of the absolute passivity of God is clearly such a subversion, one which is wholly alien to the Bible itself, and one which could have only a purely negative relationship to the primary New Testament symbol of the Kingdom of God. While scholasticism intended to know the eternal life of the Godhead, it knew that life as the *ipsum esse* or "existence itself" of God or Being (*Summa Theologica* I, 4, 2), an existence which eternally remains "impassible" (*Summa Theologica* III, 46, 12), and which eternally is and only is itself. No such identity of God is present at any point in the Christian epic tradition, except as a wholly negative identity, a negative identity which becomes ever more comprehensive in that tradition, until in Blake it passes into a fully Satanic identity. But the God whom Blake could imaginatively know as Satan is conceptually known by Hegel as "Being-in-itself," a Being which is "evil" itself, and evil in its absolute solitude, that very solitude which Milton envisioned as the solitude of God. This is that God who undergoes self-annihilation or self-negation in a uniquely Christian apocalypse, an apocalypse which is the ultimate embodiment of the God of love, and is, indeed, that unique and absolute act which the Christian knows as the act of redemption. But that is the very act which is most alien to Christian scholasticism, and most alien to that Christian orthodoxy which knows only the purely transcendent God, a transcendent God who can be immanent only in His transcendent identity, and who can be known as a "living" God only insofar as Godhead itself is known and envisioned as an absolute impassivity.

But scholasticism itself is a historically evolving scholasticism, one which historically begins with Philo and historically ends with Spinoza, and one whose initial philosophical ground is an ancient Neoplatonism and whose later philosophical ground is a medieval neo-Aristotelianism, and even as each of these grounds is transformed in nominalism, scholasticism itself therein undergoes a deep transformation. That is a transformation ending an essential relationship between the God of reason and the God of revelation, and also one which therein realizes a pure transcendence of God, a pure transcendence which is reversed by Spinoza, a reversal which is the ending of the scholastic tradition itself. Nevertheless, that tradition is a historically evolving tradition, and just as Dante could know a conceptual identity of God which could never be known by Milton, Blake could know a purely abstract and purely alien identity of God which could not be known by Milton. Accordingly, Hegel could know a purely abstract identity of deity which was not known by Aquinas, for if Hegel absorbed Spinoza's reversal of scholasticism, it was precisely thereby that he could know the scholastic God of Christian orthodoxy as a purely abstract and inactual deity, or as that very God who dies in the "death" of God. Yet that death is not simply the death of the scholastic God, it is a death occurring in the final moment or realization of that God, and thus a death which is only possible as a consequence of a fully evolutionary movement, a movement culminating in the realization of a purely abstract and thereby purely alien God.

If Christian scholasticism may be understood to have begun with a negation and reversal of Christian apocalypticism, it may be understood to have finally ended with a renewal or resurrection of that very negated apocalypticism, a philosophical apocalypticism that begins with Hegel and ends with Nietzsche, even as an imaginative apocalypticism begins with Blake and is consummated in Joyce. Scholasticism and apocalypticism alike are fully and solely grounded in God, and if scholasticism and apocalypticism have been absolutely opposing powers in our history, they are powers not only in a dichotomous relationship with each other, but their own intrinsic grounds embody a purely dichotomous relationship with one another, and one which finally is a purely dichotomous relationship between the scholastic God and the apocalyptic God. For the scholastic God is the real and actual opposite of the apocalyptic God, and even if that pure opposition does not fully realize itself until almost two millennia of historical evolution, then it realizes itself with such power as to embody the death of the uniquely Christian God. But that death itself is an apocalyptic event, and known as such by both Hegel and Nietzsche, even as it was envisioned as such by Blake, and following Blake by virtually the whole body of the modern imagination. Both Blake and Hegel finally knew that death as resurrection, the resurrection of the crucified God, and a resurrection which is a final apocalypse, and as a final apocalypse, the apocalypse of the very Godhead of God.

That is the apocalypse which Christianity has always known as redemption, or known as redemption insofar as Christianity has known redemption as a redemption occurring only in the crucifixion and the resurrection of Christ. And even as Christianity originally knew crucifixion and resurrection as one event, an apprehension and an enactment occurring in both Paul and the Fourth Gospel, so it is that Blake and Hegel finally came to know crucifixion and resurrection as one event, and as that one event which *is* apocalypse. While nothing could be further from a scholastic apprehension of God, or further from what modernity has known as Christian orthodoxy, that is an orthodoxy which itself is the culmination of a long historical evolution, for a modern orthodoxy is just as distant from Augustine as it is from Dante, and above all distant insofar as it knows a purely abstract and inactual God. A purely inactual Godhead is the pure opposite of an apocalyptic enactment, for apocalyptic enactment *is* absolute act, and is that *act* which is absolute actuality. Now even if Aquinas could know *ipsum esse* as the "act of God " or the "act of Being," that is an actuality which ever more fully passes into an abstract inactuality in the history of both that scholasticism and that orthodoxy which follow Aquinas, and even as this occurs in an irreversible history, it reverses itself in that new history which dawns with the advent of the modern world. And only now is the dominant movement of our history in absolute opposition to Christian orthodoxy, an opposition progressively freezing that very orthodoxy, for it is orthodoxy itself which ceases to truly move or evolve with the closure of the Middle Ages.

While that closure is not complete until the seventeenth century, which is precisely why the seventeenth century is the most revolutionary of our centuries, it is in the seventeenth century that a pure dichotomy first fully realizes itself at the center of consciousness, a realization which is the advent of a total energy and will. For that advent is the advent of a totally dichotomous will, a will which in *Paradise Lost* can enact a total dichotomy between Satan and the Son of God, a dichotomy which itself is the very arena of fall, and a fall so total that it erodes and dissolves every actual presence of an integral and harmonious universe. Yet the truth is that it is only now that the universe can actually be known as an infinite universe, a universe in which the *physica coelestis* and *physica terrestris* are identified and united, and unified and united in the historical birth of modern science. Nothing was a greater assault upon Christian orthodoxy than that very birth, and even as modern science is irresistible in terms of its sheer force and power, Christian orthodoxy was driven into an irresistible retreat, so that with the French Revolution that orthodoxy and the Christian Church itself passes into a fully sectarian identity. But that is the very revolution which releases a new apocalypticism, an apocalypticism that is a rebirth of that seventeenth century apocalypticism which inspired the English Revolution, and an apocalypticism which is a historical realization of the death of God. That death, too, is an apocalyptic event, and an apocalyptic event that is a rebirth and renewal of an original Christian apocalypticism.

The very beginning of a Christian and Western history is the full beginning of apocalypticism, and just as that beginning is the beginning of a total historical transformation, it is embodied in a truly new historical will. The advent of that will is the actual beginning of a universal historical transformation, and therein the beginning of a totally forward historical movement, for even if that movement is reversed again and again in our history, it nevertheless realizes a global embodiment in late modernity. That Will to Power which Nietzsche knew is at bottom an absolute historical will, and is so precisely because it is the embodiment of a purely and totally immanent power which is itself the pure reversal of everything which the Christian world had known as the absolute transcendence and the absolute sovereignty of God. Nietzsche's apocalyptic thinking and vision is the renewal of an original Christian apocalypticism, but a renewal occurring in a historical world in which God is dead, and yet that is the very death which releases a new and total immanence. An original Christian apocalypticism celebrated and proclaimed a new and total immanence which is the triumph of the Kingdom of God, a Kingdom of God which is the actual dawning of the Godhead of God, and therefore a kingdom that even now *is* that which a heavenly transcendence *was*. That heavenly transcendence is itself reversed in the very advent of the Kingdom of God, an advent which is not the advent of that sovereignty of Yahweh which the ancient prophets proclaimed, but rather the advent of the final realization of Godhead itself.

Virtually the whole body of Christian theology is grounded in the presumption that no new prophet arose in Jesus, and thus no truly new enactment of God in Jesus, no enactment or proclamation here which is not a repetition of an earlier revelation, and above all no truly new realization of God in the eschatological proclamation and parabolic enactment of Jesus. All too naturally that is a proclamation and enactment which is progressively dissolved in the Christian Church, and it is already forgotten by the second century, a negation which is the dissolution of the original Jesus. But just as it was Nietzsche who most fully knew Christianity as the total reversal of the original Jesus, it was Nietzsche who most purely apprehended that apocalyptic act which is the act of the apocalyptic God, and is that act which is most immediately present as act or actuality itself. Hence Nietzsche could know an absolute immanence which is the pure reversal of absolute transcendence, an absolute immanence which *is* that which an absolute transcendence *was,* and it is just the full realization of that immanence which is the final ending of transcendence. Even as ancient Christianity progressively came to know an absolute transcendence of God that was realized in the wake of the disappearance of an apocalyptic Kingdom of God, our history has ever more progressively come to know an absolute immanence which is realized in the wake of the disappearance of the transcendence of God. Each of these primal movements of our history is fully parallel to the other, and just as the apocalyptic ground of Christianity was only "discovered" in the wake of the uniquely modern realization of the death of God, the absolutely transcendent God of Christianity was only "discovered" in the wake of an ancient Christian dissolution and reversal of the Kingdom of God.

Yet these very historical movements make fully manifest a dichotomy between "God" and the Kingdom of God, or between the apocalyptic God and the God of Christendom, a dichotomy which is a pure dichotomy, and a dichotomy which has been actually realized in our history. All too significantly the God of Christendom is far more purely and more totally transcendent than is any epiphany or naming of God in Israel, and is even more transcendent and majestic than is any naming of God in the New Testament. But what is most missing in the orthodox God of Christianity is that very movement of actualization which is so primary in prophetic Israel, a movement which is totally realized in an original Christian apocalypticism, and there realized as the absolute triumph of the Kingdom of God. That is the triumph which Christianity originally celebrated as the resurrection, a resurrection which is the initial realization of apocalypse, and whose very occurrence is a decisive sign of a dawning apocalyptic transformation, a transformation which is the absolute transformation of everything whatsoever. Only a reversal of that transformation made possible an apprehension of the absolute transcendence of God, an absolute transcendence which is the glory of God and the glory of God alone, and therefore an absolute transcendence which is finally manifest and real as an absolutely unmoving and inactual or passive transcendence.

While we know that this is a transcendence which Aquinas did not know as such, and even a transcendence which Augustine did not know, that is the transcendence which is known by a uniquely modern Christian orthodoxy, and that is the very transcendence which Hegel could conceptually realize as the ground of the self-negation or death of God. Just as Blake could only envision the self-annihilation of God as the self-annihilation of the Satanic God, Hegel could only fully conceive the self-negation or the self-emptying of God as the self-negation of a purely alien Godhead. That alien God is a purely abstract essence wholly alienated from itself, indeed, it is that very essence which is the pure antithesis of the actualization of absolute Spirit (*Phenomenology of Spirit,* 779). Hegel can conclude this crucial paragraph of the *Phenomenology* with the affirmation that this death of "being-in-itself," a being-in-itself that is wholly alienated from itself, is "its resurrection as Spirit." That is the resurrection which is the consequence of the pure self-alienation of Spirit itself, so that that self-alienation is absolutely necessary and essential for true resurrection, a resurrection which *is* the death of that alien Godhead. Only Christianity has truly or actually known the self-alienation of God, but that is an alienation which is essential for a uniquely Christian resurrection, just as that is an alienation that is embodied in a uniquely Christian history, and there most clearly embodied in the very movement of Christian orthodoxy.

Not until Nietzsche could the Christian God be known as the deification of nothingness, for it is not until Nietzsche that the Christian God has fully historically realized an absolutely empty and abstract expression, a purely abstract expression which is a purely alien realization, and an alien realization which is the realization of an actual nothingness. Now the pure transcendence of God is absolutely unnameable, and unnameable as it never was before, for that unnameability is a realization of a real nothingness, and a fully real and fully actual nothingness that is present upon no other historical horizon of consciousness. Yet if that real nothingness is the real ending of the uniquely Christian God, that is an ending that must necessarily issue from beginning, and from the actual beginning of the Christian God. That actual beginning is the beginning of the creation itself, a creation which is the consequence of the will of God, and the consequence of that will which begins with the willing of eternal *act*. And it is precisely because that act is truly act that it necessarily must begin, and must begin in willing a creation that is not an eternal creation but far rather a once-and-for-all creation, and just for that reason a creation which must begin even as it must end. If the will of God simultaneously wills that beginning and that ending, that is a will which itself begins and ends, and even as it begins with creation it ends with apocalypse, and ends with that apocalypse which is the consummation of the will of God.

But the consummation of that will is thereby the ending of that will, the ending of that will as an actual act of the will, and that ending is the consummation of the beginning or genesis of absolute will. If a uniquely Biblical and a uniquely Christian history has known more conflicting images and identities of God or of ultimate reality than has any other revelatory tradition or traditions, then that very history may be understood as an epiphany of the will of God, and an epiphany or epiphanies recording and embodying an ultimate dichotomy which is manifest nowhere else. That is a dichotomy which realizes itself in ever diverse and conflicting expressions, but also a dichotomy which undergoes an evolutionary or forward-moving embodiment, and that embodiment may be understood to be evolutionary precisely in its ever fuller realization of a pure and total dichotomy. Just as that dichotomy now is what an earlier dichotomy was, but now more purely and more totally dichotomous than that earlier dichotomy, so, too, the consummation of absolute will *is* that which the genesis of absolute will *was*.

If the Kingdom of God which Jesus enacted and proclaimed now *is* that which a former realization of the transcendence of God once *was*, that apocalyptic proclamation and enactment can be understood as a realization of the Godhead of God, and a realization of that Godhead which *is* a forward-moving realization, but a truly forward-moving realization only insofar as it ever more fully *is* that which it once *was*. So it is that that very realization is a dichotomous realization, a dichotomous realization which is a dichotomous actualization of an antithesis between *is* and *was*, even as that antithesis is the full embodiment of an actual movement and act of Godhead itself.

The antithesis between *is* and *was* is an antithesis between an actual present and an actual past, and just as it is that antithesis which calls forth the actuality of the future, the realization of an absolute future is the de-realization or the de-activation of an absolute past, and of that absolute past which is the actual past of I AM. Now that past passes into an inactual and alien past, as recorded in both Paul and the Fourth Gospel, but it does so only in response to the full advent of that absolute future which is the Kingdom of God. Thus that alien past can be known and realized only by way of a participation in an apocalyptic Kingdom of God, just as that inactual past can be renewed only by way of a dissolution and reversal of the Kingdom of God. If that reversal is the reversal of an original Christianity, a new Church and a new Christendom can know Godhead itself as a primordial Godhead, a Godhead that is a pure passivity, and is that pure passivity which is the full reversal of the Kingdom of God. Now that is precisely the Godhead that has disappeared in our history, and disappeared in modern thinking and the modern imagination as well, a disappearance which is the disappearance of all that which Godhead *was* and only *was*. So it is that that disappearance is an apocalyptic disappearance, and an apocalyptic disappearance which is a disappearance of the will of that Godhead, and hence a disappearance of the will of the Creator.

While that disappearance may be understood as a disappearance of the will of God, that is the very disappearance which is the embodiment of the ending of absolute will, an ending which is the consummation of that will. Thus a totally apocalyptic Godhead *is* that which the Godhead of God *was*, and only the dissolution of that Godhead is the consummation of absolute will, just as only the genesis of that Godhead is the genesis of absolute will. But that is a genesis which only undergoes a real epiphany with the dissolution of the will of God, only that dissolution makes possible an epiphany of the genesis of absolute will, an epiphany that can occur only with the dissolution of the will of will. Already such a dissolution is manifest and real in the apocalyptic enactment and proclamation of an original Jesus, but as Blake and Nietzsche knew so deeply that enactment was immediately followed by its own progressive dissolution and reversal in Christianity itself, a progressive reversal which is a dominant movement in the New Testament, initially and only partially occurring in Paul, and then complete with the ending of the New Testament and the victory of the patristic Church. Now a primordial Godhead is manifest and real which precludes the very possibility of the genesis of that Godhead, but that annulment is an annulment of the forward movement of the Godhead, just as it is an annulment of a truly apocalyptic resolution of that Godhead. Now Godhead is known as that which Godhead otherwise would be, and if that is an absolute transcendence of the Godhead which never previously was manifest in history, that is a transcendence which finally disappears in that forward-moving and total history which only now is inaugurated.

The very impossibility of the genesis of the God of Christendom is now the impossibility of apocalypse itself, and if Christian apocalypticism has always been an assault upon that God, that assault is a renewal of an original Christianity, just as it is a renewal of apocalyptic Godhead itself. Hence that renewal is the renewal of an apocalyptic genesis, a genesis which is the genesis of the apocalyptic act of God, and a genesis which is an embodiment of Godhead itself in an absolutely apocalyptic act. Nowhere is that act more fully manifest than it is in the uniquely Christian vision of the absolute predestination of God, a predestination which is creation, and is creation as the absolute willing of "darkness" and "light" at once. Inevitably, that is a purely and totally dichotomous willing, and therefore a willing which must begin, and must begin in that once-and-for-all act which is creation out of "nothing." But that is the very *act* which is negated and reversed in a Christian apprehension of the absolute transcendence of God, so that the creation itself can be known by ancient Christianity as an eternal creation, and as that eternal creation which is the eternal act of God. Thereby the absolute beginning of creation itself is annulled, and annulled precisely by way of knowing a purely passive Godhead, and therefore knowing a Godhead that cannot *act*. Or, rather, ancient Christianity in knowing the Godhead as the pleroma of Being, and as that Being which is absolutely *causa sui* or "in-itself," could only know God as eternal act, and as that one eternal act comprehending every act of God, as those acts themselves are finally only one act, and that act itself occurs in an "eternal now."

There can be no actual beginning in that "eternal now," an eternal now which is present, past, and future simultaneously, so that there cannot be an act of God which is a unique and once-and-for-all act, just as there cannot be an act of God which is either a truly original or a truly apocalyptic act. We need not wonder at the immense distance between the Bible and Christian scholasticism, or between an original Christianity and "orthodox" Christianity, but it is important to realize that the "discovery" of the Bible in Protestantism and the disintegration of Christian scholasticism occurred simultaneously, and all too ironically it was Spinoza who conjoined these movements, a conjunction which is surely a decisive source of all genuinely modern theology. Yet neither theological nor philosophical thinking have been able to apprehend the genesis of God, or the unique and once-and-for-all genesis of God, a genesis of God which is an ultimate event, and is that ultimate event which inaugurates the acts of God. Only an apprehension of such a genesis could make possible an apprehension of the forward movement of the Godhead, a forward movement which is an evolutionary movement, and therefore a movement with a real and actual beginning. Just as only such a beginning could culminate in a real and actual ending, only such a beginning could make possible a real and actual act of the will, an act which must be grounded in an actual beginning, and must be so if only because an act of the will is a *willed* act, and therefore it must have an actual origin.

But that act of the will which is the act of absolute will is an act which is necessarily "other" than itself in its deepest ground, and must be other than itself if only to effect and to embody a real and actual act, an act which is absolutely "other" than the pure passivity of primordial ground. And if the will of absolute will is truly and actually a free will, then it is a totally responsible will, a will which is itself wholly responsible for its own act or actualization. Nothing more deeply deconstructed scholasticism than did the challenge of apprehending the freedom of the will of God, and even if this freedom is dogmatically affirmed by scholasticism, it could not be conceptually understood as freedom, and could not be because scholasticism as such is grounded in the absolute necessity of the will of God. Such a necessity forecloses the possibility of an actual freedom, as Spinoza came to know so deeply, and even as it was nominalism which first conceptually grasped this freedom, and did so in its new understanding of act and will itself, so that absolute will can now for the first time be conceptually apprehended as a free will, and that is an understanding which is a profound assault upon the whole horizon of scholasticism. A truly free act of the will is a totally responsible act, an act willing a total responsibility for its every act, and thus willing a total responsibility for every real consequence of its act. But in a Christian world and horizon, and above all so in that world which was a disintegration of the medieval Christian world, such a responsibility must inevitably be a responsibility for disruption and fall, and thus a responsibility for evil and death. Now predestination becomes an even more powerful dogma than it had been so before, a predestination which is finally a predestination of fall, and is so precisely because predestination is an absolutely free act, and therefore an absolutely responsible act. So it is that an actual freedom can now be known only as an actual act of the will, and ever increasingly an actually negative act, an act that is "other" than itself in its own realization, and "other" than itself precisely in realizing a pure actuality that is a free actuality, and therefore an actuality which is fully responsible for the realization of its own intrinsic otherness, an otherness which is the inevitable consequence of the realization of absolute act, or an act which is the true opposite of an absolutely passive and primordial ground.

If an absolute act must inevitably and necessarily be an absolutely free act, then that act is totally responsible for its act, a responsibility which is the responsibility of freedom, but a responsibility which is unrealized apart from an actual enactment. Insofar as Christian theology has understood creation and redemption as the one eternal act of God, it has understood God Himself to be ultimately responsible for the creation, and has even understood the act of creation as an act necessitating the act of redemption. Finally, that can only mean that fall itself is willed by God, and freely willed by God, a freedom that has been known by theology insofar as it has known predestination. But if God freely wills the fall, and freely wills an eternity of Hell as the inevitable consequence of fall, that Hell is absolutely necessary to redemption, for redemption is redemption from eternal death or Hell. Nothing could more clearly make manifest that deep and pure dichotomy which is the dichotomy of the uniquely Christian God, but that is a dichotomy which is absolutely necessary for a free and total act, an act that is the realization of an absolute otherness, and an otherness that *is* the very center of a free and total act. Only a ground in that otherness makes possible a free and actual act, an act which is free only insofar as it struggles against that otherness, and is finally free only insofar as it embodies that otherness, and now embodies that otherness as its own.

Thus that God who freely wills an eternal damnation is that God who is a free and absolute will, only that willing fully releases and embodies an absolute act of the will, and if that willing is simultaneously the willing of an eternal or apocalyptic redemption, that is a redemption which is inseparable from damnation, and precisely thereby a real and actual redemption. Only damnation makes possible an actual redemption, and if that actual redemption transcends the creation itself, so that the fall itself is ultimately a fortunate fall, then fall is absolutely necessary for redemption, which is just why the God of redemption wills the fall. That willing could only be a dichotomous willing, a dichotomous willing which is a free willing, and free precisely because it is a dichotomous willing. Not until the advent of nominalism could scholasticism apprehend such a willing, and only then does scholasticism come to understand the will of God as a free will, for even if Augustine knew the freedom of the will of God, that is a freedom which he could not know in what he apprehended as Being. Augustine fully knew the freedom of God only in knowing the predestination of God, that is the act in which an absolute freedom is most fully manifest, and if that is the act which is the willing of eternal life and eternal death at once, that is an act which is an absolutely free act.

Christianity knows the eternal act of predestination as the eternal act of redemption, for not only is predestination the ultimate source of redemption, but thereby predestination is inseparable from incarnation and crucifixion, a crucifixion and incarnation which is an inevitable consequence of the absolute will of God. For that will is an absolutely free will, and therefore an absolutely responsible will, a responsibility which is enacted in redemption, and enacted in that redemption which is the incarnation and the crucifixion of God. Now even if historical Christianity did not know the crucifixion as the crucifixion of God until the advent of modernity, that is an advent which ushers in a whole new horizon of freedom, and a truly new identity of Godhead itself. Now Godhead can be known as an absolutely free and therefore an absolutely responsible Godhead, a Godhead whose absolute will is an absolutely responsible will, and therefore a will which wills justification and judgment at once, or atonement and fall at once, or apocalypse and genesis at once. Just as that judgment is a real judgment, so likewise is that justification a real justification, each is inseparable from the other, and each is enacted by the absolutely free will of God. Yet that absolutely free will of God is absolutely other than itself, an absolute otherness which is enacted in the simultaneous act of judgment and justification, for that justification is justification only insofar as it is judgment, and that judgment is judgment only insofar as it is justification.

Now it is just the ultimate opposition between judgment and justification which embodies the very actuality of that justification and judgment, apart from that opposition judgment and justification would be actually unreal, and actually unreal because then they would not be enacted. Act is act only insofar as it is enacted, but therein enacted as the very otherness of itself, an otherness apart from which there could be no actual enactment. So it is that the uniquely Christian God can enact redemption only by enacting that damnation which is the full opposite of redemption, for a redemption which is and only is redemption would be an absolutely inactual or empty redemption, and certainly not a redemption which is the consequence of an actual act. Accordingly, the will of God in actually willing redemption, therein and thereby wills damnation; only that absolute opposition of the will could will an absolute act that is an actual act, and is a totally actual act precisely by way of its embodiment of an absolute opposition. Thereby the absolute otherness of the will of God is absolutely its own, and the actual embodiment of that otherness is an absolute decision, and an absolutely free decision, but a decision which is ultimately free only by way of its embodiment of absolute otherness. Now act is truly and fully and actually act, thereby it is a free act, but is finally free only insofar as it wills its otherness as its own.

It is just the inability to know that intrinsic otherness which is the inability to know an actual freedom, an actual freedom which is manifest only through the realization of such otherness, and a self-realization of that otherness is a self-realization of freedom. But that is precisely why true freedom can be neither an eternal act nor an eternal state, it can only be a realized freedom, and a freedom which is realized in realizing one's intrinsic otherness as one's own. That is the freedom which is absolutely realized by the absolute will of God, but that will must enact its otherness as its own, an enactment which is creation and predestination at once, but an enactment which *is* enactment only by way of a real and actual beginning. Only such a beginning could be the embodiment of an actual act of the will, a will which is itself inaugurated by way of that act, an inauguration which is the enactment of an absolute decision. That is the decision which Christianity knows as the absolute love of God, but that love cannot be a real or an actual love if it is not an enacted love, and enacted in that absolute will which is the will of God. But if that absolute will is an absolute will of love, then that love loves its otherness as its own, and loves its absolute otherness as its own, a love which is and only could be an absolute act of sacrifice.

It is the inauguration of that sacrifice which is the inauguration of the will of God, a will which wills against itself as a disembodied plenitude, or as a pure and purely inactual actuality, or as an eternal now which is eternally only itself. So it is that absolute will begins as a negation of absolute plenitude, a negation realizing its own intrinsic other, an intrinsic other which is the pure and actual otherness of a primordial plenitude. That is the negation which is the once-and-for-all act of creation, but a creation which is a willed creation, and therefore a creation which actually begins. But that very act of creation is simultaneously the act of redemption, a creation and redemption embodying the intrinsic otherness of the Godhead, and here the very enactment of that otherness is finally the enactment of redemption. So that God wills eternal life by willing eternal death, that is the willing which is a willing of the absolute otherness of the Godhead, but only that willing *is* the willing of a real and actual redemption. Now absolute otherness is willed by absolute will, and willed so as to effect its own transfiguration, but a transfiguration which would be impossible apart from the actual embodiment of the absolute otherness of the Godhead. But if that otherness is finally transfigured, a transfiguration which is an apocalyptic transfiguration, then that very transfiguration must be an embodiment of the absolute will of God, and of that absolute will which *is* the total act of absolute love or sacrifice.

So it is that the will of God finally disappears in that sacrifice, or disappears as a will which is only itself, and does so by realizing its own intrinsic otherness, an intrinsic otherness which is finally its own. If this is an ultimate transfiguration of the will of God, it can be such only as the consequence of an apocalyptic genesis, and an apocalyptic genesis releasing that ultimate movement which is a movement from genesis to apocalypse. That is a real and actual movement, and even an evolutionary movement, but it is so only insofar as its original sacrifice is finally and ultimately a total sacrifice, and a total sacrifice which is the inevitable consequence of an apocalyptic genesis, or a genesis which can only be consummated in apocalypse. Yet that is also that genesis which is a free genesis, or a genesis which is freely willed, and freely willed in that absolute freedom which is an absolute responsibility, and an absolute freedom which is and only can be an absolute act of sacrifice. True responsibility is sacrifice, the sacrifice of a will which is only its own, and a sacrifice which occurs in a free acceptance of one's otherness as one's own. That occurrence is finally a willing of one's otherness as one's own, but just as that willing cannot occur apart from a realization of that otherness, a self-realization of that otherness is a self-realization of a full and total responsibility, and that is the responsibility which *is* freedom. But it is freedom only insofar as it actually begins, a beginning which is an act of the will, and is an act negating its own impassivity, a negation which is the realization of freedom itself.

Only an apocalyptic genesis could be an inauguration of that freedom, a genesis which is a full negation of a primordial plenitude, and a genesis realizing the intrinsic otherness of that plenitude in a pure and total *act*. That realization is the inauguration of absolute will, an absolute will which is itself the pure and intrinsic otherness of a primordial "emptiness" or calm, and an absolute will which now *is* that which a primordial emptiness *was*. The "isness" of absolute will is the absolute otherness of a primordial passivity, and the advent of that "isness" is the advent of the actuality of time itself, an actuality embodying an antithesis between *is* and *was*, an antithesis that is only possible with the realization of a rift or rupture in that "eternal now" which is a primordial pleroma. That "now" disappears with the realization of a once-and-for-all and irreversible act, that act which is the act of creation itself, and with the disappearance of that "now" the simultaneity of time is shattered. Now the present is *not* the past, and now an "isness" is actual which is *not* an eternal now, and is *not* an eternal now because it is actually and immediately present. That presence is a total presence, and the total presence of the actuality of time itself, but that very presence is the negation of an eternal now, an eternal now which perishes "in the beginning."

"In the beginning" is the beginning of an apocalyptic genesis, a genesis which is the genesis of the absolute will of God, and a genesis of that will in an absolutely free act which is a free act precisely because it is a willed act, and an act transforming the simultaneity of time into the actuality of time. Now and only now the Creator *is* that which a primordial totality *was*, and even if that "wasness" is not actual as such until the realization of absolute act, the realization of that act is the realization of a gulf between *is* and *was*, and thus a gulf between the "isness" of the Creator and the "eternal now" of a primordial totality. Just as an archaic myth and ritual of eternal return is a celebration of that primordial totality, the Biblical celebration of the absolute "isness" of I AM is a negation of that totality, and a negation negating that eternal now which is an absolute impassivity. That negation is the realization of absolute will, an absolute will that now *is* that which an eternal now *was*, and an absolute will that is free precisely in that negation. The freedom of the will even as the actuality of will itself is inseparable from that gulf between *is* and *was*, only that gulf makes possible a free act which is the act of will alone, because only that gulf makes possible an *act* which is an actual movement or realization. No actual act could occur in an "eternal now" in which there is no distinction or difference between the present and the past, for that is the very difference or distinction which makes possible an act that is a new act as opposed to an eternal act, and thus an act that as such is truly different from an unending or an eternal act.

That is the very difference which is realized in an act of the will, and thus the act of absolute will is an absolutely new act, and a new act in which a pure simultaneity of time disintegrates. All too significantly there is no awareness of the freedom of the will in all ancient and primordial worlds, for those are worlds which are bound to an eternal cycle of return, and thus are closed to the full actuality of the present moment. Only that actuality makes possible an awareness of the actuality of will, but that actuality is an *is* that is wholly other than the *was*, yet an *is* that now is that which that *was* once was. Just as a Hegelian dialectical movement is a movement that is negation, transcendence, and preservation simultaneously, the act of will itself is such a dialectical movement, a dialectical movement in which will now *is* that which will itself once *was*. But that movement is possible only when there is a rift or gulf between *is* and *was*, a rift inseparable from the actualization of will, and a rift which is actualized in the *act* of creation. That is why that act is an irreversible shattering of the simultaneity of time, a shattering which is the advent of will itself, and the advent of that absolute will which is a will to an absolute future. Absolute future is wholly other than both the present and the past, and absolutely other than the pure simultaneity of an "eternal now," an absolute otherness which *is* the otherness of absolute will.

But that is an otherness which is affirmed in the act of absolute will, an affirmation which is an enactment of that will, and an actual enactment moving from an original "isness" to an apocalyptic "isness," or from an original act of the will to a final act of the will. The very difference between original act and final act is necessary and essential to the realization of will itself, a realization not only actually moving from *was* to *is,* but a realization in which the fullness of *is* is all that which once *was,* but it *is* that fullness only by way of the absolute negation or emptying of that *was.* Thus if genesis is identical with apocalypse, or if the act of creation is identical with the act of redemption, it is so only insofar as apocalypse now *is* everything which genesis once *was.* Yet that is a dialectical identity which is inseparable from a dialectical difference, or an ultimate identity of genesis and apocalypse which is inseparable from an ultimate difference between genesis and apocalypse. Only that difference makes possible an actual realization, just as only that difference makes possible an actual act of the will, and if that act is finally a full or apocalyptic realization of that difference, that is a realization in which an original act or an original will is dissolved.

So it is that that dissolution is the disappearance of the will of the Creator, a disappearance which is the death of God, yes, but nevertheless a disappearance or dissolution which is the fulfillment of absolute will itself. Therein it is the fulfillment of an apocalyptic genesis, and is that fulfillment because it is the fulfillment of the original act of God, an act which could only truly be enactment if it is an enactment which comes to an end. That is an ending which is inevitable in every act of the will, and if absolute will is absolute act it can truly be so only insofar as it realizes an absolute ending, or that ending which is apocalypse. But in that ending apocalypse *is* all that which genesis *was,* so that the absolute act of beginning itself passes into the absolute act of ending, and even if there is an ultimate difference between beginning and ending, that is a difference which *is* an identity, and an identity of absolute genesis and absolute apocalypse.

Yet that is an identity which can be realized only when apocalypse *is* that which genesis *was,* or only when Spirit *is* that which Godhead *was,* or only when an absolute future *is* that which a primordial past or an "eternal now" *was.* That is the future which is the consummation of absolute will, yet a future that is already actual in the ultimate act of genesis, a genesis that is the genesis of God, yes, but precisely thereby the actualization of that apocalypse which is finally the total disappearance or dissolution of God.

That dissolution is the final realization of genesis itself, a genesis which is both an actual and an absolute genesis, and therefore a genesis which is wholly other than an inactual or "empty" totality. But just as an original genesis is a dissolution or reversal of an undifferentiated pleroma, a final apocalypse is a dissolution or reversal of that very origin, but a reversal in which apocalypse *is* all that which genesis *was*. Only a realization of that identity could make possible a consummation of genesis itself, but that very realization calls forth the apocalyptic identity of genesis, a calling forth which is the epiphany of the absolute triumph of the Kingdom of God. Just as that triumph is the apocalyptic realization of Godhead itself, a realization in which Godhead perishes as "God" even as world perishes as "world," that creation which is "new creation" is the consummation of creation itself.

While historical Christianity has ever been impelled to know that consummation as the original or primordial glory of Godhead itself, that is clearly an impulsion which is a revulsion from an apocalyptic Kingdom of God, and thus a reversal of original Christianity itself. Only a reversal of that reversal makes manifest an apocalyptic genesis, a genesis which is an absolutely new act, and therefore an act which actually and inevitably begins. That beginning is the beginning of the will of God, and thus the beginning of the love or sacrifice of God, a sacrifice and a love which is fully actual precisely by way of a fully actual and real beginning. Thus a refusal of that beginning is a refusal of that sacrifice, and just as "orthodox" Christianity evolved by way of an ever progressive refusal of the crucifixion of God, and hence an ever progressive exaltation of the transcendence of God, that refusal and that exaltation are one movement, and that one movement which is a flight from the genesis of God.

Only a realization of crucifixion is finally a realization of genesis, even as only a realization of the crucifixion of God is a full realization of the genesis of God, or the realization of that genesis which is the absolute sacrifice of God. That sacrifice is embodied in the will of God, and is embodied in that will which wills eternal life and eternal death at once, thereby and necessarily thereby willing its own eternal death in willing its own eternal life. And that willing is an actual willing, even as it is an actual enactment, and therefore an enactment which does begin. But just as that beginning is an actual beginning, so, too, the ending of that sacrifice is an actual ending, an ending which is the dissolution of God, but thereby and precisely thereby the consummation of the eternal act of genesis.

If that act *is* the absolute act of sacrifice, its consummation can only be crucifixion, and only that crucifixion which is finally apocalypse. Yet that apocalypse *is* genesis, or, rather, that apocalypse *is* all that which genesis *was,* hence it is as absolutely new as was genesis itself, and is once again that absolute sacrifice which genesis *was.* And if genesis is the inauguration of the will of God, apocalypse is the consummation of that inauguration, and the very actuality of apocalypse now *is* that actuality which genesis once *was.* Hence the dissolution of God is the consummation of the inauguration of the will of God, an inauguration which is an actual genesis, even as an apocalypse is an actual apocalypse. For it is the actuality of apocalypse itself which perishes with the dissolution of the actuality of genesis, even as the actuality of the apocalypse of God perishes with a dissolution of the genesis of God.

APOCALYPTIC CREED

I believe in the triumph of the Kingdom of God, in that Kingdom which is the final life of the spirit, a life incarnate in Jesus, and consummated in his death. That death is the self-embodiment of the Kingdom of God, and a death which is the resurrection of incarnate body, a body which is a glorified body, but glorified only in its crucifixion, which is the death of all heavenly spirit, and the life of a joy which is grace incarnate. That joy and grace are all in all, offered everywhere and to everyone, and invisible and unreal only to those who refuse them, a refusal which is everyone's but a refusal which is annulled in the death of the incarnate and crucified God, and transfigured in that resurrection, a resurrection which is the actual and present glory of the Kingdom of God. Amen.

BIBLIOGRAPHICAL NOTE

A vast literature has come into existence exploring the worlds which are the arena of *The Genesis of God*. Only a small fragment of that literature will be cited here, but these citations will I hope include those non-theological works which have most shaped the contours of this inquiry. There is first and foremost the problem posed by the Christian epic tradition itself, and all too unfortunately there is only one book which is explicitly given to that topic, and that is my *History as Apocalypse* (The State University of New York Press, 1985), a book which could not possibly bear such a weight of responsibility. The truth is that this tradition is so vast and comprehensive that it simply cannot be understood from a singular perspective, but even if this is so, there is an extraordinarily rich and exciting literature exploring Dante, Milton, Blake, and Joyce, much of which is profoundly theological. All of us are indebted to Charles S. Singleton's translation of and commentary on *The Divine Comedy* (Princeton University Press, Bollingen Books, 1970–75), even if theologically his is a purely Thomistic interpretation which no longer can critically be sustained, as witness Etienne Gilson's *Dante the Philosopher* (Sheed & Ward, 1952) and, even more forcefully, the chapter on Dante in Ernst H. Kantorowicz's *The King's Two Bodies: A Study in Medieval Political Theology* (Princeton University Press, 1957). Erich Auerbach's *Dante: Poet of the Secular World* (University of Chicago Press, 1952), which made possible his *Mimesis,* is an Hegelian study of Dante with nevertheless calls forth Dante as the inaugurator of modernity, and this is the Dante who is now established for us as our deepest modern precursor.

Our understanding of both Milton and Blake has been revolutionized in the past half century, and while the critical literature on each is vast, the theological interpreter of Milton might best begin with Milton's *Christian Doctrine,* as translated by John Carey and with an excellent introduction and editing by Maurice Kelly, in the sixth volume of the Yale Milton

(1973). That this glorious theological work, which is perhaps our only systematic theology which is a fully Biblical theology, is unavailable to the common reader is as great a scandal as anything in Protestantism today. Although chosen somewhat arbitrarily, the following books are invaluable to the theological interpreter of *Paradise Lost:* Walter Clyde Curry, *Milton's Ontology, Cosmogony, and Physics* (University of Kentucky Press, 1957); William Empson, *Milton's God* (London, 1965); Harris Francis Fletcher, *Milton's Rabbinical Readings* (Archon Books, 1967); Christopher Hill, *Milton and the English Revolution* (Faber & Faber, 1977); William Kerrigan, *The Prophetic Milton* (University of Virginia Press, 1974); C. Patrides, *Milton and the Christian Tradition* (Oxford University Press, 1966); Regina M. Schwartz, *Remembering and Repeating: On Milton's Theology and Poetics* (University of Chicago Press, 1993); and Don Marion Wolfe, *Milton in the Puritan Revolution* (Humanities Press, 1963). Of special interest to lovers of Milton are *Milton on Himself* (Oxford University Press, 1939), edited by John S. Diekhoff, and *Milton and His England* (Princeton University Press, 1971), edited by Don M. Wolfe. Yet it must be confessed that we still lack a full and genuine theological exploration of *Paradise Lost.*

My colleague, David V. Erdman, has been our most important Blake scholar for two generations, and his edition of *The Poetry and Prose of William Blake* (Doubleday, 1985) is the definitive such edition, and this is also true both of his *The Illuminated Blake* (Doubleday, 1974) and of the *Notebooks of William Blake* (Oxford University Press, 1973), even as his *Blake: Prophet Against Empire* (Doubleday, 1969) deeply advanced literary scholarship itself by drawing forth the deep historical, political, and social ground of Blake's language and images. A miracle of modern publishing is the Trianon Press's edition of Blake's illuminated books, which so beautifully embody the original editions, and two of these have now been published in relatively inexpensive editions by the William Blake Trust and the Princeton University Press, *Songs of Innocence and Experience* and *Jerusalem*. In 1978, Shambhala (Boulder), in association with Random House, published fascinating illustrated editions of *The Book of Urizen* and *Milton,* edited with commentary by Kay Parkhurst Easson and Roger R. Easson. Our first great Blake scholar was S. Foster Damon, and his *A Blake Dictionary* (Brown University Press, 1965) is invaluable to all lovers of Blake. The Blake bibliography is in the extraordinarily capable hands of G. E. Bentley, Jr., and Martin K. Nurmi, whose *A Blake Bibliography* (University of Minnesota Press, 1964) launched this scholarly venture. Other deeply important studies are G. E. Bentley, Jr., *William Blake's Vala or The Four Zoas* (Oxford University Press, 1963); Martin Bidney, *Blake and Goethe* (University of Missouri Press, 1988); Bernard Blackstone, *English Blake* (Archon Books, 1966); Mark Bracher, *Being form'd, thinking through Blake's Milton* (Station Hill Press, 1985); S. Foster Damon, *William Blake* (Peter Smith, 1958), Northrop Frye, *Fearful Symmetry* (Princeton University Press, 1969); A. L. Morton, *The Everlasting Gospel* (Haskell House, 1966); Milton O. Percival, *William Blake's Circle of Destiny* (Octagon Books, 1964); Albert S. Roe, *Blake's Illustrations to the Divine Comedy* (Princeton University Press, 1953), and Joseph H. Wicksteed's *Blake's Vision of the Book of Job* (London, 1910) and *William Blake's Jerusalem* (London, 1954). All too unfortunately, my own *The New Apocalypse: The Radical Christian Vision of William Blake* (Michigan State University Press, 1967) remains our only fully theological study of Blake.

The critical studies of Milton, Blake, and Joyce are simply overwhelming, and one might well begin a critical study of Joyce with Richard Ellmann's great biography, *James Joyce* (Oxford University Press, 1982). But it is the actual reading of Joyce which is the supreme challenge, and above all so the reading of *Finnegans Wake*. A wise beginning would be to read the final book, pages 593–628, aloud, in our only real edition of the *Wake* (Viking-Penguin, 1967). This is the easiest language in the work, and despite appearances to the contrary, it becomes overwhelmingly real when read aloud. But the simple truth is that only deeply dedicated scholarship has brought real meaning to the *Wake*, and every reader should employ both Roland McHugh's *Annotations to Finnegans Wake* (The Johns Hopkins University Press, 1980) and Clive Hart's *A Concordance to Finnegans Wake* (University of Minnesota Press, 1963). Other invaluable studies of Joyce and the *Wake* are James S. Atherton, *The Books at the Wake* (Viking Press, 1960); Bernard Benstock, *Joyce's Again Wake* (University of Washington Press, 1965); Norman O. Brown, *Closing Time* (Random House, 1973); Vincent John Cheng, *Shakespeare and Joyce, A Study of Finnegans Wake* (Pennsylvania State University Press, 1984); Umberto Eco, *The Aesthetics of Chaosmos* (University of Tulsa Monographs, 1982); John Gordon, *Finnegans Wake: A Plot Summary* (Syracuse University Press, 1986); Clive Hart, *Structure and Motif in Finnegans Wake* (Northwestern University Press, 1962); Hugh Kenner, *Dublin's Joyce* (London, 1955); Roland McHugh, *The Sigla of Finnegans Wake* (The Johns Hopkins University Press, 1980); Louis O. Mink, *A Finnegans Wake Gazeteer* (Indiana University Press, 1978); William T. Noon, *Joyce* and Aquinas (Yale University Press, 1957); Margo Norris, *The Decentered Universe of Finnegans Wake* (Johns Hopkins University Press, 1976); and Mary T. Reynolds, *Joyce and Dante* (Princeton University Press, 1981).

Princeton University Press is now publishing what should become the finest critical edition of the collected works of Spinoza in English, as edited and translated by Edwin Curley, and its first volume (1985) includes the *Ethics*. H. A. Wolfson's *The Philosophy of Spinoza* (Meridian Books, 1958) is an exciting and masterful historical study demonstrating both Spinoza's continuity with and his radical break from the scholastic philosophical tradition, both Jewish and Christian. Paul Wienpahl's *The Radical Spinoza* (New York University Press, 1979) is itself a radical venture, attempting to correlate Spinoza's God both with the Biblical God and with Mahayana Buddhism. Henry M. Rosenthal's *The Consolation of Philosophy* (Temple University Press, 1989) is a brilliant philosophical, political, and theological correlation of Spinoza and Hobbes. Leo Strauss's *Spinoza's Critique of Religion* (Schocken Books, 1965) launched Strauss's philosophical career, following his study of Maimonides, for Strauss was persuaded that Spinoza's dissolution of the Mosaic authorship of the Pentateuch was a dissolution of the deepest ground of the order and authority of the West. E. M. Curley's *Spinoza's Metaphysics* (Harvard University Press, 1969) is perhaps the best of the analytic studies of Spinoza, and Errol E. Harris's *Salvation from Despair* (The Hague, 1973) is a study fully integrating a philosophical and an ethical study of Spinoza.

But it is Hegel who most profoundly understood Spinoza, and his dialogue with Spinoza is a constant motif in his work, just as his exposition of Spinoza in his lectures on the history of philosophy is unsurpassed. J. N. Findlay's *Hegel* (London, 1970) is still the best critical introduction to Hegel, and Findlay profoundly wrestled with Hegel throughout his philosophical career, finally realizing a primordial Neoplatonism by way of a reversal of Hegel in the second volume of his Gifford lectures, *The Transcendence of the Cave* (London, 1967). But perhaps the best way to begin a critical study of Hegel is by way of H. S. Harris's *Hegel's Development Toward the Sunlight* (Oxford University Press, 1979), and *Night Thoughts* (Oxford University Press, 1983). The State University of New York Press is now our major publisher of Hegel studies, and these include Joseph C. Flay's *Hegel's Quest for Certainty* (1984); *Essays on Hegel's Logic* (1990), edited by George di Giovanni; Quentin Lauer's *Hegel's Concept of God* (1982) (which perhaps could only have been written by a Jesuit, for it both demonstrates the totality of Hegel's understanding of God even while dissolving its Christian theological ground); James Yerkes, *The Christology of Hegel* (1982); and Donald Philip Verene's *Hegel's Recollection* (1985). The great French Hegel scholar, Jean Hyppolite, has given us not only the *Genesis and Structure of Hegel's Phenomenology of Spirit* (Northwestern University Press, 1974) but also *Studies of Marx and Hegel* (Basic Books, 1969). Perhaps the clearest critical introduction to Hegel's *Phenomenology of Spirit* is by Howard P. Kainz, Part I (University of Alabama Press, 1976) and Part II (Ohio University Press, 1983). Karl Löwith's *From Hegel to Nietzsche* (Holt, Rinehart, & Winston, 1964) remains the best scholarly study of Hegel as the inaugurator of a radically new cultural and human world, just as George Lichtheim's *From Marx to Hegel* (Herder & Herder, 1971) is perhaps our best political study of Hegel, even as Herbert Marcuse's *Reason and Revolution* (Beacon Press, 1964) remains our deepest political re-thinking of Hegel. But Eric Voegelin's violent political and theological assault upon Hegel cannot be ignored, as most forcefully present in *The Ecumenic Age* (Louisiana State University Press, 1974). Mark C. Taylor's *Journeys to Selfhood* (University of California Press, 1980) is extraordinarily important theologically if only because it so fully correlates the thinking of Hegel and Kierkegaard. Edith Wyschogrod's *Spirit in Ashes* (Yale University Press, 1985) correlates Hegel's and Heidegger's understanding of death in the perspective of the Holocaust, and Heidegger himself records his own deep ground in Hegel in *Hegel's Concept of Experience* (Harper & Row, 1970), a ground which is reenacted by a Christian Heideggerian, Hans Georg Gadamer, in *Hegel's Dialectic* (Yale University Press, 1976). Nowhere is Hegel more profoundly embodied than in D. G. Leahy's *Novitas Mundi* (New York University Press, 1980), although this is an embodiment which is a reverse embodiment, and finally a Catholic apocalyptic reversal of Hegel. There is a spirited Hegel Society of America, which publishes its own journal, *The Owl of Minerva,* and their first conference was on Hegel's philosophy of religion, which, as edited by D. E. Christensen, was published at The Hague in 1970. But more recently Hegel has been having a deep impact upon literary studies, as brilliantly embodied in Janine D. Langan's *Hegel and Mallarmé* (The University Press of America, 1986). Even Mark C. Taylor's *Disfiguring: Art, Architecture, Religion* (University of Chicago Press, 1992) is simultaneously an Hegelian and a Kierkegaardian celebration and reversal of postmodern art and architecture.

Hegel and Nietzsche studies threaten to transcend all limits, but it is Nietzsche who is that thinker who has had the most ultimate impact upon our world, and surely it would be difficult if not impossible to name a major imaginative expression of our century which is unaffected by Nietzsche. And this impact is not confined to the West, as witness *Nietzsche and Asian Thought* (The University of Chicago Press, 1991), edited by Graham Parkes, and dedicated to Nishitani Keiji as "the major precursor," for Nishitani, along with the Kyoto School as a whole, has called forth a uniquely modern Buddhism which is fully correlated with Hegel, Kierkegaard, and Nietzsche, and which can fully be encountered in Nishitani's *Religion and Nothingness* (University of California Press, 1982). Perhaps only in that perspective can the Christian realize the deep unity of Nietzsche and Hegel, although such a unity has been deeply embodied in the most radical thinking of Lacan, Foucault, and Derrida. But among the vast body of Nietzsche studies, perhaps these are the ones which deserve mention here: Martin Heidegger, *Nietzsche* (Harper & Row, 1979); Erich Heller, *The Disinherited Mind* (Barnes & Noble, 1971); Karl Jaspers, *Nietzsche* (University of Arizona Press, 1965); Walter Kaufmann, *Nietzsche* (Princeton University Press, 1968); Lawrence Lampert, *Nietzsche's Teaching: An Interpretation of Thus Spoke Zarathustra* (Yale University Press, 1986); Bernd Magnus, *Nietzsche's Existential Imperative* (Indiana University Press, 1978); George Allen Morgan, *What Nietzsche Means* (Harper & Row, 1965); Joan Stambaugh, *Nietzsche's Thought of Eternal Recurrence* (The Johns Hopkins University Press, 1972); John T. Wilcox, *Truth and Value in Nietzsche* (University of Michigan Press, 1974); and perhaps above all, David Allison, editor, *The New Nietzsche* (MIT Press, 1985), although my essay here is so badly edited as to be all but unreadable.

INDEX

192

Index

Index

197